# Literary Genius

OF THE

# New Testament

By

## P. C. SANDS

HEAD MASTER OF POCKLINGTON SCHOOL, AND LATE FELLOW OF
ST. JOHN'S COLLEGE, CAMBRIDGE

## GREENWOOD PRESS, PUBLISHERS
WESTPORT, CONNECTICUT

Originally published in 1932
by the Clarendon Press, Oxford

First Greenwood Reprinting 1970

Library of Congress Catalogue Card Number 74-109837

SBN 8371-4328-4

Printed in the United States of America

# PREFACE

LONG study of the manner of Biblical writers tempts one to begin this Preface in the style of St. Luke: 'The former treatise have I made, O Theophilus', of the Literary Genius of the Old Testament, and now encouraged by the publishers and the reception of the 'former treatise', I have attempted another volume concerning the Literary Genius of the New Testament.

For this second attempt I must beg the indulgence of my readers, who will be well aware of the peculiar difficulties of analysing the beauty of the Gospels. Not only is their text read almost exclusively for devotional purposes, so that some people may resent any other aspect of them being stressed, but the mass of criticism that has accumulated on the subject of the Gospels and Epistles is so great that one can scarcely put into writing an appreciation of a single verse without conflicting with the published opinion of some scholar either upon the correctness or genuineness of the text or its interpretation. For instance, it has grown difficult to think of St. Paul's last days except in the terms of the second letter to Timothy: 'I have fought the good fight, I have finished my course, I have kept the faith. . . . At my first defence no one took my part . . . but the Lord stood by me . . . and I was delivered out of the mouth of the lion.' Famous words these, and long admired as characteristic of St. Paul, as full of his blended humility and egoism, his hope and pride, his metaphors and oratory. But to admire them as St. Paul's own words is to risk the censure of those who contend that the letter to Timothy was not Paul's, but a later composition by an imitator. Yet imitations, however clever, excite quite a different kind of admiration.

In these days, however, when we are urged to 'live dangerously', risks must be taken, and when literary appreciation is not only taught in schools but is the subject of wireless talks, no excuse is needed for offering a literary appreciation of the greatest collection of books ever made, and for devoting a special volume to them.

The writer would like to acknowledge his debt to the New

Commentary (Gore), and to Peake's Commentary, Hastings's Dictionary, and the Westminster Commentary on the Acts of the Apostles (Rackham). He is also very grateful to Dr. W. H. Rigg of Beverley for revising the manuscript and making many corrections and suggestions. There is one more debt to acknowledge, that to Dr. T. R. Glover, his former director of studies at Cambridge. If this volume had seemed sufficiently important to dedicate it to anybody, it would have been only fitting to dedicate it to him, since it was his generous article upon the Literary Genius of the Old Testament in a leading London journal that secured it a wide and favourable reception and encouraged the production of a companion volume.

P. C. S.

POCKLINGTON SCHOOL,
E. YORKS.

# CONTENTS

# I

## INTRODUCTORY

Memoirs—the literature of a single fact—limits of literary ability in these memoirs.

THE literature of the New Testament is founded on that type of record which we call 'memoirs' or 'memoranda', things to be remembered about some person. Good memoirs are those which give the vividest impression of the person concerned, his personality. A lively memoir is likely to survive a complete biography, simply because it can be memorized better. As a condensed collection of incidents and sayings, it lends itself to quotation, and repetition, as proverbs, epigrams, and short songs do, the kind of literature which lives longest.

It was then providential that the only attempt to help people to remember Christ, and to catch the spirit and life of his personality should have been by memoirs, brief selections of things he did, and things he said. The longer the work, the greater the difficulty of transcribing and circulating, and the fewer people it could reach; also the less able to be remembered.

Memorizing was in fact the main consideration when the record of Jesus was first begun. When the disciples made converts, it was necessary to teach them the main facts about the one who was preached to them as risen from the dead and able to save them from sin. The acts of Jesus were presented and learnt in separate little stories, and formed one part of the memoirs. The sayings of Jesus, quoted like oracles, formed the other part. It has been suggested that the *stories* as given to the converts were grouped round certain events, viz. the resurrection, the trial and death, the ministry, the baptism and John the Baptist, and the childhood of Jesus. Of these, the last would not be prominent at first; the resurrection would be all important as it confirmed men's wistful hopes of a future life. The form in which the *sayings* were taught is fairly clear from the papyrus discovered at Oxyrhynchus in A.D. 1897, and another discovered in A.D. 1903, which give series of sayings introduced by the mere phrase: 'Jesus saith ...';

'Jesus saith ...' The fourth chapter of Mark presents the same feature, sayings loosely put together, see vv. 21, 24, 26, 30, though usually the occasion of the saying is given. The papyri referred to give not only some of the sayings of our Gospels in an altered form, but some new ones equally striking.

The literature of the New Testament arose, however, out of a single fact. But for the resurrection, there could have arisen no such account of Christ as we have. It is all an expansion of 'Jesus rose again and we are witnesses'. The second part of the New Testament, the Letters, are reflections upon the fact, and here the scope for literary genius to display itself is at once broadened. Philosophy and oratory are admitted, and letters, which, expressing the writer's personality and displaying peculiarities of style, constitute in themselves a separate branch of literature proper. Even in the Acts there is much more scope for literary ability of an historical kind, where the author's scheme embraces peoples and countries from Ethiopia to Rome, the events of many years, and the spread of a sect from a city over a continent. But in the Gospels the influence of the manifesto or motto 'We are witnesses' imposes narrow limits upon the editor or composer of these records. In the faithful repetition of the sayings of Jesus, and the bare recital of what the disciples claimed to have seen, there seems little scope for literary genius. If the account comprises sayings and doings, the literary merit of the sayings, for example of the parables, must be partly that of the original speaker;[1] the claims of the writer are confined to any art which may be shown by a story-teller, whose first duty is to confine himself strictly to the truth.

But this, of course, is just where the genius of the various gospels comes in. Story-telling, even of true stories, is not a simple business. It is significant that the most popular Gospel, that of Luke, is that which shows the greatest literary qualities, and for these qualities and for skill as editor, credit has actually

---

[1] 'A tradition as to the sayings and deeds of Jesus, based ultimately upon the oral teaching of the Apostles, would tend to crystallize in each of the leading centres of Christian missionary work. Especially would this be the case in regard to the teaching of Jesus.' Rawlinson, *Mark* (W.C.), xiii.

been assigned to Luke. But to assign credit is less our concern than to examine the literary beauty of the narratives as they stand. It is also, of course, acknowledged that besides the deep truths that they contain, the parables of Jesus display the greatest literary art, and that the appeal to millions of such a parable as the Prodigal Son depends, in part at least, upon the skill and genius which chose and arranged the words as well as originated the ideas.

Truth has a habit of finding beautiful forms in which to express itself. Keats said beauty and truth were the same thing. The enormous and evergrowing sales of the Memoirs in all languages is due not only to the stupendous truth which they contain but to the beauty of its expression. They have also not only influenced but totally changed the lives and conduct of thousands of readers in all countries without any commentary and in many cases without any contact with teachers. It is doubtful whether they could have done this except for their unique literary qualities, that is to say, unless an inspired simplicity of composition, and the choicest diction and the sound editorship of those who composed the Gospel narrative, had kept the truth clear, bright, and attractive. How many conversions to Mohammedanism could be attributed to the unaided reading of the Koran? In the New Testament the personality of Christ is admittedly a world above that of other religious leaders like Mohammed, but that personality had to be expressed, and, just because of its divine claims, it needed inspiration of a special kind for the disciples and their pupils to be able to express it in teaching and writing. Of this inspiration Pentecost was perhaps the explanation so far as the unlettered disciples were concerned. But no one who carefully compares the different qualities of the narrative of Mark and Luke, the graphic power of Mark, and the grace and beauty of Luke can doubt that this inspiration encouraged each narrator, except where the actual words of Jesus were concerned, to develop his own excellences of form and style.

It is these excellences, and those of the language used by Jesus himself, and the very different literary genius of John and of Paul that suggested the adding of another small volume to all the volumes that have been already written about the New Testament.

Within what limits could literary ability affect the memoirs about Jesus Christ?

As their aim is evidently to depict the personality of Jesus, the efforts of the authors would be directed to the outlining of that personality, and to the filling it in as far as they could without conveying wrong impressions: in fact to present the truth about him, 'the whole truth and nothing but the truth'. To tell the whole truth about such a personality involved a difficulty connected with choice of material. Though Mark gives the truth, a truthful picture of Jesus as man and Messiah, yet Luke and John put new lines, new touches into the portrait that add to the total impression. They do it not only by including additional matter as editors, for example, Luke by including incidents showing tenderness to outcasts, John by including intimate conversations. There are differences of composition as well. And though it is true, as was said in another sense, that 'Christianity is always supreme over the means of its expression', yet the personal outlook of its various reporters has given a distinct character to their records. John's Gospel is marked by deep spiritual reflection, Matthew's is largely Hebraic, while Luke's reflects the broader outlook of the West.

Again, in John's Gospel, it has been pointed out, Jesus appears rather as the Eternal Word, the idea of what God is. In Matthew's, he is the son of David and Abraham fulfilling Old Testament prophecy. In Luke's he appears as the son of Adam, the perfect Man, the Saviour of all men and friend of the poor. In Mark's he is before all things 'the Son of God, moving among men with his gift of miracle and making the things of nature the servants of his grace'. If we indulged the fancy so far as to picture the evangelists existing to-day, and having suitable spheres of work allotted to them, we should say that John would go to the Universities, Luke to Polynesia or the Eskimos, Matthew to the Ghetto, and Mark to write versions of the scriptures as an agent of the Bible Society.

## II

## ST. MARK'S GOSPEL

**Prefatory Note.** Main feature of the Gospel—healing of the Lunatic Boy—
the Deaf and Dumb Man—the Blind man healed—a typical day—human
expressions and feelings of Jesus—journeys, and special incidents in each, as
framework of the narrative—looks, gestures, and actions of Jesus—the crowd
portrayed—the 'great refusal'—the words of Jesus—Jesus as the Son of God—
his power—realism of Mark—portrait of the disciples—their training—
interest in the movements of Jesus from place to place—brevity and vigour
of Mark's style—the Gospel of action—its correspondence with the character
of St. Peter.

### PREFATORY NOTE

In examining the literary qualities of the Gospel of St. Mark,
especially those of the narrative portions, the question is bound
to obtrude itself sooner or later how one is to regard that main
feature of the Gospel, the realism and graphic detail of its
stories. For instance, when Mark tells the story of the healing
of the deaf and dumb man, what does it represent? Did some
one such as Peter originally tell the story in that vivid form,
recalling what he saw himself, while the incident was fixed in
his memory, and in that form did the Christians receive it and
memorize it, and did Mark, who was associated with Peter,
write it down much as he received it? Or did the story, as some
modern scholars assert, gain these extra vivid touches 'through
frequent telling and re-telling in early Christian preaching'?
Or again, as others suppose, did Mark give such a graphic
reconstruction of the incidents out of his own vivid imagination?

It was difficult to discuss these stories for their literary
interest without revealing the definite point of view, at which
one arrived in examining them. 'The literary quality of the
Gospels', says an objector, 'is what it is, whatever their
historical value.' This is surely doubtful, and it is not possible
to discuss the literary quality of history, historical romance,
and fiction in the same terms. It is not the same kind of
literary genius that sets down what it is told by a witness and
that reconstructs scenes from imagination.

The point of view from which the following chapter was

written is the older view, namely that Mark's account closely depended upon St. Peter, and that his vivid and graphic narrative is derived eventually from that Apostle's actual observation. It is a begging of the question to call this view antiquated, as some modern scholars do, when it still commands the support of scholars of eminence. It has been re-stated in clear terms by Turner in the *New Commentary*, S.P.C.K., 1928, pp. 45 ff.: 'It is as a disciple of St. Peter that Mark left his impression on tradition. . . . The Gospel is the unique record, objectively stated, of an eyewitness, an intimate companion of Jesus . . . We would rather have had Peter's story direct from his own pen, but we have it in a form, which, so far as analysis can tell us, has suffered *comparatively little blurring* of the sharpness of the outlines.' . . . 'Peter's mind was narrower in its range (than John's), but it was extraordinarily tenacious.'

Rawlinson, on Mark, Westminster Commentaries, 1925, Introd., p. xxiii, says: 'it is possible to exaggerate the extent of the direct dependence of Mark upon Peter'. Yet he says later, 'It remains true that the Gospel itself conveys the impression *at innumerable points* of just such contact at first hand *with historic tradition* as is claimed for St. Mark *in the earliest statements* about the authorship and origin of the Gospel.' What can 'historic tradition' mean here but that of Peter, who is the subject of those earliest statements, namely those of Papias and John the Elder? Elsewhere he says of certain incidents, 'No doubt it is true that the ultimate source of these stories is Peter.'

He believes, however, that 'the gift of *dramatic visualization*, which enables Mark to call up so vividly the setting and circumstances of a story . . . is the Evangelist's own'. This is a very great faculty to attribute to Mark's genius. But when he discusses the particularly vivid incident of Bartimaeus, he refers the vividness to the *memory*, not to dramatic visualization or imagination, 'This episode of Bartimaeus was *vividly remembered* and precisely located in the tradition.'

Streeter, *The Four Gospels*, states that the narrative gained its vividness through the telling and retelling in early Christian preaching. But a story may gain or lose detail in retelling. It depends on the kind of story, and on the retailer. A man trying

faithfully to repeat incidents as told him by a witness loses
details, especially those that are not vital, if he is aiming at
repeating the truth, and the Christians made much of the truth
of their records. A man trying to repeat a good story for enter-
tainment will perhaps replace lost details by others of his own
invention, if he is clever enough. But the circumstances of the
circulation of the Gospel story were rather of the former kind,
and its tendency to shed details is shown by the versions of
Luke and Matthew, when they used Mark. Streeter himself
says: 'How any one who has worked through these pages (of
*Horae Synopticae*, J. Hawkins) can retain the slightest doubt
of the original and primitive character of Mark, I am unable to
understand.'

Three things must be borne in mind, the emphasis the Gospel
writers lay upon truth, the importance of memory in the teaching of those days, and the unlikelihood that Mark should have
possessed the requisite originality to draw upon, even if he had
been disposed to do so.

Remembering always that 'we are witnesses' is the motto of
the first disciples, and that Mark is agreed to have been in
touch with the earliest traditions of the disciples, and was
connected with Peter,[1] we are not surprised that the first
official account that we have shows the closest observation of
Jesus as he worked and taught, those small details that impressed the first wondering eyewitnesses, who were trying to
place him ('What manner of man is this?'), his actual words
and gestures when he healed, his expression of emotion that
showed him man, his words of power that showed him God.
'This particular Gospel is singularly destitute of literary skill
and grace.'[2] That is true, if we think of style, diction, or
imagination. But fidelity to truth, memory, and the selection
of memoranda that would express the man, were parts of the

---

[1] 1 Pet. v. 13: 'It is as a disciple of St. Peter that Mark left his impression on
tradition,' Turner, S.P.C.K., *New Commentary*, Mark, p. 43 b. See also Prefatory Note above.

[2] Gore, *Belief in God*, p. 190. Rawlinson, *Commentary on Mark*, p. xxxi, says:
'The writing all through is colloquial, unpolished, and characterized by a
singular monotony of style.' For some peculiarities of the Greek, see p. 25.

literary art of Boswell. The main charm of Mark's account, as distinct from the other synoptic gospels, is the faithful reproduction of scenes where the disciples watched Jesus at work, a charm that also appears in some degree in that of John.

*Healing of the Lunatic Boy.*

The healing of the lunatic boy immediately after the Transfiguration would have excited the keenest interest of the disciples, and especially of Peter. This problem of healing, his baffled colleagues and the excited crowd would be remembered vividly as a contrast to the recent exhilarating experience on the mountain,[1] and the account given in Mark is more graphic than that of any other miracle.

Mark ix. 14–29.

(The parts peculiar to Mark are in italics)

And when they came to the disciples, they saw a great multitude about them, and *scribes disputing with them.* And straightway all the multitude, when they saw him, *were greatly amazed,* and *running to him, saluted him.* And he asked them, '*What question ye with them ?*' And one of the multitude answered him, 'Master, I brought unto thee my son, which hath a *dumb* spirit; and wheresoever it taketh him, it dasheth him down; and he foameth, and *grindeth his teeth,* and pineth away; and I spake to thy disciples that they should cast it out, and they were not able. And he answereth them and saith, 'O faithless generation, how long shall I be with you? How long shall I bear with you? Bring him unto me.' And they brought him unto him; and when he saw him,

Luke ix. 37–43. Matt. xvii. 14–21.

Matt. 'When they came to the crowd, a man came . . .'

L. 'When they had come down from the mountain, a man from the crowd . . .'

*Symptoms* of the boy:

Matt. 'A lunatic and sore vexed . . . falls into fire and water.'

Luke, with the interest, as some think, of medical knowledge, gives them more fully, 'he shrieks . . .'—convulsions, foaming . . .—'it wears him out.' Luke also mentions the further convulsion as the boy is brought to Jesus.

These words are also in Matthew and Luke and show they used the same account as Mark, or followed Mark.

[1] See note on p. 10.

straightway the spirit tare him grievously; and *he fell on the ground and wallowed foaming. And he asked his father, 'How long is it, since this hath come unto him?' And he said, 'From a child.* And often it hath cast him into the fire, and into the water to destroy him; *but if thou canst do anything, have compassion on us and help us.' And Jesus said unto him, 'If thou canst!' 'All things are possible unto him that believeth.' Straightway the father of the child cried out, and said with tears, 'I believe; help thou my unbelief.' And when Jesus saw that a multitude came running together,* he rebuked the unclean spirit, *saying unto him, 'Thou dumb and deaf spirit, I command thee, come out of him, and enter no more into him. And having cried out and torn him much, he came out: and the child became as one dead: so that many said, 'He is dead'. But Jesus took him by the hand, and raised him up: and he arose.*

And when he was come into the house, his disciples asked him privately, 'Why could not we cast it out?' And he said unto them, 'This kind can come out by nothing but by prayer.'

Matthew does not mention this epileptic fit and Luke does not emphasize its continued violence, as Mark does.

Luke omits this question. Matthew has it, and as he sometimes does, inserts a passage which occurs in another connexion (v. Matt. xxi. 21, and Luke xvii. 6).

This is one of the best instances of the primitive tradition, in which the minuter details reflect the personality and methods of Jesus much more completely than the shortened accounts of the other two Gospels, Matthew and Luke. In Mark we see everything that Peter would see, as he approached the scene, the crowd in the distance round a knot of disputing men, who turned out to be the disciples and the scribes. The dispute seems to have been so warm that the cause of it had been left

C

out of immediate view, on one side. Before Jesus reaches the scene, the crowd leaves the dispute, in the way crowds have, and runs towards him. Their *amazement* at the sight of Jesus is not explained. It may have been because his face kept some of the radiance of the Transfiguration. The word used (translated by Moffat 'thunderstruck') is strong for mere surprise at his coming into view, though of course Mark has a way of using strong expressions.[1]

The father tells his trouble and rehearses the boy's symptoms, including the dumbness and the grinding of teeth, which the other Gospels omit. Jesus cannot help giving vent to his disappointment at his disciples' failure and at the wrangling, which would jar his spirit all the more after his recent experience. The father is very lifelike. The question of Jesus starts him off again with a tale of further symptoms. In a most natural bit of dialogue his appeal, 'If you can do anything' provokes the 'If you *can*, indeed!' of Jesus (R.V.) ('It depends on yourself, not on me. Can *you* rise to it?'), and the father tries desperately to respond.

The boy had had a paroxysm when brought to Jesus, which had prompted Jesus' question. Seeing more people gathering, Jesus cuts short his observation of the boy, and speaks the word of release. Not only are the actual words given, in the direct speech preferred by Mark, but the effect of the cure is most realistically noted, the last spasm and the deathlike stupor that followed, the crowd pronouncing the boy dead. The detailed observation does not end there. Jesus 'took the boy by the hand', and roused him, so that he stood on his feet.

How natural, too, the sequel! The question in private, 'Why could not *we* do it?' and the answer, 'Spiritual concentration is needed', are perhaps the most interesting things in the account. A surprising candour is shown, when the chief disciple is willing to leave on record such a failure, and with the other detail stamps the account as true. The narrator is thinking of the

---

[1] See pp. 13, 25. Rawlinson, *Mark*, p. 123, suggests that Mark has specially attached the incident to that of the Transfiguration, but it is easier to believe that the memoir came to him already fixed in the tradition as a sequel to the Transfiguration, as the text has it.

scene, not of the disciples' credit with the early Church. Luke, with that credit in view, omits the discussion, and makes a characteristic addition instead about the crowd praising the power of God.

### The Deaf and Dumb Man.

Equally striking are the details in another healing, as if Jesus had been closely watched. The other Gospels record the healing of the deaf and dumb, but Mark alone gives a typical case, and in the same careful manner as he preserves the healing of the lunatic boy. Matthew and Luke both omit the story 'probably because they thought the use of material means like spittle unworthy of the Lord. Mark is closer to the peasant atmosphere of Galilee'.[1]

'And again, coming out of the borders of Tyre he came through Sidon to the Sea of Galilee, through the midst of the borders of Decapolis. And they bring to him a deaf man with an impediment in his speech, and they beseech him to lay his hand upon him. And (1) taking him away from the crowd apart (2) he put his fingers into his ears, and (3) spit and touched his tongue, and (4) looking up to heaven (5) he groaned and (6) said to him, "Ephphatha" (which is, "Be opened"). And his ears were opened and the binding of his tongue loosed, and he began to speak plain.' (vii. 31–7.)

This narrative conveys to us what must have been the first wondering interest of the disciples in the cures of Jesus. Each sentence in the above gives some detail of the method of healing. Mark records one miracle which was actually done in stages, on a man whom Jesus again led away from the crowd, 'out of the town', when, after the same actions, the use of saliva on the part affected, and the putting of the hands upon the patient, he asked him if he saw anything. The man could 'see men as trees walking'. A second application of the hands on his eyes made him see clearly. Mark's boldness has here been commented upon in allowing it to be inferred that the power of Jesus did not act successfully at once (viii. 22–6).

These details and minute touches tended to disappear in subsequent accounts. Yet they have a close bearing upon the

[1] Rawlinson, *Mark*, p. 102.

proper representation of Jesus the Man. A hundred similar touches, showing the feelings and little actions and gestures of Jesus, have disappeared from the later portraits, removed perhaps as small lines are removed by a photographer who desires a smoother effect. It has been suggested that as the Divinity of Jesus became the dominant and only thought in the Church, and the Son of Man became exclusively called the Lord Jesus,[1] these traces of human feeling were consciously removed by Luke, and, except in Gethsemane, by Matthew. 'Either timid desire to set a fence round our Lord's person, or deference paid to prejudices of Christians who had been educated as Stoics, and had been taught that a good man is never surprised, angry, or agonized... that perfect calm was essential to his character', led to such removal.[2] Peter and John, on the other hand, 'who had known Jesus intimately in the flesh', had no hesitation in ascribing such emotions to him, and the portrait in the fourth Gospel agrees in this respect with Mark's, inspired by Peter. But it always happens that minute touches disappear from an oft-told story.[3] What was regarded as insignificant would be discarded. Only intimate friends treasure the looks and sighs as personal memories. Those who bow in homage to the great, and only know them as Lord and at a distance, demand the big things.[4] Luke, for instance, records gestures of Paul, with whom he was intimate, but rarely of Jesus, though he found them in Mark, or the account they both used. The charm of Mark for us is that he paints this close, intimate picture of Jesus as man, and that without any loss, as we shall see, of the impression of his divinity. In that first chapter of Mark one can almost hear Peter retailing his memories of a typical day in our Lord's ministry:

'I remember a Sabbath early on in the ministry when Jesus was so good as to use my house, and his visit to the synagogue

[1] This title is not used by Mark of Jesus except twice in the last twelve verses, which are judged to be a later addition, but it is used sixteen times by Luke and twelve by John. Good instances of its introduction by Luke are Luke xxii. 61, vii. 19.                [2] Wright, *Synopsis of the Gospels*, p. 27.

[3] See prefatory note to the chapter.

[4] For other evidence of Mark's circumstantiality see Hastings, *Dict. of the Bible* (Mark), vol. iii, p. 254.

in the morning, when a lunatic startled the congregation, as our Lord was speaking. It was no less startled at the reply to the lunatic, "*Be muzzled* and come out of him'', and immediately the spirit obeyed, and the man was cured. Then Jesus came home to a meal, and heard my wife's mother was ill, and went up and cured her. Later on, as the sun set, we saw the street filling up with sick cases—he was soon famous—and Jesus was kept busy all the evening. A wonderful day it was, and to our surprise our Master, tired out though he was with healing, rose from bed early, and walked to the hills to pray by himself. The crowds asked us where he was, and we had a search for him.' (Gk. 'they pursued him'.)

*Human Feelings.*

'You say he looked tired?' 'Yes, often, and disappointed sometimes, and angry, and surprised. You should have seen the look upon his face when he healed that first leper, full of pity; and he put out his hand and touched the very place. And he was quite stern with the man afterwards, to keep him from talking about it.' [1] Strong expressions are used for these feelings, as that he '*marvelled* at their unbelief' (vi. 6), 'sighed deeply in spirit' (viii. 12).

*Special Incidents.*

In the same way the record seems to follow the journeys of Jesus, and to dwell on some outstanding incident that occurred in each. This, in fact, will be found to be the framework of a large section of Mark's Gospel, if we follow the text. For instance, in the long tour described in chapters vii and viii, the first stage is to the borders of Tyre, and one chief memory stands out, the healing of the daughter of the Syrophoenician woman. Then the way is traced to the Sea of Galilee and Decapolis, where the deaf and dumb man is cured; from there by ship to Dalmanutha, where the outstanding memory is a challenge from the Pharisees; again by ship to the other side, and during the sail the question of the shortage of bread cropped up; back to Bethsaida, where the only memory is the cure of the blind man. Yet again, mentioned next in order, comes the tour of the towns of Caesarea Philippi, where every

[1] Matt. viii. 1–4, and Luke v. 12–16, omit this.

memory is overshadowed by the momentous question, 'Whom say ye that I am?'

*Looks and Gestures.*

As some special incident is given of each journey, so some vivid detail is given of each incident, some look or gesture of Jesus, some action of the crowd, the notable words Jesus used, or the feelings aroused in him. He 'looked round on all things' in the Temple the day before he cleansed it. 'He looked round about him with anger,[1] grieved at their hardness of heart', when the Scribes objected to the cure on the Sabbath. When the woman touched his garment, he 'looked round' to see who it was, and when his brethren sought him, 'he looked round on those who sat about him' and called them his brothers. He 'looked up to heaven' when curing the dumb man, and when blessing the loaves for the Five Thousand.

*Actions.*

A special memory was the occasion when he had a rebuke for Peter and his brethren, who were disputing about precedence, and when he entered the house and '*sat down*' before addressing them, and asked them what they had been discussing. They were afraid to say. And 'he took a child in his arms'[2] . . . What little touches are added to that scene at the treasury,[3] where Luke has merely ' Jesus looking up saw' the people casting gifts into the treasury, while Mark says so graphically ' Jesus *having sat down opposite the treasury* was *watching how* . . .' And the coins, he points out, were copper or brass, and the rich would need to 'cast in many' to make a decent gift. They were the current coin used by the Jews without the idolatrous symbol of the Romans engraved on them. Luke has simply 'gifts'. Again, when the chief priests challenged Jesus,[4] Jesus '*was walking about* the Temple', where Luke says 'as he taught in the Temple', and Matthew 'when he had come into the Temple'. For one action that Mark alone records special gratitude is due; he not only records the *indignation* of Jesus, when

---

[1] Luke omits 'with anger' but keeps the words 'looked round' and 'grieved'.
[2] ix. 33-7.      [3] xii. 41-4.      [4] xi. 27.

children were kept from him, but that he 'took them up in his arms' to bless them. Both the action and the feeling have been refined out of the later versions of Matthew and Luke.

### The Doings of the Crowd.

Nor does Jesus monopolize the observer's attention. His eye seems to pass to the patients and to the crowd. He remembers Jesus calling the crowd to him for a special warning or explanation, or the crowd sitting round about him; and Mark thinks these details worth mentioning. Now the crowd, by its pressure, makes Jesus keep a boat ready by the shore, and on one occasion teach from it sitting (iii. 9, iv. 1); now it hurries round the lake, when it sees Jesus going off in the boat, and forestalls his desire for retirement (vi. 33: Luke says simply, 'it followed him'); now it rushes to get near him to touch him for their plagues (iii. 9 f.), or presses into the house and interrupts his meals, whereupon the family of Jesus questions his sanity, a usual attitude of philistines to genius, and Scribes, who had 'come down from Jerusalem' to investigate, accused him of being an agent of Satan (iii. 22). This accusation Luke says was made by some of the crowd, but Mark is particular to state by which section, as he also names all the districts from which the crowd had collected, in fact from the whole length of Palestine, following him, when the hostility of the scribes and Herodians caused him to withdraw from his head-quarters (iii. 7).

Usually Jesus took his patients away from the crowd to heal them, as is duly noted, but on one occasion the record describes the crowd's interest in the case. 'A *good number* of people' (Gk. ὄχλος ἱκανός) was following Jesus, when a blind man, sitting begging at the roadside, called after him as the Son of David. Mark records his name, the crowd's fussy attempt to silence him, and the brief dialogue between Jesus, the crowd, and the man. 'Call him', says Jesus to the crowd. 'Cheer up. He is calling you', says the crowd to the man, and he 'throws away his cloak' in his eagerness, and 'jumps up', and is cured. The scene is ready for 'filming'.[1]

[1] x. 46-52.

A good example of this 'moving picture' is the account of 'the great refusal'.

Luke [1] has the section that occurs in Mark practically as it stands, but where he shortens it, he does so by leaving out just the graphic touches that belong to the *setting* of the story, the local colour and the drama. These are:

> '*Jesus was starting out on a journey.* A man *ran up,* and *kneeled before him.* After his avowal that he has kept the law, Jesus *looking upon* him *loved him.* The man's face at the saying of Jesus *clouded over,* and he *went away* grieved. Jesus then *looked round about,* a disappointed look at his followers, as the young man withdrew, "How hardly shall they that have riches enter into the kingdom of God!" Their *astonished* look leads him to repeat the words "*Children,* how hard it is to enter into the Kingdom of God."[2] And they were *astonished out of measure.*'

Six little actions and changes of expression have by Luke been refined out of the first official narrative. They are exactly the details that the eye-witness must give, because he saw them with the rest and he cannot help mentioning them. Every detail is precious that he remembers. The next narrator at second hand lightly omits details that do not affect the point of the story. Matthew's narrative of this incident shows a different kind of refining process:

> 'Good Master, what shall I do . . . ?' 'Why callest thou me good?' becomes 'Master, what good thing shall I do . . . ?' 'Why speakest thou to me about the good?'

This alteration reflects the mind of the later teachers or transcribers, who thought it dangerous to teach converts that Jesus rejected the title 'good'. They need not have been anxious. Jesus was only checking what we call 'gush', as he habitually did. He objected to complimentary titles carelessly offered. 'Not every one that saith to me, Lord, Lord . . .'

### The Words of Jesus.

In this episode the remark repeated to the disciples and introduced by 'Children' brings us to our next point, for this earliest

---

[1] Luke xviii. 18–27.

[2] Mark x. 17–22 (omitting the words 'for them that trust in riches' which are not in the best MSS.).

tradition of our Lord treasures not only his expressive looks and glances but his actual words.

Both Luke and Matthew in their editions have left out the striking 'Listen!', the first word of the address from the boat, with which Jesus prefaced the parable of the Sower.[1] In the miracles, especially, the word of command is given, 'Be muzzled' (silent) to the lunatic,[2] and again, 'Be silent, be muzzled' ('Peace, be still') to the storm, while Luke and Matthew say simply 'he rebuked the sea'.[3] The word, colloquial as it is, is probably a close rendering of the actual Aramaic word used by Jesus, for sometimes this Aramaic word is given, and explained in Greek, 'Taleitha, Koum', 'which is', says Mark, 'Maiden, arise'; or, to the dumb man, 'Ephphatha', 'that is, Be opened'.[4] Again we have, 'Deaf and dumb spirit, I charge thee, come out of him, and enter no more into him'.[5] For the words to the Syrophoenician woman, '*For this saying* go thy way, the devil is gone out of thy daughter',[6] Matthew substitutes more theological language, 'O woman, great is thy faith; be it unto thee as thou wilt',[7] but Mark preserves the note of pleasure that Jesus took in the woman's clever reply.

Whenever there is any difference in the synoptists in quoting the sayings of Jesus, we may expect that Mark's version is nearest to the original tradition. For instance, in the parable of the Sower[8] Mark closes with 'Some fell on good ground and bare fruit, some thirty, some sixty, and some a hundredfold'. Luke, though using the same account, shortens this to 'a hundredfold'; Matthew inverts the order. Both lose the effect of the 'crescendo', which we may be sure from his other sayings and parables Jesus understood and used. Again, when his brethren sent him a message through the crowd that 'was sitting about him', Jesus, says Mark, looked about on 'those that sat

[1] Mark iv. 3; Matt. xiii. 3; Luke viii. 4. Cf. Mark vii. 14: 'Listen, all of you, and understand.'
[2] Mark i. 25.
[3] Mark iv. 39; Matt. viii. 26; Luke viii. 24.
[4] Mark vii. 34. Cf. Turner, *Mark*, p. 76, S.P.C.K., Commentary. 'The actual Aramaic word with which our Lord accomplished the miracle impressed itself on the memory of the hearers.'
[5] ix. 25.                     [6] vii. 30.
[7] Matt. xv. 28.              [8] Mark iv. 8.

D

round about him' and said, 'Behold my mother and my brothers.' The look and the phrase are omitted by Luke, and Matthew applies the words to the disciples only. But Jesus called the *crowd* brothers.[1] The tendency of Matthew and Luke to shorten or omit dialogue has been mentioned; Mark, like the Old Testament narrators, found direct speech most economical in the end and richest in its effect.

If we have to thank Mark's Gospel for this vivid first-hand impression of Jesus the Man, his looks and gestures, his wonder, grief, and indignation, sitting in the boat teaching, asleep on a pillow in the ship's stern, walking round the Temple taking in the scene, watching the gifts dropping into the Temple box, taking up children in his arms—as man, not knowing the time of his second coming, feeling the need of prayer and solitude, suffering agony in the garden—as man again, unable to give seats in Heaven to his personal friends,[2] yet we have also to acknowledge the convincing picture that Mark presents of his superhuman works. For the energy and power of the Son of God are just as vigorously depicted.

### The Power of Jesus as the Son of God.

The style of Mark, its vigour and rapidity, and even his diction, help the impression of power moving among men. 'It belongs to the genius of this gospel that it is distinctively the gospel of action.'[3] 

The preface, brief as it is, stresses this power of Jesus; John said, 'There cometh one *mightier* than I.' And the very first chapter plunges us into the heart of the matter. (Mark's favourite word 'immediately', which occurs ten times in this chapter, heightens the impression of compelling force.) Specimens of his power are given over every kind of disease, leprosy, paralysis, deafness, blindness, and even over death itself. He calms the storm, and walks on the sea. Twice he multiplies bread. He claims power to forgive sins, the special prerogative of God. He claims power over the sabbath, modifying the

---

[1] iii. 31–5.  [2] x. 40.
[3] Hastings, l. c. See p. 12 note.

commandment, and he abolishes the tradition of defilement.
All is told without comment, but the compelling effect upon
the crowd and the disciples is shown. The wonder of it all is
conveyed to us by the impression made upon *them*—the crowd's
confidence that his touch will heal, their pressure driving him
into the boat, their invasion of his lodgings, so that they 'had
scarce room to stand or sit, or leisure even to eat', their awe
and wonder, the marvelling even of the Pharisees at his skilful
reply, the awe of him that fell on all his enemies. The disciples
are equally affected with fear and sore amazement, with terror
when they see him on the water, with astonishment when he
calms the storm, 'What manner of man is this?'

The serenity and the majesty with which this power was
exercised are conveyed by the terse phrases with which Mark
reports the commands of Jesus, sometimes in the common
idiom of the countryside. 'I will. Be thou clean.' 'Son, thy
sins be forgiven thee.' 'Daughter, thy faith hath saved thee.
Go in peace', to the trembling woman. Calmly he soothes the
violent maniac with a question, 'What is thy name?' Nothing
conveys the sense of power better than the words to the storm,
and the next phrases of Mark at his briefest, 'Peace; be still',[1]
and there was *a great calm*. And he said to them, 'Why are ye
timid? Have ye not yet faith?' This passage has made us
see Christ more vividly than any other, 'in the stern asleep on
the cushion', the tired son of Man, and 'Peace; be still', the
majestic son of God. How calmly he accepts the confession of
Peter, 'thou art the Christ ...', the truth to which the centurion
bears witness at the cross.

His greatness forbids familiarity, 'they were afraid to ask
him', as he walked before the disciples in the way. And note
the significant comments of the people on his miracles, as reported by Mark and Luke. 'He hath done all things well', they
say in Mark; their attention is upon Jesus. 'They glorified the
God of Israel', says Luke, not 'they glorified Jesus'. Luke's
version represents the crowd's afterthought. Mark gives their
first impression, that of the power of Jesus himself.

[1] Or more literally 'Silence; be muzzled', a colloquialism. So also to the man
with the unclean spirit (i. 25).

It is this superhuman power, rather than his teaching or his purity of life that is the main interest in this gospel. It was left to Luke to bring out the connexion between the power and the purity, in his account of the draught of fishes, where Peter says, under the effect of the powerful miracle, 'Depart from me, for I am a *sinful* man, O Lord.'

### The Nature of Mark's Realism.

In admiring the realism of Mark, we are not crediting him with the realistic power of a novelist, who has also to imagine his scenes and dialogues. We are crediting him, and his informants, with the apt Jewish memory which all Jewish disciples sought to cultivate, according to their saying: 'The good disciple is like a cistern, built of concrete, which does not lose one drop.' The realistic power of one who invents his situations and persons, and makes them real to his readers, was not a faculty of the Jew of the first century, and if Mark had been artist enough to invent and make real the person of Christ, his art, one may expect, would have shown itself also in his style, which happens to have little literary skill or grace.[1]

### Picture of the Twelve.

The picture of the disciples is equally faithful and human. The lines in their portraiture preserved by Mark are often smoothed out by Matthew and Luke, as a concession to those who wished to exalt the persons of the Twelve, and thought the mention of their failings derogatory. From Mark one could gather that the Apostles themselves admitted these failings. 'How dull we were! the simplest parable was beyond us then.' 'Know you not this parable?' says Jesus. 'Then how will you know all parables?'[2] Again, 'So *you* don't understand either

---

[1] Quoted by Gore, *Belief in God*, p. 192, who points out that even a modern novelist 'would describe for us ordinary human nature. He would not succeed in producing out of his imagination a lifelike image of so supernaturally conceived a person as Jesus'. Ibid. 190. See also prefatory note, *supra*.

[2] iv. 13.

(what defiles man and what does not)?'[1] The proper inference about Jesus from the feeding of the Five Thousand they were very slow to draw. They could worry soon after about having no bread for themselves.[2] 'Why are you discussing being without bread?' Here Jesus was most insistent, because it was a vital lesson he wished them to learn, to trust him present or absent, and the miracle of the loaves was so obvious an object lesson even for men of ordinary grasp. And so we get, 'Don't you see? Don't you understand even yet? Are you still dull of heart? You have eyes. Do you not see? You have ears. Do you not hear? And don't you remember how many baskets you took up?' Then follows a catechizing about the two miracles. Then 'Don't you understand now?'

When Jesus walked on the sea, they still did not grasp what he was, for 'their heart was dull'.[3] When he foretold his resurrection, they 'questioned what it meant', and they 'did not understand what he said, but were afraid to ask him', and soon after were arguing about precedence, and were rebuked by Jesus. Miracles of course were not easy to grasp, and it was natural that the disciples should only learn from them very gradually. But it is a great feature of Mark's account that it dwells frankly on this dullness of the Twelve, which they themselves could look back upon with humility, but which their successors perhaps thought it unwise or unnecessary to put before converts. Mark makes the disciples 'abnormally stupid', say some critics. But it may be said that the happenings were abnormal, the personality of their Master was abnormal, and the spiritual lessons they were learning abnormally difficult.

The time spent by Jesus in training the disciples to take his place has been shown at length by Latham in his *Pastor Pastorum*. It is in Mark that we find most hints of this, and it has been called the disciples' gospel. 'To the crowd he spoke in parables . . . but when they were alone, he expounded all things to his disciples.'[4] Sometimes the disciples were questioned and attacked behind the Master's back, and Jesus answers for them.[5] They report to him after their first mission: 'They

[1] vii. 18.  [2] viii. 14.  [3] vi. 52.
[4] iv. 34.  [5] ii. 16, 18.

gathered together to Jesus and told him all things, what they had done, and what they had taught.' [1] He then invites them to take a period of rest with him.

Their early morning search for him, already mentioned,[2] the rebuke they suffer for hindering children being brought to Jesus,[3] are two more of a number of details which give the disciples' point of view or experience, 'toiling in rowing', 'hungry in the cornfield', 'indignant with James and John', for their ambitious request, or asking questions about their own prospects, 'Master, we have left all, What shall we have therefore?', and reminding their Master of the late hour, when he had been speaking to the multitude, and asking him to dismiss them.

A special word Mark uses suggests that Jesus had some difficulty even with his disciples on this last occasion, when the miracle had inspired the crowd with the idea of making him king, as we learn from John. By using the word 'constrained', 'he *constrained* his disciples to take boat . . .', Mark suggests that Jesus feared the Twelve might seize upon this erroneous idea of 'the Kingdom', and that he hurried them off the scene, and then calmed the multitude himself.[4]

*Movements of Jesus.*

There is the same intimate interest in the *movements* of Jesus, which are so frequently referred to in Mark. It is in the order of these movements that Mark's authority seems to have recalled his impressions, and so gives us an outline of part of the ministry. They receive more attention in this Gospel than in Luke's. The acts and sayings of our Lord are of general interest. But his many withdrawals into privacy could only interest those who shared them. To the disciples they were as important as the public ministry, and Jesus himself thought them so for the purpose of training them. Here then is further private domestic detail of the programme followed. First there is the tour of the country on all sides from the base at Capernaum,

---

[1] vi. 30.          [2] i. 36.          [3] x. 14.
[4] vi. 45. Cf. John vi. 15; Latham, *Pastor Pastorum*, p. 367; Rawlinson, *Mark*, 89.

with special notice of the work in the synagogues. Hostile encounters are shunned as likely to distract and perplex the disciples, and, on the other hand, popularity that might tax his physical strength in cures. Several times he returns to his base, the cities by the lake, the home of at least five of his band, then he sends out the disciples to experiment themselves, then he gradually withdraws from the public eye, and is more intent on preparing the band for his departure, of which he warns them on three distinct occasions, and the ministry is brought to a close in Jerusalem, where, though previous visits are omitted, the account now gives what happened each day in full and with details.

*Vigour of Mark's Style.*

The first great feature, then, of Mark's Gospel is that the narrative has allowed the personality of Jesus to shine clearly through the facts, and has not obscured or dimmed it; that it has given a graphic intimate picture of our Lord at work with his disciples. There are also features of style which may warrant us in speaking even of the literary genius of this Gospel, for it is marked by the same speed, vigour, and restraint that are characteristic of the story-telling of the Old Testament.

The account of the temptation consists of four graphic strokes in a couple of lines:

> 'he was forty days *in the desert, tempted by Satan,* and was *with the wild beasts,* and *angels ministered unto him.'*[1]

The subjective nature of the temptation is omitted (and that is typical of Mark), but again one objective detail is inserted, which is not in the picture of Luke and Matthew, 'he was with the wild beasts'.

The description of the Scribes is as terse, all done by objective details:

> 'Beware of the Scribes, who like to walk about in long robes, and greetings in the markets, and chief seats in the synagogues, and chief couches at dinner, who eat up widows' houses, and for a show make long prayers. They shall receive a severer judgment.'[2]

[1] i. 13. Mark also has 'the spirit *driveth* him forth', where Matthew and Luke have 'he *was led*'.                [2] xii. 35-40.

The words are the words of Jesus, but Mark, instead of a long series of denunciations, which Matthew has recounted,[1] selects the main objective items and compresses five pictures of the Scribes into one sentence, *in the street* parading their garb, *in the market* using solemn salutations, *in the synagogue* or *the dinner party* pushing rudely forward, and in the Temple or *public places* praying for all to see.

While it finds time for graphic details, as already illustrated, for instance, time to describe Jesus not only as asleep in the boat, but in the stern and on the cushion, this narrative uses an economy of words that can compress language like this:

> 'Which is easier, to say to the paralytic, "Thy sins are for-given", or to tell him, "Rise, take up thy bed and walk?" *But that you may know* that the Son of Man hath power on earth to forgive sins'—*he saith to the paralytic*—'I say unto thee, "Rise, take up thy bed and go home".'[2]

Here Jesus in the same sentence addresses two sets of people in the second person, 'But that *you* (Pharisees) may know ... I say unto *thee* ... (the paralytic)', but the dramatic direct speech to both sets of people is preserved without any confusion by a slight stage direction ('he saith to the paralytic').

Nothing could be simpler than the Greek of 'What is this? A new teaching?'[3] or 'Whom say ye that I am?',[3] nothing briefer than, 'Lord, I believe, help thou mine unbelief', of which the shortest paraphrase is 'Help me out of my despair, though my faith is weak.'[4]

The connexion of the sentences is of the simplest, almost in-variably by the use of 'and'. Participles, which are a part of speech used to save time and words, and which leave the main thought of a paragraph for the one main verb to deal with, are used by Mark in abundance and in quick succession:

> 'And there was a certain woman *having* an issue of blood for twelve years, and *having spent* all that she had, and *been benefited* nothing, but rather (*having*) *grown* worse, *having heard* of Jesus, *coming* in the crowd behind she touched his garment.'[5]

Such a sequence of participles and such sequences of sentences joined by 'and' are condemned as monotonous, and Mark uses

---

[1] Matt. xxiii.    [2] ii. 10.    [3] i. 27 (R.V.), viii. 29.
[4] ix. 24.    [5] v. 25–28.

faulty, irregular constructions, his Greek style being the most ungrammatical in the New Testament except that of Revelation. As many of these are eliminated in a translation, they do not trouble the English reader. Latin expressions are also imported to reinforce his limited Greek vocabulary. But the style is certainly vigorous, that of one who is engrossed with transcribing actions, and thinks more of matter than of form. Brief as he is, he has frequent redundancies, '*At even, when the sun did set*', '*he had need* and *was an hungred*', '*all that she had, even all her living*'.[1] But some of these seem due to a desire to add vigour and life to the story:

'he began to *publish it much* and *to blaze abroad* the matter.'
'the (good) seed *sprang up* and *increased* and *brought forth* ...'
'I *know not neither understand I* what thou sayest',

which well renders the emphatic denial of Peter.[2]

It is tempting to draw a relation between the nature of this Gospel and the character of St. Peter. It is the Gospel of action, and Peter was the disciple of action, who tried walking on the water, who went straight into the tomb, who jumped into the sea to get to the risen Master.[3] It is the Gospel of one whose interest was lively and quick, and Peter was of quick intuition, rather than a thoughtful reasoner. 'Blessed art thou, Simon,' commended a flash of intuition, which told him what 'flesh and blood' were slow to grasp.[4] It is the Gospel of one who was emphatic, and Peter before and at his denial was essentially this. Finally it is objective, that is, the account of one who *saw* things, rather than of a philosopher who conceives ideas.

NOTE. For the monotonous use of 'and' see x. 33 ff. In the last twelve verses of the Gospel, believed to be an addition by a later editor, a different Greek particle for 'and' is preferred. For a typical irregular construction see ix. 20: 'And they brought him to (Jesus), and *having seen* him, immediately the spirit tare him (the boy), and falling on the ground *he* wallowed foaming.' Here Mark in his haste leaves one particle in the air ('having seen'), and changes his subject without having noted the change with a pronoun, as is the rule in good Greek, a thing which people telling a story often do, assuming that the audience will understand in spite of the quick transition.

---

[1] i. 32, ii. 25, xii. 44. Cf. also xiv. 30, xvi. 2.
[2] i. 45, iv. 8, xiv. 68.     [3] John xxi.     [4] Matt. xvi. 17.

# III

## ST. MATTHEW'S GOSPEL

Excellence of editorship—the Sermon on the Mount—collections of matter of the same type—impressiveness and force of sayings of Jesus preserved in St. Matthew—influence of Old Testament—special features—Hebrew outlook.

WHEN we turn to St. Matthew, we find the simple vivid memoirs have undergone a change. They have been re-arranged, expanded, and to some extent re-edited. Some suggest that the re-arrangement was to make sections suitable for special readings or instruction at certain times. There appear to be seven such sections, five of them clearly marked by the phrase, 'And it came to pass, when Jesus had ended all these sayings . . .'

We miss in this gospel many of the signs of the eyewitness, for the narrative portion depends on Mark, though the writer edits Mark's material freely, re-writing it more smoothly, and even interpolating and cutting out many picturesque details. The other material, mainly a collection of discourses which may have been edited by the Apostle Matthew (and a version of which was used by Luke), is fitted into the Marcan narrative along with additional matter by a later compiler. This is at present the most widely accepted view. The result is that, though some of the matter is new, there is not such a striking difference between it and St. Mark's Gospel, as that presented by Luke's and John's with their large amount of entirely new material.

If then we look for literary excellence in this Gospel, apart from that of the words of Jesus himself, it will be the excellence of *editorship*. There is an obvious way of estimating this. Imagine the Gospel without the Sermon on the Mount. Luke has a shorter sermon that is in some particulars identified with it. Almost certainly Matthew's Sermon on the Mount contains matter delivered on other occasions, and Matthew made a collection of sayings like his collection of parables in chapter xiii, and the charge to the Twelve in chapter x. No doubt it comprises some special nucleus, which has been expanded by similar material connected with other occasions.[1] If so, it was a mark of genius on the part of the editor, who thus expanded a genuine talk of Jesus, delivered on a mountain-side, into this great manifesto, an epitome of Christ's teaching and the Christians' book of reference; who set this manifesto right at the beginning of the ministry, with its striking opening, the Beatitudes, and its equally effective ending, no doubt recalling the actual art of Jesus. We cannot think of the New Testament or indeed of Christianity at all without this Sermon on the Mount.

### The Sermon on the Mount.

'And seeing the multitudes, he went up into a mountain, and when he was seated, his disciples came unto him, and he *opened his mouth and taught them*, saying . . .'

The stage is set quickly and simply as usual in these Gospel narratives, and the sermon is linked to the previous chapter.

The next ten verses with their nine blessings and the command to 'rejoice and be exceeding glad' are the most revolutionary declaration the world has ever heard. Luke has only four blessings (on the poor, the mourners, the hungry, and the reviled), and then four corresponding 'woes', to the rich, &c., and the effect is greatly lost. But he, too, puts them at the beginning of the sermon, and evidently they formed the striking beginning. But Matthew, in keeping the nine blessings, which include the meek, the merciful, the pure in heart, and the peacemakers, gives a greater effect to the crescendo and the climax in vv. 11 and 12, actual hardships of persecution, reviling and slander 'for my sake'. The great personal claim of Jesus comes in as a surprise in this last phrase. It must have been a greater surprise to the crowd.

### Collections of Matter.

It is a real convenience to the reader to have a number of miracles brought together in chapters viii and ix, and a collection of parables in chapter xiii. Another chapter (xviii) offers

[1] Luke confirms this, but says that Jesus came down to a level place to deliver the address, after calling the disciples.

a fairly well connected talk on offences and forgiveness, illustrated by suitable parables. A specially skilful combination of matter is that of chapter xxi. 12 to chapter xxiii. 39, which brings out the full tragedy and pathos of the struggle between Jesus and the religious leaders of the Jews in their Holy City. In order, we have the challenge which Jesus offers by cleansing the Temple, the fig-tree incident as emblematic of the Jewish people's condemnation, the counter-challenge of the Pharisees to Jesus, checked by his counter-question, and the three parables following to complete their discomfiture (the Two Sons, the Vineyard, and the Wedding Feast). Then come the further attacks of the Pharisees, the Herodians, and the Sadducees, and the question of Jesus, 'What think ye of Christ?', again reducing them to silence. Then are placed the terrible denunciations of the Pharisees at great length, most impressive with their refrain, 'Woe unto you, Scribes and Pharisees, hypocrites!...' The section closes with the beautiful lament over Jerusalem, which Luke puts in another setting, but Matthew welds very happily with xxiii. 31–6, 'Ye are the children of them which killed the prophets'...; 'upon you shall come all the righteous blood...; all these things shall come upon this generation . . .'

> 'O Jerusalem, Jerusalem, that killest the prophets, . . .
> Your house is left unto you desolate . . .'

The next section shows continuity, too. After the charge to the disciples, combining all the sayings appropriate to the occasion, the fall of Jerusalem is foretold and the coming of the Son of Man (ch. xxiv), and then come most appropriately the parables that specially bear on these events, the Foolish Virgins, the Talents, the Sheep and the Goats, though there is nothing to indicate that they were delivered on the same occasion. We must count it a happy thought of the editor to insert them here.

### Prophetic Force of the Sayings of Jesus.

The beauty of the *balance* of the speech of Jesus and the happy effect of the *refrains*, the impressiveness of *repeated* words and phrases—one cannot credit to editing without knowing how far the actual order of the words of Jesus has been preserved in Matthew, but these features, the qualities of the great line of Hebrew prophets, are more in evidence in Matthew than in the other Gospels. Nowhere else do the words of Jesus carry such force and dignity, though in Luke they surpass in grace and tenderness. To quote once more the denunciation of the Pharisees, as an instance of the way in which Matthew presents this feature of our Lord's speech, if we compare it with the denunciation in Luke, we find that Luke gives some of the censure to the Scribes and some to the Pharisees separately, in a different arrangement, but Matthew by repeating the 'Woe unto you . . .' six times, and combining the censures against both, has made one sustained and powerful piece of rhetoric. As Luke's method is to keep intact the verses in the source or authority which he followed, it is thought that the editor of Matthew has here at any rate shown his special skill.

We have to thank Matthew's Gospel for preserving at least one jewel of a saying:

'Come unto me, all ye that labour or are heavy laden, and I will give you rest. Take my yoke upon you and learn of me, and ye shall find rest unto your souls. For my yoke is easy, and my burden is light.' [1]

## Hebrew Outlook.

It is also of interest that in Matthew the *Pharisees are treated with more severity*, women are kept in the background, and *Samaritans* are only mentioned once, and that for nothing creditable, when Jesus tells the disciples *not* to enter their villages. *Widows*, so prominent in Luke, are not mentioned in Matthew, even the widow's mite being omitted. It is suggested that widows were so numerous, and often young, in the early Church, that they were a charge and a difficulty for the Church, but the explanation perhaps is the thoroughly Hebrew outlook in this Gospel, which tells of the birth of Jesus from the man Joseph's standpoint in distinction to Luke's, which tells of it from the woman's point of view; which traces his genealogy to Abraham, when Luke traces it to Adam; which again

[1] xi. 28–30; cf. also xxv. 40.

has the distinctively Jewish title for Christ, 'the Son of David'.

In this Gospel *dreams* are the channel of God's communications instead of visions and angels as in the other Gospels, though the Hebrew belief in angels is prominent in several passages. Five dreams occur in chapters i and ii, while that of Pilate's wife is peculiar to this Gospel.

# IV

## ST. LUKE'S GOSPEL

New features in this Gospel—effect of new matter—new outlook—notice of
women, Samaritans, Publicans—buoyant temperament of St. Luke—the
happiness of Jesus—historical sense and literary gift of St. Luke—his Preface—the story of the birth of Jesus—literary beauties of the story in the
A.V.—modern poems on the same.

IF in a limited degree we could speak of literary genius in Mark
or Matthew's Gospel, we can far more freely attribute it to
Luke for the following reasons: first, because the large amount
of additional matter gives him more scope for its display, as the
Acts too come from his pen; secondly, because the nature of his
new matter, even in the Gospel, gives his work a different com-
plexion; thirdly, because the wider sympathies of Luke, his
particular temperament, and his historical sense affect his work
through many new touches and editorial links. It is these
qualities that make his Gospel most popular with modern
western readers, and in conjunction with his literary gift have
caused the book to be styled by Renan the most beautiful book
in the world's literature.

The persecution of the Scribes and Pharisees, pursuing Jesus
even to Capernaum and threatening to cut off his work prema-
turely, bulks largely in the story of Mark and Matthew. Mark's
second and third chapters are full of it, and Jesus has to leave
the district. It is continued in chapter vii, and again he leaves
the district. In chapter viii there is more opposition, and Jesus
'sighs deeply in spirit', and has to warn his disciples twice about
it (vv. 15 and 31). He finds them troubling the disciples when
he comes down from the mount of transfiguration.[1] In chapter x
we find further 'heckling' and a further warning. Chapters xi
and xii are full of it again, and a third warning of impending
death at the Scribes' hands is given. Chapter xiii forecasts
similar persecution for the disciples, and it casts a shadow of
impending doom over the story of Mark and Matthew. The
story of the birth of Jesus in Matthew is clouded in the same

[1] ix. 14.

way by the murder of the children of Bethlehem and the flight into Egypt.

*Effect of New Matter.*

The new material that Luke has gleaned has quite changed the spirit of the drama. The peaceful prelude of the first two chapters, the beautiful picture of the countryside and of the simple piety of the people, the fine collection of fresh parables and incidents that make a respite half-way, especially the mission of the Seventy in chapter x, whose success so gladdened the Master, the parable of the Prodigal Son with its joyful ending, and the beautiful closing picture of the walk to Emmaus told at length in chapter xxiv—all these show an editor with a new outlook.

*New Outlook of Luke.*

Mark and Matthew were members of the suffering nation, and to them Jesus is the Man of Sorrows, and the persecution of the Scribes repeats the traditional persecution of the old prophets. Luke belongs to the world outside, and is absorbed in other aspects of Jesus and his message. He is interested, too, in other classes of people, for whom the message was a more joyous thing—shepherds, soldiers, taxgatherers, women and widows and outcasts, and, what were to the Jew real 'outsiders', the Samaritans. His world is of course the non-Jewish world, whose battle the Apostle Paul, his friend, fought so hard to win in the Acts. He sees the Scribes and Pharisees with more sense of proportion, as he views them from the other end of Europe. He can even afford to be more tolerant of them. It is strange how he makes John the Baptist address to *the crowd* words which in Matthew he addresses to the Pharisees, 'O generation of vipers', and on three occasions makes the crowd challenge or cast aspersions on Jesus, when Matthew says it was the Pharisees, who did so.[1] Luke loved humanity, but not the behaviour of rabbles. Three Pharisees in Luke's Gospel ask Jesus to a meal.[2] Pharisees warn Jesus of Herod's designs, and

[1] Luke iii. 7; Matt. iii. 7; Luke xi. 29, xxxi. 14, xii. 54; Matt. xii. 38, ix. 34, xii. 24, xvi. 1.　　[2] vii. 36, xi. 37, xiv. 1.

a Pharisee asks him a genuine question for information.[1]
Though Luke preserves the denunciations of the Pharisees, it
is only in part.

Much matter that would appeal to Jews and not to Gentiles
is omitted, for instance the teaching about the old Law in the
Sermon on the Mount, while the appeals to the Old Testament
are few, and occur chiefly in the sayings of Jesus which Luke
quotes from his authorities. Contrast the constant refrain in
Matthew, 'that it might be fulfilled which was spoken by the
prophet'. Not that Luke was anti-Jewish. Had he been so, he
might well have omitted passages in which observance of the
Jewish Law is commanded.[2]

His attitude to *women* is non-Jewish. He gives them unusual
prominence; he has listened to them, used their accounts of
incidents, and not forgotten the domestic side of the story.
Such a domestic incident of feminine interest as Martha's com-
plaint about Mary, and the mention of women supplying the
household wants of Jesus and his band on their preaching tour,
are peculiar to Luke. What feminine points of view colour the
first two chapters! Their comments on the strange events,
events belonging to their own sphere, their private thoughts;
'the Lord hath taken away my reproach'; 'her neighbours and
cousins rejoiced with her'; 'Mary kept all these things and
pondered them in her heart'; the reminiscence of the lost boy,
and the thoughts it aroused, which once more she kept to herself; Luke would hardly have reported these thoughts unless
he had the story from Mary's lips. It was natural for her to
mention them, but not for any one else. 'His mother said, "Son,
why hast thou dealt so with us? Thy father and I have sought
thee sorrowing"'—surely Mary's own reminiscence. Widows
are mentioned nine times, but only once in Mark, and not in
Matthew at all. Only Luke records Christ's word to the women
on the way to the Cross: 'Daughters of Jerusalem, weep not
for me.' [3]

Mark does not mention *Samaritans*, Matthew mentions them

---

[1] xiii. 31, xvii. 20.
[2] v. 14, xvii. 14, xvi. 29, xviii. 20, and cf. ii. 21, and xviii. 38.
[3] xxiii. 28.

once, John shows the prevalent contempt for them in the bitter taunt of the Jews, 'Say we not wel¹, Thou are a Samaritan, and hast a devil?'¹ But Luke has made them famous by the parable of the Good Samaritan, shows the tenderness of Jesus towards their intolerance,² and in a miracle peculiar to his Gospel records the only grateful leper in ten as a Samaritan. So in the Acts he records the evangelizing of their villages.

So it is with the outcast *Publican*. One of the most delightful episodes is the honour paid to Zacchaeus.

But if one wishes to gauge the specially wide interest and sympathy of Luke, it is worth while to note the account of the mission of John the Baptist in all four Gospels. In describing this event Mark specifies the *localities* influenced by the mission; that is *his* way: 'All the land of Judaea, and all the men of Jerusalem went out. . . .' Matthew adds to this the mention of the *Pharisees and Sadducees* as going out to see the Baptist. As usual, they alone interest him. John adds that there was *an official delegation from Jerusalem* of priests and Levites, but Luke names not only the multitude, but two classes, *publicans* and *soldiers*, their faults and the special advice to them. While all the evangelists quote Isaiah, 'The voice of one crying in the wilderness', only Luke pursues the quotation to the end, '*all flesh* shall see the salvation of God'. Nothing could better illustrate Luke's wide sympathies, that claimed the Gospel for the whole of humanity, than this piece of editorship, and the search for and selection of material that it implies. In things Roman he is always interested, and in fact the whole Gentile world, its governors and officials, is constantly before his mind.³ While therefore of the three hymns which he introduces in his first two chapters, the first, Mary's, is full of *personal* feeling, and the second, that of Zacharias, is full of *national* aspirations, the third, Simeon's, is full of *cosmopolitan* hope:⁴ 'all people' are to share, and 'the Gentiles' to see the light. The first teaching of Jesus, which Luke records, is on the subject of the outside peoples, and the last utterance embraces 'all nations'.⁵

¹ viii. 48.   ² ix. 52.   ³ See Rackham, *Acts*, p. xlv f.
⁴ Wright, *Syn. of the Gospels.*   ⁵ xxiv. 47.

*Temperament of St. Luke.*

Along with this wide sympathy, like a breeze from the outer world blowing into the haunts of Judaism, there goes quite a different temperament, a really joyous one.

Joy is the first note struck; joy is to mark the birth of John the Baptist, 'Thou shalt have *joy and gladness*, and many shall *rejoice* at his birth.' It is the mark of the coming of Christ, and Elizabeth is at once conscious of it when Mary crosses her threshold. Into Mary's mouth is put a song of joy, 'My spirit hath *rejoiced*. . . .' The neighbours' joy is mentioned too, and songs of thanksgiving are put into the mouth of the father Zacharias and of Simeon, when he sees the child Jesus in the Temple. It is to this radiant Luke that we must credit our merry Christmas. The rejoicing in these two chapters was and is its inspiration, and one can hardly imagine Christmas having been ever celebrated but for the watch of the shepherds, the choir of angels, the good tidings of great *joy*, the 'Glory to God in the highest', and the return of the shepherds *glorifying* God. From Mary's first outburst, 'My soul doth magnify . . .', to Simeon's 'Now lettest thou thy servant . . .', it is one long, glad prelude to the coming of the Light of the Gentiles and the Glory of Israel.

A Scotchman and a southerner hearing the news of the armistice after the Great War would no doubt equally have felt satisfaction and wonder, but the southerner's face was far more likely to be wreathed in smiles. The Gospels of Mark and Luke give us a similar impression. Mark's conveys the impression of wonder and amazement and solid satisfaction at the great doings of Jesus, Luke's of an exuberance of smiling happiness. In Mark when Jesus does a miracle, the crowd is 'amazed exceedingly', the disciples 'astonished beyond measure'; in Luke their wonder and that of the healed resolves itself into rejoicing, and they praise and glorify God, even when fear is present.[1] The Seventy returned with *joy*. The *joy* of the Father in heaven and among the Angels over the repentant sinner is emphasized in three parables. Zacchaeus receives Jesus

---

[1] iv. 15; xiii. 13, 17; xvii. 15; xviii. 43; xix. 37; v. 25 f.; vii. 16.

*joyfully.* Even after his Resurrection, when our Lord appeared among them, the disciples believed not for *joy*,[1] and after his ascension they returned to Jerusalem with *great joy* and were continually blessing and praising God. This joy goes on all through the Acts. Luke himself must have radiated gladness.

There is, finally, more of a glow on the face of Jesus himself in Luke's picture. He alone records the happiness that the seventy disciples brought to Jesus. The new parables are particularly cheering ones with their happy endings, the Prodigal Son, the Good Samaritan, Lazarus the beggar comforted, the humble Publican justified at prayer; the friend knocked up at midnight, putting his head out of the window to argue, but brought down by the knocking; the widow sitting on the judge's doorstep, so to speak, till she is heard. Luke has added to his collection of sayings many that dwell on the happiness reserved for his followers, 'Blessed are the eyes that see the things that ye see', 'Blessed are those servants whom the Lord shall find watching', 'Blessed is that servant whom the Lord shall find so doing'; [2] and that delightful 'Fear nor, little flock, it is your Father's good pleasure to give you the kingdom' is one of the jewels that make Luke's collection sparkle. It is as if, when Jesus turned away from the hard, set faces of the religious rulers, his face lit up again as he thought of the experiences and natures of his humbler fellow creatures, and the goodness to be found in the world at large. And it has struck Luke forcibly. No one sees the good and bad in people so well as a doctor. A doctor is rarely a pessimist or a cynic. If Luke, as there is ground for thinking, was a doctor, it is natural that he should have noticed gladly this outlook of the great Physician, which so richly justified his own.

### St. Luke's Historical Sense and Literary Gift.

That other feature of Luke's genius, his historical and literary faculty, will best be shown by a comparison of three passages from the first chapters, two of which passages are entirely his own composition as editor (i. 1–4, ii. 1), while the third he compiled from information that was almost certainly

[1] xxiv. 41.                              [2] x. 23, xii. 37 and 43.

oral (ii. 8–20). They present three aspects of Luke as an author, and at least two distinct styles.

The first is purely literary, a preface to his book:

> '*Forasmuch as* many have undertaken to draw up a narrative about those things that have been fulfilled among us, *even as* they delivered them to us, who from the beginning were eye-witnesses and ministers of the word, IT HAS SEEMED GOOD to me also, *having followed* the course of all things most carefully from the first, to write them down for you in order, most excellent Theophilus, *that you may determine* the certainty of the accounts in which you were instructed.'

Notice first the structure and balance of this sentence, a proper 'classical period', or complex sentence stating facts in logical, that is chronological, order, cause before effect, 'Since many . . ., just as . . ., therefore it seemed good . . .'—ending with a sentence expressing purpose, 'that you may. . .'

It is built up on the main verb in the centre—'it seemed good' —and on one side of this is a causal clause dependent on it, with another sentence in turn depending upon *it*, whose subject again is a participial clause (in English rendered by a relative clause); on the other side of it is a participial clause agreeing with 'me', an infinitive clause expanding the main verb, and a 'final' sentence.

Only an author with a knowledge of classical style could frame a sentence like that; a sentence that keeps the interest of the hearer to the very end, because it is not complete till the last word rounds off the sentence and the sense—a sentence in which contributory ideas are subordinated by the syntax to the chief conclusion, in this case the author's resolve.

The diction is also classical, that is to say (i) exact, and (ii) carefully arranged. (i) The verbs are compounded with pre-positions that give finer shades of meaning; for instance, the word for 'determine' is more than 'know' (as rendered in the A.V. and R.V.), it means 'coming to a judgement', and so 'acknowledge' or 'approve' as Paul uses it (1 Cor. xvi. 18).[1] (ii) The words are arranged with a view to emphasis and rhythm; for instance, (a) the words 'carefully' and 'in order' are in the

---

[1] Cf. Thucydides, i. 70, ii. 65, iii. 57.

Greek put against one another at the end and beginning of their respective clauses (by a figure called Chiasmus); when words of similar or opposite meaning are so placed, they each bring out the strength of the other, like strong men in opposition. (b) Again, whereas we usually open, 'Dear Sir', the person addressed is not even put early in the sentence, but his name is *built into* it by a most happy introduction when the needs of the sense and the sentence demand it and not before, 'unto *thee*, most excellent Theophilus'. Placed where it is, it makes a rhythm preserved even in English, but pleasanter still in Greek after the two previous spondees, 'to write to thee in order, excellent Theophilus'. (c) The last word of the sentence, the crowning word in a classical sentence, not only has the rhythm (in the Greek) which was Cicero's favourite for his closing word, that cadence of a long and a short syllable followed by a spondee, which gives the ear the right sense of finality, a kind of repose after the somewhat strenuous exercise of pursuing the complex sentence; it also drives home the main thought in Luke's mind, and, as the last word, gives it additional emphasis, 'that you may be convinced . . . of their (absolute) certainty' (or 'reliability'). 'I want you to feel absolutely safe about it', as our modern slang would render it.

Moffat's translation seems to lose this effect. After opening in the more formal style '*inasmuch as* a number of writers have *essayed* to draw up a *narrative*', he ends with a staccato effect, 'the solid truth of what you have been taught'. The A.V. is much nearer to the style and balance of the original, and keeps the rhythm better, 'the certainty of the things wherein thou hast *been instructed*'. Moffat's Anglo-Saxon words at the end are more suitable to the rendering of the simple narrative that follows.

The preface then is that of a polished writer.

Take next the prelude of the ministry of John the Baptist in chapter iii. 1:

'Now in the fifteenth year of the reign of Tiberius Caesar, Pontius Pilate being governor of Judaea, and Herod being tetrarch of Galilee, and his brother Philip tetrarch of Ituraea, and of the region of Trachonitis, and Lysanias tetrarch of Abilene,

Annas and Caiaphas being the High Priests, the word of God came unto John. . . .'

Only a historian would have written like this, a man with an orderly mind, giving in a series of clauses duly subordinated to the main verb that is to follow, the names of all the officials of the country round in a particular year, and in order: first the year of the emperor's reign, then the Roman provincial governor, then the princes appointed by Rome, in order of their importance, then the Jewish High Priests, the first counted permanent by the Jews, the second nominated by Rome. This orderly historical mind is evidenced by a hundred other touches in the Gospel and in the Acts.[1]

The number of officials, named with an accuracy only possible to one writing in the period that he describes,[2] shows Luke's carefulness to prove that his narrative may be tested by reference to contemporary official records. In chapter ii. 2 in the same way he brings his story of the birth of Jesus into relation with a particular Roman census, 'the *first* census held when Quirinius was governor of Syria', a statement thought to be a mistake till recently, as Quirinius was governor later on, but now confirmed by a newly discovered papyrus, from which it appears he was governor twice or had a predecessor of the same name.

The Roman system was a great one, and destined to last for centuries, and when Luke wrote this sentence, he defied critics for ever to divorce his account from secular history and turn it into a romance of remote Judaea. As he reports in the words of Paul, in the Acts, 'this thing was not done in a corner'. Judaea might be distant, but the Roman magistrate was there, and Jerusalem was much in the Roman eye, as much as Ireland was in ours before the War. In these sentences then, ii. 2 and iii. 1, Luke at the outset claims to be judged as an historian, not a novelist. This is what constitutes the wonder of Luke's Gospel, when those passages are considered along with the following passage:

'There were in the same country shepherds, abiding in the

---

[1] Some of Luke's dates have been disputed, but the point here is that he gives the political background with such care.

[2] Rackham, *Acts* (W.C.), p. xlv.

field, keeping watch over their flocks by night. And lo, the angel of the Lord came upon them, and the glory of the Lord shone round about them, and they were sore afraid. And the angel said unto them, "Fear not; for behold, I bring you good tidings of great joy, which shall be to all people. For unto you is born this day in the city of David a Saviour, which is Christ the Lord . . .""

From Roman officials to angels in the same chapter, almost in the same breath! And this admittedly is a serious history ('I want you to know the absolute reliability, Theophilus'), and Luke is not only a historian, but ranks high among them,[1] not merely a transcriber but a polished writer, as his preface showed, a careful inquirer and an artist at the same time. From such a man, one who would know the difference and weigh it between legend and history, we can take it that these marvels had foundation in fact. Shepherds were scarcely people of sufficient importance to be brought unnecessarily into the account of a King's birth. Mary would vouch for the visit of the shepherds and their report of the mysterious lights and sounds.[2] In what way they were described to Luke, we don't know, but the revelation observes the same limits as the other revelations of the Old and New Testaments, a voice from heaven with a message, and a light round about.

But the language in which Luke has clothed it, is Greek of great simplicity and beauty of rhythm. Luke, in spite of the culture which enabled him to write fine periods, at once falls into the simple Aramaic style suited to the reports of shepherds and Hebrew witnesses. The sentences are simply constructed and the style recalls the Old Testament narrative at its best. In the monosyllabic English the language is still more simple, and for this reason perhaps even more effective, and whether it is this surprising skill of the translators, or the glamour of the anthem strains to which the words have been set, and the associations of Christmas, this passage has come

[1] 'A competent historian' (Gore, New Commentary, S.P.C.K., p. 210), though not, of course, impeccable. Streeter, The Four Gospels, p. 548, pronounces Luke artist rather than historian, but the evidence collected in Rackham's Introduction to the Acts, pp. xliv–xlvii, is sufficient to justify both titles.

[2] See p. 33, and cf. ii. 19: 'Mary kept all these sayings in her heart.' See also the note at the end of this chapter, p. 44.

to be considered one of the most melodious in the New
Testament.

It is a passage in which the rhythms of the A.V. are so sur-
passing. Notice for instance the similar rhythm of:

abídǐng ǐn thĕ fiēld,
the Ángĕl ŏf thĕ Lōrd,
the glóry ŏf thĕ Lōrd,

or again the regular dactylic effect of:

súddenly there was with the *Ángel a múltitude* of the *heávenly*
host. . . .
*glóry to Gód in the* highest.

In these the shorter syllables preponderate, and the stress is
less frequent. As a contrast, the second part of the verse has
more frequent stresses, and long and short syllables alternating,
with an iambic effect:

and théy were sóre afraíd.

or trochaic:

praísing Gód and sáying,

or even spondaic:

on eárth peáce, goodwíll towards mén.

Ver. 9 with its close balance recalls the parallelism of Hebrew
poetry:

And lo, the Angel of the Lord came upon them,
And the glory of the Lord shone round about them.

Notice the crescendo of strong words in ver. 10:

'Behold, I bring you *good* tidings of *great* joy, which shall be
to *all* people,'

the 'leap', as Dr. Walford Davies calls it in musical sounds,
from one emphatic word to another still more so.

Yet again notice the order of words in ver. 11, leading up to
a climax of interest. The A.V. has put 'in the city of David'
earlier in the sentence, not at the end as the Greek does, so that
the facts of the revelation work up to their crowning point:

Unto you—is born—this day—in the city of David—a
*Saviour*—which is *Christ the Lord.*

Itself a lyric in prose, the passage has inspired many lyrics,
from the simple ballad to classical odes. We often turn our eyes

with pleasure from a mountain to its reflection in a lake. The old ballad-writer and Milton in their different ways reflect Luke's anthem: both meditate upon it, one with the aid of a simple simile, the other with the more elaborate and artificial play of fancy and personification. The spirit of the first is closer to Luke:

He came al [all] so still,
   There [where] his Mother was,
As dew in April,
   That falleth on the grass.

He came al so still
   To his Mother's bour [bower]
As dew in April,
   That falleth on the flour [flower].

He came al so still,
   There his Mother lay,
As dew in April
   That falleth on the spray.

Mother and maiden,
   Was never none but she.
Well may such a lady
   Goddes [God's] mother[1] be.'

It was the winter wild,
   While the heavenborn child
All meanly wrapped in the rude manger lies:
   Nature in awe of him,
   Had doffed her gaudy trim,
With her great Master so to sympathise:
It was no season then for her
To wanton with the Sun, her lusty paramour.

   .   .   .   .   .

No war or battle sound
   Was heard the world around;
The idle spear and shield were high uphung;
   The hookèd chariot stood
   Unstained with hostile blood:
The trumpet spake not to the armèd throng:
And kings sat still with awful eye,
As if they surely knew their sovran Lord was by.

   .   .   .   .   .

The shepherds on the lawn
   Or ere the break of dawn
Sat simply chatting in a rustic row;
   Full little thought they than
   That the mighty Pan
Was kindly come to live with them below:
Perhaps their loves or else their sheep
Was all that did their silly thoughts so busy keep.

---

[1] Quoted by Quiller Couch, *Art of Writing*.

When such music sweet
Their hearts and ears did
greet
As never was by mortal fingers
strook,
Divinely warbled voice
Answering the stringèd noise,
As all their souls in blissful rap-
ture took:
The air such pleasure loth to
lose,
With thousand echoes still pro-
longs each heavenly close.

. . . . .

But see! the Virgin blest
Hath laid her Babe to rest.
Time is our tedious song should
here have ending:
Heaven's youngest-teemèd
star
Hath fixed her polished car,
Her sleeping Lord with hand-
maid lamp attending:
And all about the courtly stable
Bright-harnessed Angels sit in
order serviceable.

We have quoted the above verses to show the wide range of imagination and fancy inspired by Luke's simple narrative. Only a few stanzas of Milton's Ode have been given, which he wrote at twenty-one, but each shows the imagination playing upon the simple fact. 'Nature doffs her gaudy trim' in sympathy with the occasion, the air *takes pleasure* in the melodies, the stars attend *as handmaids*. Milton's Ode was pronounced by Hallam the finest in the English language; the ballad, too, has a delicate beauty that would place it high among carols. But both poems are reflections only, and send us back with the greater enjoyment to the clearer outlines of the original:

She . . . laid him in a manger, because there was no room for them in the Inn,
And there were . . . shepherds abiding in the field, keeping watch over their flocks by night.

And lo, the Angel of the Lord came upon them,
And the glory of the Lord shone round about them, and they were sore afraid.

And the Angel said unto them, Fear not: for behold, I bring you good tidings of great joy, which shall be to all people. . . .

And suddenly there was with the Angel a multitude of the heavenly host, praising God and saying,

Glory to God in the highest, and on earth peace, among men of His goodwill.[1]

[1] Dr. Plummer points out the triple balance; glory, peace; in the highest, earth; God, men. (*Commentary on St. Luke*, ii. 14.) Of this Christmas story Gore says: 'All the world loves it. Some consider it beautiful romance and some true history. Our verdict will depend on how far we believe the Spirit of truth "brooded over" the record of the Christian origins, and how far we believe that there was an inventive genius in the earliest Jewish Church capable of an imaginative effort of such a high order.' *New Commentary*, Luke, p. 214.

# V

## ST. JOHN'S GOSPEL

*General appreciation—critical difficulties—literary features—its conception of Christ—composition and style—style of the preface—style of the discourses—the narrative, its preciseness of detail—the dialogues.*

To the average reader of to-day this Gospel, as distinct from the other three, is the Gospel of 'the disciple whom Jesus loved', and of the great phrases which voiced our Lord's claim to be the Bread of Life, the Light of the World, the Good Shepherd, the Resurrection and the Life; it is the Gospel of the miracle of the raising of Lazarus; and, as the Gospel read in church on Good Friday and Easter Day, it is the one in which Pilate showed Jesus to the crowd ('Behold the Man!'), and in which the two disciples are seen running to the Tomb. If he has ever been a mourner, he will remember it for its fourteenth chapter, 'the best thumbed leaf in the cottar's Bible'. More constant readers of the New Testament will have come to appreciate some of the claims made for this book, its 'simplicity, subtlety, sublimity', 'its sublime themes handled with a simple dignity of language',[1] 'that singular beauty of the Johannine picture, which may be easily overlooked in the microscopic scrutiny of details'.[2] 'It holds in equal poise', says another scholar, 'sides of truth which are often placed in opposition to each other', for instance the humanity and the divinity of Jesus, and the individual's relation to God and Saviour on the one hand, and institutional religion on the other.[3] It was especially when meditating on the Gospel of St. John that Wordsworth the poet declared that his creed 'rose up of itself with the ease of an exhalation, yet a fabric of adamant'.[4]

But one who ventures to discuss the literary features of this Gospel must walk warily indeed. At any moment the question may arise whether the qualities under discussion belong to the writer of fact or the writer of a philosophical study, or, again, to

[1] Howard, *The Fourth Gospel in Recent Criticism*, p. 243.
[2] Ibid., p. 235.
[3] Lock, *New Commentary*, St. John, p. 240.
[4] Ibid.

one who is blending history with an interpretation of history. At any point he may fall foul of some critic among the host of commentators whom this Gospel has both delighted and distracted. A recent review of books and articles on the Fourth Gospel in the last thirty years, in English alone, prints a list, confessed to be incomplete, of 109 books and essays, besides articles in magazines, encyclopaedias, and commentaries, and a library of German, French, and American works. The Gospel is well worth all this attention, for those who analyse it rarely fail to add their homage to its genius. Unfortunately the grounds of one scholar's admiration often conflict with those of another scholar's. If after reading the Gospel through you conceive a love for the personality whose authority is claimed for its 'witness', if you say that behind this supreme study of Jesus there must be a great heart and mind, one who must have been intimate with our Lord, and derived from him the necessary inspiration, and that this must surely have been the disciple who 'leaned on his breast at supper', then there are many to deny to the book that authority and who point even to the second century for the author. There are some who will even assert that the 'disciple whom Jesus loved' was an unreal title for an ideal, unhistorical person. If one scholar praised the unity of the book, 'woven without seam' like the garment of Jesus, to this unity another will object that three persons had a hand in its compilation, an oral witness, a writer, and an editor. If one admires the composition of the book as a harmonious whole, a blend of narrative and discourse, the commentators point to sections apparently out of place and needing transposition. The discourses of Jesus in this Gospel, to many scholars so full of the authority of our Lord, are to others the clever composition of a later genius. Where some praise the preciseness of the narrative, and see history in its close detail and circumstantial fact, the evidence of an eyewitness, others say that the writer never meant to write history at all, and that the details are the inventions of romance, the numbers merely symbols, the raising of Lazarus a parable, and the whole an allegory. It need only be added that, to complicate the issues, and make a point of view difficult to achieve, scholars have sometimes changed their minds, and that what Dr. Bacon thought of the authorship in 1910 was the opposite of what he thought in 1900, and Dr. Abbott found in 1917 that 'the Fourth Gospel in spite of its poetic nature', in which he had till then believed, was 'closer to history than he had supposed'. The conservative reaction of 1900–5 in favour of the Apostle's authorship was followed by a sudden revolt from traditional belief in the next decade, but a partial reaction has again set in. Stress is now laid by many [1] on the authority of an eye-witness for the main narrative of the Gospel, and that authority is given with more hesitation as that of the Apostle John. The writer was a disciple of this eyewitness, and one who had him-self seen the Lord, and lived at Ephesus, and wrote the Gospel in his old age. This writer is supposed by some to have been John the Elder.[2] Whoever he is, he seems to be appealing, in xxi. 24, on behalf of the Ephesian elders to the witness of John the Apostle. 'The Gospel', declared Bernard, 'represents faith-fully his (the son of Zebedee's) picture of Jesus Christ and re-produces his teaching.' 'It is the Gospel *according to* St. John, relying in many instances on the reminiscences of the Beloved Disciple.' [3] The study of the literary qualities of the Gospel has led the present writer to emphasize this authority of the original witness, John the Apostle, to see that authority im-printed on both narrative and discourse, to think of him as an old man dictating his memories, the specially vivid memories which an old man has of his youth, those sayings and doings of Jesus which, moreover, have been the subject of his meditations and preaching and teaching for a generation—to think of him as dictating these memories to a disciple who translates them into Greek, and edits them, and adds the special memoir of chapter xxi, also heard from the same witness. Not all the evidence he has been able to read, much of it extremely fanci-ful, has shaken this impression, but rather confirmed it.

[1] Scott Holland, *The Fourth Gospel* (1920); Armitage Robinson, *Historical character of the Fourth Gospel* (2nd edition, 1929); Dr. Nolloth, *The Fourth Evangelist* (1925); Lock and Harris, *New Commentary* (1928); Bernard, *International Critical Commentary* (Clark, 1927); Howard, *The Fourth Gospel in Recent Criticism* (1931).
[2] Bernard, and Streeter in *The Four Gospels* (1924).    [3] *I.C.C.*, p. xciv.

The matter of this Gospel is in a large measure supplementary to that of the Synoptic Gospels. In Mark we have the ministry in Galilee, in John more especially the ministry in Jerusalem. In the Synoptists we find short sayings, and talks, which with one or two exceptions are very brief, in John longer talks, usually in the form of conversations. In the Synoptists we get parables, in John such allegories as that of the Good Shepherd. John develops the hints of the Synoptists, and emphasizes what they lightly touch upon, especially in respect of the claims made by Jesus. 'What is implicit in the Synoptists is explicit in John . . . a clearer statement evoked by the lapse of time, and by the needs of the time.' [1]

The Synoptists record very briefly the call of the first disciples. John gives a fuller and more intimate account of it. They mention that Jesus prayed, and Matthew gives a prayer a few verses long. John records a prayer that fills a chapter. They record miracles briefly. John records special miracles at length with circumstantial accounts of the feelings that they roused and the talk that they caused, and he also relates the crowning miracle of the raising of Lazarus. The appearances of Jesus after the Resurrection, briefly recounted in Matthew, are told circumstantially in John with conversations. The Synoptists mention the unbelief of the disciples. John gives the supreme instance of it, that of Thomas, and again with details and conversation. They state the claims made by Jesus on one or two occasions, 'Come unto me, ye that are weary . . .' (Matthew) ; 'Art thou the Christ ?' 'I am' (Mark). John gives many more instances of such direct claims, and a full discussion of these claims with the disciples. Lastly, the book of the Acts has been called the 'Gospel of the Holy Spirit', and without the long talk of Jesus on the Holy Spirit, the Comforter, in John xiv, there would be a serious gap in the history, and his relation to Christ's ministry would be hard to understand.

The most striking literary features of the Fourth Gospel are to be found in its conception of Christ, its style of composition, blending incident and discourse, its precise and circumstantial narrative, and its dialogues.

[1] *I.C.C.*, p. cxxxv.

Its conception of Christ as Christ the Lord, a dominant conception from the first page to the last, is one of the sources of its unity.[1] 'I saw and bare record that this is the Son of God', is the witness of the Baptist. 'We have found the Christ', says Andrew, also in the first chapter, and Nathaniel confesses: 'Master, thou art the Son of God, thou art the King of Israel.' The wonder of the Samaritan woman, 'Is not this the Christ?', and the worship of the Blind Man are followed by the declaration of Martha: 'I believe that thou art the Christ the Son of God.' The original record ends with the worship of Thomas: 'My Lord and my God.' This impression of Christ is subtly conveyed in the talks of Jesus, and his prayer to his Father (ch. xvii). In Mark men are making up their minds about the Son of Man. In John men are judged for unbelief in the Son of God. 'The Synoptists draw a picture of Jesus as viewed by his contemporaries. The Fourth Gospel brings into full view what may not have been clearly discerned at the first.'[2]

The style of composition increases the impression of the book's unity, its appearance of being 'woven without seam', as Strauss said, in spite of certain dislocations of sections in our present text and in spite of the comments interspersed by the evangelist. When Luke turns from his preface to the narrative, his style changes at once, and when he reports the talks of Peter and of Paul, these again have nothing in common with the style of the preface. But it is part of the subtlety of John's style that incident and talk, narrative and editorial comment show the same features and are blended into a unity. The style is one throughout, and what appear to be the evangelist's own comments are so merged with the other matter that it is not always easy to say where they begin and end. 'For God so loved the world . . .' has been attributed to Christ himself, but commentators now see in this verse the beginning of a short commentary of the author or editor upon the reply of Jesus to Nicodemus.[3] Further, the sections of the Gospel are linked

---

[1] Lock, *New Commentary*, St. John's Gospel, speaks of this unity as 'carefully planned . . . the end is in view from the beginning (i. 19, xix. 36) . . . Within this unity two threads intertwine, one of incident, the other of spiritual idea.'

[2] Bernard, *I.C.C.*, p. cxxxv.       [3] iii. 16. Cf. v. 20–9.

together while the links remain concealed to the casual reader. Embedded in the preface are references to John the Baptist,[1] with whose witness the story is going to open,[2] and the message of John the Baptist is in turn linked up with the call of the first disciples,[3] as it is certainly not connected in the Synoptists. With these calls notes of time link up the first miracle recorded: '*The day following* Jesus would go forth into *Galilee* . . .', 'And *the third day* there was a marriage in Cana of *Galilee*.'[4] From the next two miracles, the healing of the lame man, and the feeding of the Five Thousand, arise respectively, quite naturally, the discussions of the authority of Jesus, and of the true Bread of life.[5] Two references to Jesus as the Light of the world prepare the ground for the story of the healing of the blind man, while the raising of Lazarus is linked up with the Triumphal Entry into Jerusalem and with the plot for the arrest of Jesus, and his Passion.[6] If chapters xv and xvi should come immediately after xiii. 30, and, as some think, are misplaced, then the final words of Jesus to his disciples, followed by his prayer to the Father and entry into the Garden, are similarly linked up with his arrest, which immediately follows.[7] With conscious or unconscious art the parts of the story are to this extent 'fused' together.

The qualities of the style are best illustrated by the prologue or preface. It deserves perhaps more than any part of the Gospel the three epithets sometimes applied to John's style, as mentioned above: simple, subtle, sublime. It is not a formal address to the reader like Luke's. It is one that 'introduces us at once into the central mysteries of God's existence, and prepares us for the teaching that is to follow.' It has been called a hymn to the Logos, and the supposed comments of the writer (in vv. 6–9, 12, 13, 15–17) have been detached from the hymn proper.[8]

Simple as it is in diction and phrasing, it digs deep into the mysteries of the Gospel. It is an expansion of 'Jesus was with God, and became flesh to reveal God', but it touches on

(i) the ideas of *Fatherhood and Sonship* being always in God from the beginning,

---

[1] i. 6, 15.    [2] i. 19.    [3] i. 35.    [4] i. 43, ii. 1.    [5] v. 31, viii. 14.
[6] xi. 10, 17, 47.    [7] xiv. 30, 31; xviii. 1.    [8] Bernard, *I.C.C.*, p. cxliv f.

(ii) Christ as the source of *light*,
(iii) God as the source of *life*,
(iv) the mysterious connexion between life and light,
(v) the incarnation of Jesus and his rejection,
(vi) the doctrine of *grace* or 'regeneration', that is, the power, from a belief in Jesus, to become new men and women,
(vii) the doctrine of 'revelation' (as opposed to the modern idea of unaided evolution).

These are the very subjects illustrated in the Gospel itself,[1] so that this fine preface, though no one would be conscious of it as he reads it, takes the place of a dry table of contents, and then moves quietly on to merge in the narrative.

Its simplicity is astonishing. The more profound the thought, the simpler becomes John's language:

'In him was life, and the life was the light of men.'
'The word became flesh, and dwelt among us ("lived as in a tent").'
'Of his fullness have we all received."

Syntax and grammar, as well as diction, contribute to this simplicity. Simple sentences are used, complex ones are rare, and, as in the dialogues, simple forms of verbs are used, rarely verbs compounded with prepositions, which are much commoner in Greek authors. Particles are conspicuously absent. Instead of these and of relative pronouns, repetition of a noun or the mere order of the words makes the connexion clear. This simplicity of language, not a syllable wasted, has a wonderful effect, as in the dialogues.

A study of the verbs and nouns is interesting. How limited is their range and number! The writer plays upon ten nouns, 'word' and 'world' four times each, 'God' six times, 'light' five times, 'darkness', 'life', 'flesh', 'glory', 'man', and 'will' (all repeated), and upon five verbs, 'was', 'became', 'witness', 'receive', 'believe', of which 'was' comes nine times, and 'became' eight times. On this small range of words he builds up this stately paragraph.

[1] (i) as in ch. viii, x. 15–30, xiv. 1–14. (ii) as in ch. ix. 5, xi. 9, 10, xii. 35, xvii. 21. (iii) as in ch. vi, xi. 22–7, xii. 44–50, xvii. 7. (iv) as in ch. viii. 12, xii. 46, 50. (v) as in ch. iii. 16, ix. 35, xi. 27. (vi) as in ch. iii. (vii) as in ch. xvi. 25, xvii. 6.

This repetition of a noun or phrase is the source of the impressiveness, directness, and vigour of John's style. Replace some of these repeated nouns by relative pronouns, and note the weaker effect:

> 'He was in the world, *which* was made by him, but *which* knew him not.'

The impressiveness, the music have gone. Contrast

> 'He was in the world, and the world was made by him, and the world knew him not.'

Or again,

> 'He came unto his own, *who* received him not.'

Then read

> 'He came unto his own, and his own received him not.'

And again,

> 'In him was life, *which* was the light of men, and shineth in darkness, *which* overtook it not.'

Read now

> 'In him was life, and the life was the light of men, and the light shineth in darkness, and the darkness overtook it not.'

Relative pronouns are substitutes to speed up the style, but the essence of John's style is stateliness and simplicity, and it recalls the stateliness of the opening of Genesis. In fact the opening of the Gospel was no doubt suggested by Genesis. Note the striking resemblance of form and thought:

| Gen. i. 1. | John i. 1. |
|---|---|
| '*In the beginning* God *created the heaven and the earth.* . . . | '*In the beginning* was the word; . . . *all things were made by him.* . . . |
| And God said, Let there be *light* . . . and God divided the light from the *darkness.*' | In him was life and the life was the *light* of men, and the light shineth in *darkness.*' |

Simple and transparent as the style is, it is also elusive. In the first place each fresh thought seems to be suggested by a word in the previous sentence, as though the writer had no settled design:

> 'The true light was the one that, coming into the *world*, lighteth every man. In the *world* he was, and the world was made through him, and the world knew him not.'

Then 'world' seems to suggest that part of the world, *his own*
land, where 'his own received him not'. This suggests by contrast others who *did receive* him, and so were able to be made
'*sons* of God'. 'Sonship' suggests *birth*, 'these were *born* not of
*flesh*. . . .' Then, as if 'flesh' had suggested it, the paragraph
concludes 'the Word became *flesh*'. But meanwhile he has
picked up the first idea of all, 'the Word', which he seemed to
have forgotten.

This is a second characteristic of the Evangelist, this habit
of picking up again what seemed a lost thread, and weaving it
in again. Noun echoes noun, and verb echoes verb. This must
be intentional, in order to drive home certain main ideas. It is
done with a quiet persistence that leaves certain outstanding
truths firmly fixed in the reader's mind, as will be seen from
the following example.

i.  1. The Word was with God
    4. . . . and was the *light* of
       men.
                                    6. John came from God (he
                                       was not the *light*)
                                    8. to *bear witness* of the light.

    14. The *Word* was made flesh
        . . . full of *grace and truth*.
                                   15. And John *bare witness* of
                                       him,
                                       'He . . . is *preferred before
                                       me*'.

    17. *Grace and truth* came by
        Jesus Christ.
        (This first mention of
        'Christ' is soon echoed in
        ver. 19.)
                                   19. And this is the *witness* of
                                       John (R.V.) when the Jews
                                       sent to ask him,
                                       'I am not the Christ (cf. "he
                                       was not the light", ver. 8).
                                   27. 'He it is who is *preferred
                                       before me*' (cf. ver. 15).
                                   29. The next day John seeth
                                       Jesus coming, . . . 'This is
                                       he of whom I said, He is
                                       *preferred before me*'.
                                   32. And John bare witness
                                       saying (R.V.) 'I have seen
                                       and have *borne witness* that
                                       this is the Son of God'.

Even in chapter iii, this thread of the narrative is picked up once more, 'Ye yourselves *bear me witness* that I said, "I am not the Christ"' (ver. 28), and a last echo comes in chapter v, this time from Christ's lips, 'Ye sent unto John, and he *bare witness.* . . . He was a burning and a shining lamp, and ye were willing to rejoice in his *light.*' (Cf. above, i. 6.)

This same feature will be found in the talks of Jesus in chapters v, x, and xv, and in the prayer of chapter xvii, this recurrence to certain thoughts, and repetition of certain words to form the thread of the argument.[1]

Before leaving this preface notice that justly famous verse:

'And the Word was made flesh, and dwelt among us (and we beheld his glory, glory as of the only begotten of the Father), full of grace and truth.'

Grace and truth are the two words most adequate to represent Christ, for grace includes love, and these two words present the Gospel from the favourite aspects of Paul and John. But the words in parenthesis are interesting. As the sentence was being framed, did the memory of the vivid personal experience on the mount of Transfiguration stir the speaker and make him glow, so that the end of the sentence had to wait for this precious

[1] St. John v. gives the best example of this, one of the talks of our Lord, the recurring ideas being 'judgment' and 'the dead shall live'. It should be compared with I John iv. 1–10, where the phrase 'of God', contrasted with 'of the world', is a kind of hinge, on which the talk swings from one topic to another. The similarity of the Gospel and of the first Epistle of St. John is well known. Both have the same balance of phrase and sentence, the same quiet and persistent way of recurring to the main points, the same playing upon certain words to form the thread of the argument, the same summing up in phrases remarkable for simplicity and depth of thought. Both Gospel and Epistle dwell upon the same favourite expressions and ideas:

John iii. 36.

'*He that believeth on the Son hath everlasting life, and he that believeth not the Son, shall not see life.*'

I John v. 10–12.

'*He that believeth on the Son* of God, hath the witness in himself. . . . And this is the witness, that God gave us *life eternal,* and this life is in his Son. *He that hath the Son, hath life. He that hath not the Son, hath not life.*'

John iii. 11, 12.

'We speak what we do know and *testify what we have seen.*'

I John i. 2.

'*We have seen and testify.* . . . *What we have seen* and heard, we proclaim.'

memory? 'The Word . . . tabernacled among us. . . .' 'And Peter said, "Let us make three tabernacles".'

When we turn to the narrative of the Gospel, the outstanding feature from a literary point of view is its particularity of detail. It reminds us in this respect of Mark, but with a difference. Mark's account is distinguished by graphic details of action and gesture, especially of Jesus himself. This Gospel gives details rather of time, place, numbers, names of speakers, even where not specially important, and explanatory circumstances.

*Time.*

It carefully notes the historic sequence of events, especially of the incidents which impressed themselves on the memory when Jesus first came upon the scene. Five distinct days are given in the first week of the ministry: 'On the morrow John seeth Jesus coming. . . .'; 'On the morrow John was again standing and two of his disciples . . .'; 'On the morrow Jesus was minded to go forth. . . .'; 'And on the third day (giving time for the journey across country) there was a wedding in Cana. . . .' [1] Whether notes were made at the time, is not known, but they are set down later with the confidence of a diarist.

Special mention is made of the feasts in Jerusalem which Jesus attended, and of special incidents in connexion with them. These visits are not mentioned in Mark, but John carefully distinguishes two earlier visits to the Passover besides the last one, and visits also to the feast of Tabernacles and the feast of Dedication. [2] He connects two great sayings of Jesus with two special days of the feast of Tabernacles. [3]

The first two miracles in Galilee are noted as such, and the first two appearances to the Eleven are also dated. [4] Other days particularized are 'on the morrow' in vi. 22; the anointing of Jesus' feet six days before the Passover, correcting Mark's two days for the same incident; [5] 'on the next day much people' in xii. 12; and the timing of the Last Supper as *before* the

[1] i. 29, 35, 43; ii. 1.
[2] ii. 13, vi. 4, xi. 55; vii. 2, x. 22.
[3] vii. 14, 37.
[4] ii. 11, iv. 54, xx. 19, 26. Cf. also xxi. 14.
[5] xii. 1. Cf. Mark xiv. 1.

Passover, instead of at the Passover itself, as in Mark, apparently a deliberate correction, just as the 'sixth hour' for the
Crucifixion corrects Mark's 'third hour'.[1]  The stay of Jesus at
Capernaum 'not many days' and at Sychar 'two days' are also
noted.[2]  This is a remarkable number of details of time for so
short a narrative, a great deal of which is discourse or dialogue.

*Place.*

Places are inserted with equal deliberation, and even added
at the end of an incident, when not previously specified: 'these
things were done in Bethabara beyond Jordan, where John
was baptizing'; John the Baptist moves to Aenon, *'near to
Salim'*, because there was plenty of water there; Sychar is
'near to the parcel of ground which Jacob gave to Joseph', and
the pool 'called in Hebrew Bethesda' is defined as 'near the
sheepmarket'. These and other instances show anxiety to
make the topography clear to readers Jewish and Gentile.[3]
Especially interesting is the fixing of the place as well as the
time of the long talks of Jesus, most of which revolve upon
some striking saying, as the discourse in v. 17 arises out of the
curing of the infirm man on the Sabbath, and leads up to the
saying, 'the dead shall hear the voice of the Son of God and
live'. For instance, 'These things he said in the synagogue,
teaching at Capernaum' (notable saying, 'I am the Bread of
Life'); 'when the feast was *half-way through*, Jesus went *into the
Temple* and taught. . . . Then cried Jesus *in the Temple*, as he
taught . . .'; 'on the *last* day, the *great day* of the feast (of
Tabernacles), Jesus stood and cried, "If any man thirst, let him
come to me . . ."'; 'these things he spake *in the Treasury*,
teaching *in the Temple*' (notable saying, 'I am the Light of the
world'); 'and it was at Jerusalem, the feast of Dedication, and
it was *winter*. And Jesus was walking *in Solomon's Porch*'
(notable saying, 'I and my Father are one').[4]  By taking such
pains to label the occasion of these speeches the evangelist

---

[1] xviii. 28, xix. 14. Cf. Mark xv. 26.
[2] ii. 12, iv. 40.
[3] i. 28, iii. 28, iv. 5, v. 2.
[4] vi. 59; vii. 14, 28; vii. 37; viii. 20; x. 22.

evidently wished the nucleus of each discourse to be attributed to Jesus.

## Quantity and Measure.

His habit of recording quantities and measures is part of the same exactness, and not to be explained by symbolism or an effort of fiction. When Jesus walked on the sea, Mark says the boat was 'in the middle of the sea', and Matthew says the disciples had rowed '*many* stades', but John has '25 or 30 stades'. At the wedding feast at Cana 'six' waterpots held 'two or three' firkins apiece. At Bethany Mary took '*a pound* of ointment of spikenard, very costly', and the fish caught by the sea of Galilee in the last chapter were 153 'great' fishes, and therefore, as has been suggested, were not put into heaps for division but laid out and counted. In the same incident they 'were not far from the land, but *about* 200 *cubits off*'. Many fanciful interpretations of those 153 fishes have been offered, but though some of the numbers in this Gospel have lent themselves to symbolism, the literary methods of the evangelist do not encourage the idea that they were introduced into the narrative intentionally for that purpose.[1]

## Persons.

There is the same preciseness about persons. 'The Greeks came to Philip, Philip told Andrew, Andrew and Philip told Jesus.'[2] Philip is a Greek name and the passage about the Greek inquirers coming to their fellow Greek would interest the Greeks amongst the evangelist's readers. But in the first enlisted disciples, the group from Bethsaida, the writer seems to have felt a special interest, and members of this group are frequently mentioned. He shows them following Jesus before the formal call of the Twelve. Thus 'Philip was of Bethsaida, the city of Andrew and Peter', 'Philip found Nathaniel', and Philip and Andrew are specially mentioned at the feeding of the Five Thousand.[3] What we know of Thomas, whose character

---

[1] vi. 19, ii. 6, xii. 3, xxi. 8, 11, and see Howard, *Fourth Gospel in Literary Criticism* (1931), Part III, ch. i, and Appendix G.
[2] xii. 21.　　　　　　　　　　　　　　[3] i. 44 f., vi. 5-8.

is so consistently indicated, we get from John; of Judas as keeper of the common purse, and denounced beforehand; of Nathaniel's call and his connexion with Cana, and his interesting contempt for Nazareth, the little neighbouring town.[1] The movements of Peter, his importance as leader and spokesman, come out even more clearly than in Mark, in many a reference showing him singled out by Jesus. Especially interesting are the details about him after the arrest of Jesus.[2] In fact the references to the disciples have that intimate domestic touch which might be expected from the memoirs of John the Apostle. Simon Peter '*nods to him*' as he reclined against Jesus at supper, to ask Jesus whom he meant as his betrayer. And John, '*leaning back* on Jesus' breast said . . .'. The evangelist not only gives the names of those who ask Jesus questions,[3] but knows what was in the disciples' minds, and explains their comments, motives, and ignorance. For instance, the disciples, after seeing the Temple cleansed, recalled the quotation 'the zeal of thine house hath eaten me up', and he notes that they did not at first see the meaning of the Triumphal Entry, or of their Master's warning to Judas.[4] His account of Peter at his denial explains several details of St. Mark. His entry into the palace is explained as due to the 'other disciple's' influence, and this explains his first denial, for the maid questions him on admitting him. Her surprise that he should seek admission would be natural, as ours would be, if we did not know from this Gospel that the other disciple had the requisite influence to secure his safe entry. The third challenge to Peter is also explained as that of a kinsman of the Malchus whom Peter had wounded.[5]

### Explanatory Remarks.

The explanations of small points are another feature of this particularity, as when it is shown that the buffeting of Jesus before the High Priest followed upon the answer which Jesus gave to the High Priest, while the Synoptists mention a buffeting

---

[1] xi. 16, xiv. 5, xx. 24–9; xii. 4–6, vi. 70; i. 46.
[2] xviii. 10, 15–27.     [3] xiii. 36, xiv. 5, 8. Cf. xi. 16.
[4] ii. 17, xii. 16, xiii. 28.     [5] xviii. 26.

by the onlookers generally. Many of these explanations are added apparently as if due to queries that suggested themselves while the memoirs were being dictated or revised: 'He (the ruler of the feast) knew not whence it (the wine) was; but *the servant which drew the water knew.*' 'The Galilaeans received him, having seen what he did at the feast, *for they also went unto the feast.*' '*But there did come other boats from Tiberias*', answering the question, 'How did the crowd get back?'[1] Some of these 'afterthoughts', like the last one, are thought by some critics to be later comments added by editors after the Gospel was finished, since they differ in style from the text. But the majority are John's own comments, explaining words of Jesus, 'But he was speaking about the temple of his body';[2] or a misunderstanding by the Jews, 'they did not know that he spake to them of the Father'; or the motives of the actors, 'this (Judas) said, not because he cared for the poor. . . .' Points are made clear to non-Jewish readers, 'For the Jews have no dealings with the Samaritans', and the identity of persons is noted, 'Judas saith unto him (*not Iscariot*)', 'he (Annas) was father-in-law of Caiaphas'.[3]

To all this particularity of detail add the constant references to the attitude of the audience, as if this witness were keeping his finger, so to speak, on the pulse of the audience of Jesus, and drawing a chart of their belief.

After every striking discourse or miracle he takes stock of its effect on the crowd or the disciples, as on the first disciples,[4] the Samaritans,[5] the Galilaeans,[6] the nobleman,[7] the crowd wanting to make Jesus king,[8] the Jews murmuring,[9] and so on through the Gospel. So he notes, too, the impression the crowd's attitude made upon Jesus, 'he did not trust himself to them'.[10] He watches for new adherents, and has firsthand information about them, men who dared not declare themselves—Nicodemus, Joseph of Arimathaea (both members of the

---

[1] ii. 9, iv. 45, vi. 23.  [2] ii. 21. Cf. vii. 39, xii. 33, xvii. 3.
[3] viii. 27, xii. 6, iv. 9, xiv. 22, xviii. 14, 26.  [4] ii. 11.
[5] iv. 39–41.  [6] iv. 45.
[7] iv. 53.  [8] vi. 14.
[9] vi. 43. A score of instances besides may be collected.
[10] ii. 24.

Sanhedrim), and others of the rulers who 'loved the praise of men more than the praise of God'.[1]

To sum up, we may notice that to almost every incident John contributes some striking additional touch that completes the picture and explains what might have been a difficulty, as when in the feeding of the Five Thousand he says, 'Now there was *much grass* in the place'. Mark says the disciples made the people sit down on the grass, but grass would not be common in those wild parts, and there were 5,000 to be seated. Or again, 'there is *a lad* here' . . . the boy with the loaves is remembered by John as part of the scene. John alone tells us that the loaves were of barley, the cheaper bread of the poor.[2] In the cleansing of the Temple John has the picturesque addition 'when he had made *a scourge of small cords*', which would be a help for driving out the cattle. When Jesus was anointed by Mary, John alone says that 'the house was filled with the scent of the ointment', as if it were the recollection of one who had been present.[3]

The peculiar interest of the narrative of John will be best illustrated by taking a complete incident exhibiting many of the features just mentioned.

### Healing of the Blind Man.

The healing of the blind man in chapter ix and the raising of Lazarus in chapter xi, are a contrast to all the accounts of miracles in the Synoptists. There the actual healing is the sole interest, closing with the briefest comment about the effect on the crowd. To John the miracle is not only a 'sign', it is a light playing upon the faces of the onlookers, and under that light he watches their expressions and judges the feelings they reveal.

All therefore that is said before, during, or after the miracle is important to him.

Among the few miracles he relates, that of the blind man is included because of the exceptional stir it made, and its illustration of Christ's claim to be the Light of the world. The special

[1] iii, vii. 50, xix. 38, xii. 43.
[2] Bernard, *I.C.C.*, vol. i, p. 178; vol. ii, p. 418.

stir arose from two causes; first, the man was blind from birth, not merely a victim to eye-affections caused by the conditions of climate and country; secondly, he was cured on the Sabbath. Very rapidly John shows how differently people's minds work when some great fact bursts upon them. The *disciples* are of the class that, when they see suffering, always want to fix the blame. 'Some one must have sinned.' This was the long-established Jewish notion. The desire to blame somebody and sit in judgment swallows up sympathy. Job's friends came to rake up his past rather than sympathize. Jesus replies to his disciples that the purposes of God are too deep and wide to be solved so simply. It is in the treatment of suffering, the compensations for it, and the healing of it, that the 'works of God' are most clearly shown. The *neighbours* display the usual curiosity, and little else. 'Can it be the same man?' 'How did He do it?' Pure curiosity, no special sympathy, a case for the Pharisees to look into. How will *they* take it? The *Pharisees* represent the prejudiced class that, when a good thing is done or a great man appears, is never satisfied till the goodness or greatness is explained away. They prefer to think that bad men can do good works rather than accept an explanation they don't like. The *parents* come out badly. Frightened out of sympathy for their son when up against society leaders, and adopting a mean-spirited neutrality, they put the responsibility on some one else.

But the *patient* himself is the most interesting study. The growth of his conviction is so realistically traced. He starts with pure sensation—he can see—that is enough for him. 'Whereas I was blind, now I see.' He is hardly able to realize his sudden experience. Then he is interviewed, and has to tell the same tale again and again, pleasant at first, perhaps, afterwards monotonous, so that before the Pharisees the second time he loses patience, 'I have told you already.' Then, to his surprise probably, he is taken along to an inquiry and finds there is apparently some disgrace in recovering his sight. Now for the first time perhaps he really has to face the question, 'What do you think of the man who did it?' He had not worried about him till then. Common sense comes to his

rescue. He must be 'a prophet', a great man. And he holds
on to his solid fact, 'One thing I know . . . I can see.' Their
talk rouses him at last, attempts to shake him only bring more
conviction to him. His eyes begin to open in another sense.
His cure was wonderful. Then so must his benefactor be! The
nagging of the Pharisees provokes him. He suffers for his
obstinate common sense, and is made a social outcast.

Jesus heard of it, 'and when he had found him' (delightful
brevity, implying a search),[1] he gave him what he only gave to
one or two, the truth about himself as Son of God. (The woman
at the well was an outcast, too, John iv. 9, 26.) The question,
"Dost thou believe on the Son of God?"[2] prepares him for the
revelation, and the man now knows where to place this wonderful healer. Only one attitude is possible now, that of worship.
His eyes are really opened at last.

It was not the miracle, it should be noted, that convinced
him. That took him only part of the way. It was the sense of
authority in Jesus himself, as he claimed his allegiance.

Jesus' own comment on the case in the hearing of some
Pharisees gives an artistic finish to the incident. The cure of
the blind man had only emphasized the blindness of the
Pharisees.

So John treats this important case and traces the growth of
belief. He is as careful as Mark when it comes to concrete details, 'he spat on the ground, made clay of the spittle, and
anointed the eyes of the blind man with the clay,[3] and said
unto him, 'Go, wash. . . .' It was his usual way to arouse ex-
pectancy in the patient and then his faith, by some such means,
and give his spirit a chance of responding to the spirit that was
healing. But besides this, in the few miracles he relates, he gives
the whole setting of the miracle, its atmosphere, and the actions
and reactions it produced in the minds of witnesses. Those who
find a difficulty in accepting the miraculous in Mark have a still
greater difficulty to meet in John. So far from the difficulty of
the miracle being hurried over, it is carefully stressed in the

[1] Cf. John i. 43: 'Jesus findeth Philip . . .', and vv. 41, 45.
[2] Or 'Son of Man,' as some read.
[3] Cf. Mark vii. 33, viii. 23.

account itself. It is advertised. The fact of healing is fiercely contested. The conversation about it is as realistic as the concrete details, and as little likely to be invented. Who would have invented clay mixed with spittle for a great man's way of healing? Realistic is the man's attitude, its subtle changes, the growing irritability as the lack of sympathy all round from parents and rulers drives him to desperation. The psychology of the disciples, of the curious crowd, of the parents, of the Pharisees, and of the man himself, is all in keeping. It is a wonderfully faithful picture. And all will admit that it was like our Lord to make an exception in his practice in favour of the lonely outcast, and tell him expressly who he was, as a consolation for the disgrace that his loyalty had brought him on the very day which should have been the happiest of his life.

*Raising of Lazarus.*

Another realistic picture is the account of the raising of Lazarus (ch. xi), the most discussed miracle in the New Testament, but one which is given much dramatic significance in the Gospel itself, as crowning the ministry of Jesus just before his death, and showing Jesus to be 'the Resurrection and the Life'.[1] It is given historical significance, too, as the act which roused the enthusiasm of his followers and caused the Triumphal Entry (which in the other Gospels is not too clearly explained), and finally as the act which drove his enemies to take summary action against him.[2] This evangelist's care for the historical sequence of the incidents of Jesus' life, for cause and effect, in contrast with the more detached memoirs of the Synoptists, deserves to be given full weight as one of the literary features of the Gospel.

In all these senses then the raising of Lazarus is the crowning miracle. But there was not time for it to be widely known, since it was done in the last few weeks and in the privacy of the home at Bethany. It is true many friends of the family were there,[3] the disciples and others, and of course rumour soon noised it abroad, and the Pharisees had a report of it from some

---

[1] xi. 25. Cf. v. 24-8.      [2] xi. 46, 47-53, xii. 19.
[3] xi. 19, 31.

of the Jews present at the time,[1] but the comparative privacy of the miracle, a special act of tenderness to his friends Martha and Mary, and the immediate retirement of Jesus,[2] will account for its omission from the material taught by Peter to his catechists and published by Mark. Bernard accounts for this more simply by supposing that Peter was absent, and gives good reasons. Nor could it have been Jesus' wish that Lazarus should be the object of a pilgrimage and embarrassed by questioning (see xii. 9 for the reason to fear this), but when John's record was published, Lazarus would be dead and the need for silence removed.

The miracle agrees with the rule by which Jesus did all his miracles, that is, its motive was compassion (xi. 3, 5, 33, 35, 36) and the instruction of his disciples (xi. 15).

It is the method of the evangelist that again concerns us; here as elsewhere some of the details affect but little the miracle itself and suggest that love of circumstantial detail which the aged show in telling a story. Note especially ver. 31, which states the place where Jesus met Mary, and indeed all the movements of the sisters, also the comments of the Jews on Mary's leaving the house. These details help to complete the picture. The narrator's method is to describe the position on the stage, so to speak, of the bystanders, to note their movements, and report their remarks, mostly on the case, but sometimes not. 'If the witness is romancing,' says Dr. Garvie, 'he must be one of the most consummate realists in fiction, for so vivid is the impression he makes of reality.'[3]

Here there are two groups, on the one hand Martha and Mary, on the other the Jews who came to offer sympathy. And then there is Jesus himself.

As usual there is a careful explanation of the identity of the sisters, and the affection of Jesus for the family is referred to in the message they send, ver. 3, and emphasized in ver. 5. The first tidings of Jesus draw Martha from the house, Mary

---

[1] xi. 46.   [2] xi. 54.
[3] Cf. Bernard, *I.C.C.*, p. clxxxv: 'The Raising of Lazarus cannot be treated as a mere invention or as a parable. . . . The literary method of John is quite different.'

sits still inside. This detail is consistent with Luke's picture of the two.[1] Martha's talk is given at some length. She goes back, calls Mary out, and gives her Jesus' message to come. She gives it '*secretly*', and Mary rises '*hastily*'. Note these details, not affecting the main issue but filling in the picture. Mary's attitude of deeper worship than Martha's ('fell down at his feet') is again true to the impression which Luke gives of her. Her weeping leads to a general outburst of feeling. Martha has returned in Mary's wake (ver. 39).

The Jews who come to show friendship and sympathy have a great deal of notice. They are with Mary in the room and follow her to the grave. This explains their presence at the miracle. They weep in sympathy with Mary, they remark on Christ's weeping, and wonder why he did not prevent the death of his friend. Their final attitude is stated, some impressed so far as to believe, some only so far as to report to the Pharisees (ver. 45). Information is added of their secret counsels, since they concern the miracle and its sequel.

About Jesus himself John here supplies one of his most illuminating records. In face of a miracle of supreme difficulty, as the reported conversation does not disguise,[2] John carefully indicates the humanity of Jesus and the human limitations of his knowledge, as he waits for the leading of his Father,[3] even though elsewhere, like Mark, he emphasizes his divinity. Thus (ver. 4) when Jesus hears the news of the sickness of Lazarus, he has an intuition how it will end, and result in a great work, but does not see his course of action clearly at once. He seems to have waited for guidance, for 'I am glad I was not there' implies that to some extent he had not felt able to go, while vv. 5, 6 suggest that he would have liked to go to the help of the family. Verses 8 and 16 show there was danger in going, and ver. 54 shows that Jesus needed further time to instruct his disciples, and agrees with x. 40 and xi. 6, and he could not risk arrest till this work was further advanced. 'My hour is not yet come', used several times elsewhere, suggests that Jesus waited for such intimations from his Father.

[1] Luke x. 40–2.      [2] See especially John xi. 39.
[3] Cf. 'I do the works of my Father'.

In this uncertainty he waits for two days, then seems to get the leading he awaited. 'I am going to awaken Lazarus out of his sleep.' The knowledge of the death of Lazarus may have come by the same intimation, or it might have reached him through friends. John's care to show Jesus resigned at having to wait, and then glad because he realizes the possibility of the great work he may do for the disciples' faith, leaves no ground for the idea that he stayed away longer on purpose to let Lazarus die. He 'accepts the delay with resignation, and even finds cause for joy in what had been a sorrow to him, i.e. in not going to his friend's help'.[1]

Besides this dependence upon his Father other signs of his humanity are given. He has to ask where the tomb is, and his human feelings are vividly described, as when, at the sight of the others weeping, he '*straitly charged*' or '*sternly admonished*' his spirit,[2] evidently feeling great emotion and trying to control it. Again he '*was troubled*' just as he was before speaking to the traitor Judas at the Last Supper. Then '*he wept*', which Moffat renders 'burst into tears', which expresses the Greek tense used of a sudden action, but is rather violent for the word used. Lastly, in the actual working of the miracle, 'he *lifted up his eyes*', as man naturally does in prayer. As he prays, he feels the answer and that his power will be sufficient, and utters his thanks aloud 'for the sake of the people that stood by'.[3]

The distress, too, of Jesus near the grave and the loud voice of command suggest perhaps the greater strain upon the

---

[1] Brooke, in Peake's *Commentary*, Gospel of St. John.

[2] So in Matt. ix. 30, Mark i. 43, where it can mean nothing else, and also governs the dative case, '*charged* the leper not to tell any one (ἐνεβριμήσατο). Elsewhere the word means 'indignation', cf. LXX, Lament. ii. 6, where its noun form occurs, and in Aeschylus, *Septem contra Thebes*, l. 461, the verb applies to horses snorting or chafing. 'This description of the agitation of Jesus is not what a romancer would have ventured to set down.'

[3] For this humanity of Jesus coupled with intimate relationship with God, compare xii. 27: 'What am I to say? "Father, save me from this hour?" but for this cause I came unto this hour. Father, glorify thy name.' Compare the struggle in Gethsemane, the spirit of which John brings out here, since the other Gospels had told of Gethsemane, and he avoids overlapping, relating instead this other incident and meditation of Jesus, in which Jesus' humanity questions, though only for a second, the means of accomplishing his mission. Cf. Latham, *Pastor Pastorum*, on the temptation, p. 147 ff.

powers of Jesus in recalling to life Lazarus after four days, when corruption had begun, than in recalling the daughter of Jairus, a few hours dead. To make it clear that it was not a case of trance, John gives Jesus' conversation with the disciples beforehand, 'our friend Lazarus sleepeth', calling death 'sleep' as his followers did later invariably. The disciples reply, 'Lord, if he sleeps, he will recover.' This literalness of the disciples is called dullness in Mark. Then said Jesus plainly, 'Lazarus is dead'.

## Conversations or Dialogues in John's Gospel.

Few chapters are more attractive than the fourth chapter of St. John, the account of the meeting with the woman at the well, perhaps because the homely wants and private conversations of Jesus are mentioned so rarely in the Gospels. Those who have read the charming openings to the Dialogues of Plato may have derived as much pleasure from the glimpses of Socrates caught, so to speak, 'off duty' or in his leisure moments, as from the dialogues themselves.

The memoir in John iv is of a scene vivid in the witness's mind, one that struck him powerfully at the time, one of the early impressions made upon him in the first months of the ministry, and few memoirs seemed more worth preserving, whether for the striking saying that emerged from the conversation, or for the striking incident, the Master talking with a woman, and a Samaritan too; then there was that curious declaration about his 'meat', the simile about the harvest, and his invitation to John and his fellows to share in the harvest of souls. And as their journey was broken for a day or two, by a stay in the neighbouring village, what more natural than that this eager disciple [1] should question the woman about what was said between the Master and herself, for she was quite willing to talk of it (vv. 29, 42).

So after his usual careful explanations of *place*—Jacob's

---

[1] Dr. Sanday, *Criticism of the Fourth Gospel*, p. 86, suggests that John as a youth 'with something of the fidelity of the dog for his master, who does not want to be long out of his sight', did not go with the disciples but 'sat a pace or two away', drinking in the conversation.

Well, Sychar—of *time*—the sixth hour, the heat of noon—and of *circumstances*—the reason for leaving the south, and for the route through Samaria, the weariness of Jesus, and the absence of the disciples in quest of food—John unfolds the eastern scene, in which the water, as usual, was drawn by a woman; the religious feud, Jew against Samaritan; the eastern tradition, the attitude to women (ver. 27). Then in a wonderful précis he reveals his Master's great manner, as he sweeps away all these false restrictions and all the woman's false values, and turns away all her superficial objections by a truth that lifts the subject on to a higher plane, until the great saying that crowns every discourse in this Gospel breaks forth, 'God is a Spirit, and they that worship Him must worship Him in spirit and in truth'. What is the feud of Jew and Samaritan when there is the chance of living water? The woman appeals to the *local* hero, Jacob; but there is better water than Jacob's. Her next remark may have been ironical, 'How nice to have the better water, and not to have to come all that way to draw it!', and when she wants a safer topic than her own private life, she turns the conversation to the notorious religious dispute and the *local* place of worship. Again thwarted, she falls back glibly upon the *conventional*—belief in the Messiah. Even that last excuse for putting off serious thinking is swept away, 'I, that speak unto thee, am he.' And up come the disciples, just when they should, at the climax.

There are other good things in this conversation. 'Thou hast well said, I have no husband. For thou hast had five husbands, and him whom thou now hast, is not thy husband. That saidst thou truly.' Whether John had anything to do with the shaping of this sentence, or heard the actual words, one cannot say, but its tone is just what we might expect from Jesus, the tone of one so great that he can afford not to reprove. 'That saidst thou truly.' It is too fine for any one to call it sarcasm. It is sufficient reproof that he should *know* about it. Then there is the beautiful figure, 'The water that I shall give him shall be in him a well of water springing up into eternal life', and the one in the sequel as he sees the villagers gathering, 'Lift up your eyes and look on the fields, that they are white already for harvest. And he that reapeth receiveth wages, and gathereth fruit unto life eternal, that both he that soweth and he that reapeth may rejoice together.' There is the same vigour and distinction and beauty in all the sayings of Jesus in this conversation that there is in the more detached sayings in the synoptist accounts. 'My *meat* is to do the will of him that sent me.' There is always metaphor in his spontaneous replies, that turned them into proverbs coined and stamped for circulation.[1]

*Style of the Dialogues.*

There is a special directness in these dialogues, and the diction is reduced to its lowest possible terms. In Greek the economy is amazing, and yet it is sound Greek and transparent in meaning. The placing of the verbs saves particles, the verbs themselves are of the simplest, and uncompounded (there is only one compound verb in iv. 1–26), and most of the words are of two or one syllable, a rare thing in a highly inflectional language. Direct speech with the vivid use of the present tense contributes to this. Our own language is monosyllabic, but the condensed effect of this unique Greek may be gauged by the following version of the dialogue with Thomas:

xx. 24. Thomas, one of the twelve, called Didymus, was not with them when Jesus came.
    25. The others therefore said to him, We have seen the Lord. And he said to them,
        Unless I see in his hands the print of the nails, and put my finger into the print of the nails, I will not believe.
    26. And after eight days again his disciples were within, and Thomas with them. Cometh Jesus, *the doors being shut*, and stood in the midst, and said, Peace to you.
    27. Then saith he to Thomas,
        *Bring thy finger here*, and see my hands: And bring thy hand and put it into my side: And be not faithless, but believing.
    28. Thomas answered and said unto him, "*My Lord and my God.*"
    29. Saith Jesus to him,
        Because thou hast seen me, thou hast believed: Blessed those who saw not but believed."

[1] So we have 'Let the dead bury their dead', 'No man having put his hand to the plough and looking back is fit for the kingdom of God'.

Notice that, however brief the evangelist is, he maintains carefully the balanced utterance of Jesus (ver. 27), and uses repetition where the emphatic speech of Thomas demands it. On the other hand notice how immediately the narrative proceeds to the point in ver. 27, and how the reply exactly answers in length and weight to what Thomas said, with speaking effect. 'Brevity challenges the thought of the reader', and in ver. 26 there is not even a 'though' to call attention to the miracle, '(though) the doors were shut, Jesus came in.' Nor does he attempt to describe the feelings of Thomas, but leaves the confusion, rapture, and wonder to his own exclamation, 'My Lord and my God!' which might also indicate prostration or kneeling.

Just as simply he recounts the appearance to Mary at the tomb, and with equal pathos:

(xx. 11–18) 'And Mary was standing at the tomb outside weeping. As therefore she wept, she stooped and looked into the tomb, and sees two angels in white sitting one at the head and one at the feet, where the body of Jesus had lain.

And they say unto her, Woman, why weepest thou?

She saith to them, Because they have taken away my Lord, and I know not where they have laid him.

Saying this she turned herself back and sees Jesus standing, and knew not that it was Jesus.

Jesus saith unto her, Woman, why weepest thou? Whom seekest thou?

She thinking that it is the gardener saith unto him, Sir, if thou hast borne him hence, tell me where thou hast laid him, that I may bear him away.

Jesus saith unto her, *Mary.*

She turneth herself, and saith unto him in Hebrew, Rabboni; which is to say, Master.

Jesus saith to her, Touch me not; for I am not yet ascended unto the Father: but go unto my brethren, and say to them, I ascend unto my Father.'

Mary's gesture is only implied, not expressly stated, namely, the movement to clasp his feet. It is left to the reader's insight. And if this story had been fiction, much praise would have been given to the literary power that let the single word 'Rabboni' express the awe and rapturous recognition of a woman. As it is, that the evangelist should call attention to it as a Hebrew word and take time to explain it for his Greek readers, when he is doing his utmost to condense his matter,[1] is good evidence that he is reporting as exactly as he can an incident as told to himself.

The last dialogue between Jesus and Mary will lose half its beauty if put into reported speech:

> 'Jesus asked her why she wept and whom she was looking for. She, thinking he was the gardener, asked him if he had borne him thence, and to tell her where he had laid him, and she would remove him. Jesus then pronounced her name. She turning called him "Master" . . . Jesus told her not to touch him, because he had not yet ascended to his Father.'

The vivid drama and beauty have gone out of it. The evangelist uses direct speech on every possible occasion. We can get still nearer to the brevity of the original Greek in the following:

> 'And wine having failed, the Mother of Jesus saith to him, "They have no wine." Jesus saith to her, "What (is there) to me and thee (in common), woman? My hour is not yet come."
> 'Saith his Mother to the servants, "Whatever he saith to you, do . . ."
> 'Saith Jesus to them, "Fill the pots with water."'

Yet how carefully he uses the simple, short verbs that he prefers.[2] For instance, four verbs are used for 'see' with different shades of meaning:

i. 29. John *beheld* Jesus coming, and said, '*See* the Lamb of God. . . .'
32. 'I have *observed* the Spirit descending like a dove. . . .'
36. And as he *looked upon* Jesus walking, he saith. . . .

---

[1] The brevity of the account of the appearance to the disciples in the upper room (xx. 19, 20) is explained by referring to Luke xxiv. 36–41, who mentions what John again only implies, that the disciples were at first too afraid to be glad and did not recognize Jesus. Howard, *Fourth Gospel in Recent Criticism* (Sharp, 1931), p. 150, sees signs of severe compression in the description of the successive stages of the trial of Jesus, and remarks on the sudden introduction of the name of Barabbas (xviii. 40), as if the writer could say, 'For details see Mark.'

[2] ii. 3–5. 'Woman' is too harsh. Jesus uses it when saying something gentle and tender, and here it takes the sting out of 'What have we in common?' (or, 'You don't quite understand your son'). For the meaning of the phrase τί μοι καὶ σοί, cf. Hdt. v. 33, σοὶ δὲ καὶ τούτοισι πρήγμασι τί ἐστι; and Demos. 855, 6, τί τῷ νόμῳ καὶ τῇ βασάνῳ; (Liddell and Scott's lexicon).

This distinction is important in the account of the Resurrection:

xx. 5. Stooping down he *beheld* the linen clothes lying, but went not in.

7. Simon Peter went in and *gazed at* the clothes . . . (a speculative look of inquiry).

8. The other disciple then went in and *saw* and believed.

There is something of the artist, too, in the way in which he selects words that wed the conversations to the narrative,[1] as, for instance, when the promises of Jesus are justified by the sequel:

xiv. 27. '*Peace* I leave with you, my peace I give unto you.'

xvi. 22. 'Ye therefore now have grief, but I shall see you again, and your heart *shall be glad.*'

xvi. 7. 'The Comforter . . . will come to you; he shall convict the world of *sin*.'

'When he cometh, the *Spirit* of truth, he shall guide you into all truth.'[2]

xx. 19. And saith unto them, *Peace* be unto you.

xx. 20. The disciples therefore *were glad* when they saw the Lord.

xx. 23. Having said this, he breathed on them and said, 'Receive ye the Holy *Spirit*. Whosoever *sins* ye remit....'

*Note on the Greek Style of the Fourth Gospel.*

For those who know Greek and would examine the style more carefully, one or two main features may be pointed out:

i. Though balance is a main feature of this style, the balancing particles, which are a feature of classical Greek, are rarely used. For instance:

'*I* am the vine: *ye* are the branches,'
'If I bear witness about myself, my witness is not true;
Another is he that beareth witness about me, and I know that the witness . . .'[3]

The evangelist is fond of introducing his balance by 'as . . .', 'so . . .', or 'if . . .', 'how . . .?'

'As my Father hath sent me, even so send I you.'
'If I have spoken unto you earthly things and ye believe not, How will ye believe, if I tell you heavenly things?'[4]

[1] Brooke in Peake's *Commentary*.
[2] Cf. also xvii. 18. 'As thou didst send me into the world, I also have *sent* them.'
[3] xv. 1-7, v. 31. Cf. also v. 43-7.
xx. 21. 'As my Father hath *sent* me, even so *send* I you.'
[4] xx. 21, iii. 12.

Brevity could not go further than in the following balance:

> 'A little (while), and ye behold me not;
> And again a little, and ye shall see me.' [1]

These same words occur twice besides,[2] and were evidently actual words of Jesus.

It is not a Greek cast of sentence, and is another example of the careful preservation of the simple and more condensed Jewish language.

ii. In his syntax, besides the conjunctions mentioned above, 'as', 'even as', 'if', and 'how', his favourites are 'that' expressing purpose, and 'because' in the infrequent cases when he subordinates sentences.

iii. He can use participles as in classical Greek,

> 'Jesus, *knowing* . . ., *having loved* his own . . . loved them unto the end. And dinner *taking place*, the devil *having put* it into the heart of Judas . . . (Jesus) *knowing* that the Father . . . and that he came forth from God and goeth to God, riseth from dinner.' [3]

This kind of compound sentence is most rare, but it shows that his orderly narrative is capable of it. More often he interposes a sentence in parenthesis.[4]

iv. For examples of simple verbs where classical Greek would certainly have used compound ones, take the following, which include especially verbs of motion:

| John's Greek:[5] | where classical Greek would have had: |
|---|---|
| 'runneth and cometh' (τρέχει καὶ ἔρχεται) | 'run towards and arrive' |
| 'taken' (ἦραν) | 'taken away' (ἀπῆραν) |
| 'turned' (ἐστράφη) | 'turned round' |
| 'borne' (ἐβάστασας) | 'borne away' |
| 'put' (ἔθηκαν) | 'put down' |
| 'written' (γεγραμμένον) | 'written on' (Mark xv. 26) |
| 'took and made four parts' (ἔλαβον καὶ ἐποίησαν) | 'divided among' (Mark xv. 24) (διεμέριζον) |
| 'put (down) my life and take it (up) again' (τίθημι ἵνα λάβω) | |

---

[1] xvi. 16.   [2] vii. 33, xii. 35.   [3] xiii. 1–3.
[4] See p. 59.   [5] xx. 2, 13, 14, 15; xix. 19, 23; x. 18.

There is also the common use of λαλῶ for 'speak', φωνεῖ for 'calls', τίθησι for 'sets (wine) on', ἀντλῶ for 'draw out' (wine).[1]

v. John's repetition of nouns instead of using pronouns has been discussed. It is one of the secrets of his effective style, and is no doubt deliberate, and perhaps caught from the Master's own style, in his longer talks, when he was not speaking in parables.

John's style has been called 'simple almost to baldness, yet fascinating'. The Greek student will be impressed if he compares such passages as those already set out above and puts them side by side with any page of Demosthenes, Thucydides, or Plato, when the shorter diction of John will be noticed at once.

[1] ii. 8–10.

# VI
## LITERARY GENIUS OF JESUS

Use of illustration and imagery—oratory, instances of; balanced style—art of story-telling—parables—allegory—great sayings; epigram.

PROPHETS like Isaiah and Amos were assisted by their use of illustration. They knew that concrete instances appeal more to the audience than abstractions and generalities, and that a long address must be varied by changes of tone and even of types of sentence. The secret of good teaching is apt illustration that wakes interest and makes clear. 'Jesus may have designedly imitated the prophets', says a commentator. 'Naturally imitated' would be more correct, as he followed Jewish native traditions in many ways.

He adopts all their resources, such as, their use of *metaphor*:

'Ye are the salt of the earth,' 'I am the Bread of life',

of *simile*:

'As a hen gathereth her chickens . . .'

of *allegory*, as in the talk of the Good Shepherd;
of *hyperbole*:

'if thy hand offend thee, cut it off . . .'

of *paradox*:

'he that findeth his life, shall lose it,'

of *rhetorical question* and *irony*:

'if he ask for bread, will he give him a stone?'

of *repetition*:

'If thy hand offend thee, cut it off: it is better for thee . . . (where their worm dieth not . . .), and if thy foot offend thee, cut it off: it is better for thee . . . (where their worm dieth not . . .), and if thine eye offend thee, pluck it out: it is better for thee . . . (where their worm dieth not).'[1]

of *parallelism*:

'Heaven and earth shall pass away,
but my words shall not pass away.'

[1] Mark ix. 42 ff. The 'triplet' used by Jesus to drive his lesson home is not kept by Matthew. He has the same passage twice, but shortens it by coupling 'hand' and 'foot' in one case (v. 29), and omitting 'foot' in the other (xviii. 8).

of *apostrophe*:

'O Jerusalem, Jerusalem, that killest the prophets . . .'

of *epigram*:

'the foxes have holes, and the birds of the air have nests, but the Son of man hath not where to lay his head.'

The cast of this epigram reminds us of Isaiah's

'The ox knoweth his owner, and the ass his master's crib, but Israel doth not know, my people do not consider.'

The *analogy*, the *balance*, and the *compactness* are similar in both.

How full were the talks of Jesus of illustration by metaphor and simile, using common concrete objects to make clear spiritual and moral ideas, will only be grasped if we look closely at the Sermon on the Mount, in which illustration follows hard on illustration. After the Beatitudes in Matt. v, Jesus commences with common household objects, like *salt* and *lamps* and *corn measures*, to explain Christian influences. If they want to know what sort of goodness to aim at, it is not to be that of the *Pharisees*. Here he points to great figures of the time. *Parts of the body* are used next. *Hand* and *eye* are put for bad habits, Christian retaliation is to turn the other *cheek*, modesty is like one *hand* not knowing what the other does, hypocrisy is the same as not noticing a *beam* in your own *eye*. Then come objects of nature, to show worry unnecessary, *lilies*, *birds*, *grass put in the oven*, strengthened by an example from history, in the person of *Solomon*. Praying is like *knocking at a door*, or a son asking for *a helping at meal-times*. *Pearls* and *swine*, narrow *gates* and broad *roads*, *grapes* from *thorns* and *figs* from *thistles*— all these link the hearers' common everyday life with the moral life, and even Aesop's Fables are drawn upon for the hypocrisy of the *wolf in sheep's clothing*, while the talk closes with the fine illustration of sincerity taken from *housebuilding*. 'He *thought* in pictures.'[1] Herod he sees as a 'fox', Peter as a 'rock', his disciples as the 'children of the bridechamber', and his own suffering as a 'cup' put to his lips by his Father.

'The two chief means of teaching', said Bishop Creighton,

[1] Kelman, *Dict. of Christ and the Gospels*, vol. ii (Poet).

'are exaggeration and paradox.' *Hyperbole* or exaggeration has the same force in words as caricature in drawing. It surprises or startles the hearer into interest. It puts an improbable or impossible case to persuade belief in the more probable cases of real life. 'The hairs of your head are all numbered' is a hyperbole, or, as the Greek word means, 'shoots beyond the mark', because numbering the hairs would be a useless procedure even for Providence. But it impresses the human mind as a vivid symbol. The different interpretations found for the 'camel going through a needle's eye', viz. that the needle's eye was a small side gateway at Jerusalem through which the camel could not go without unloading, or that the word for 'camel' is a misreading for a word meaning 'rope', are ingenious but unnecessary, if we remember our Lord's fondness for hyperbole.

'If any one smite thee on the right cheek, turn to him the other also' is a hyperbolical figure of what humility should achieve. One would not actually present the cheek, but take a second blow passively. But the hyperbole is dramatic and saves words. 'You strain at a gnat and *swallow a camel*', 'Thou considerest not the *beam* that is *in thine own eye*', help to explain some hard sayings of Jesus that seem contradictory; for example, 'If any man come to me and hate not his father and mother, he cannot be my disciple' (Luke xiv. 26), put less strongly in Matt. x. 37: 'He that loveth father or mother more than me, is not worthy of me', which came from the same lips that rebuked the Scribes and Pharisees for neglecting the Fifth Commandment.

*Paradox* startles by coupling a metaphorical idea with a literal one, as in: 'Let the dead (spiritually so) bury their dead (physically so)'; 'He that loseth his life for my sake shall find it', where life again has both senses, physical and spiritual, 'he that loseth his physical life shall gain spiritual life'. When Jesus had purged the Temple, and the Jews challenged him for a sign, and he said, 'Destroy this temple, and in three days I will raise it up,' they thought he referred to the Temple building, but he 'spoke of the temple of the body'. The paradox is almost a play on words.

*Crescendo* and *climax*, as found in Isaiah and Amos, are still more remarkable in the longer utterances of Jesus. Take even the Beatitudes, as given in Matthew. The eighth one in v. 10, 'Blessed are the persecuted', is expanded into a more detailed one about persecution, which by its mere length after the eight shorter ones, and by the apostrophe, the change from 'Blessed are those . . .' to 'Blessed are *ye* . . .' provides a climax, especially with the aid of the dramatic and unexpected close—'for *my* sake'—and the emphasis laid on the joy that follows, 'Rejoice and be exceeding glad, for great is your reward in Heaven.'

The talks of Jesus never suffer from a weak ending; the argument moves in orderly and balanced phrase to an effective finish. Take one of the most beautiful instances of his talking, on worry:

Matt. vi. 25–34. (Luke has it practically identical, and we may suppose it has had very little editing.)

25 Therefore I say unto you, Take no thought for your life, what ye shall eat, or what ye shall drink; nor yet for your body, what ye shall put on. Is not the life more than meat, and the body than raiment?

26 Behold the fowls of the air: for they sow not, neither do they reap, nor gather into barns; yet your heavenly Father feedeth them. Are ye not much better than they?

27 Which of you by taking thought can add one cubit unto his stature?

28 And why take ye thought for raiment? Consider the lilies of the field, how they grow; they toil not, neither do they spin:

29 And yet I say unto you, That even Solomon in all his glory was not arrayed like one of these.

30 Wherefore, if God so clothe the grass of the field, which to day is, and to morrow is cast into the oven, *shall he* not much more *clothe* you, O ye of little faith?

31 Therefore take no thought, saying, What shall we eat? or, What

Ver. 25. Note the *balance* 'soul' (or 'life') and 'body', . . . soul more than meat? . . . body more than raiment? Each of these, 'food' and 'raiment', is then illustrated from nature, by the birds and the lilies.

26. 'a minore' conclusion in each case, 'if the birds, much more you', 'if the grass, much more you'.

25–8. Four times the argument is put as a question, as if Jesus were pleading with their common sense rather than laying down the law. The *questions* break pleasantly into the series of commands, and bring a tenderness of tone into the address.

29. The introduction of Solomon, the highest type of human splendour, is masterly. The lilies exceed Solomon. Yet they are mere grass, and perish in a day.

31. Then comes the summing up, repeating the original command. Note again the *triple* arrangement. 'What shall we *eat*? What . . . *drink*? Wherewithal . . . *clothed*?'

shall we drink? or, Wherewithal shall we be clothed?

32 (For after all these things do the Gentiles seek:) for your heavenly Father knoweth that ye have need of all these things.

33 But seek ye first the kingdom of God, and his righteousness; and all these things shall be added unto you.

34 Take therefore no thought for the morrow: for the morrow shall take thought for the things of itself. Sufficient unto the day *is* the evil thereof.

34. Matthew alone has the general conclusion, which rounds off the whole talk so effectively, a striking maxim putting the talk in tabloid form:
'Worry not for the morrow; the morrow will worry for itself; sufficient for the day is the evil thereof.'

The English diction and rhythm of the A.V. almost excel the original—especially the sentence, 'even Solomon in all his glory was not *arrayed* like one of these'. 'Array' is a fine word, always suggesting splendour, whether of battle or clothes. It makes, too, a fine rhythm in the sentence.

The passage which best shows the oratorical art used by our Lord, next after the parables, is the talk on John the Baptist:

Matt. xi. 7–19. (Cf. Luke vii. 24–35. Matthew's version is probably nearest to the original, as Luke interposes an editor's comment, vv. 29, 30, and also puts ver. 13 of Matthew in a different context, Luke xvi. 16.)

7 And as they departed, Jesus began to say unto the multitudes concerning John, What went ye out into the wilderness to see? A reed shaken with the wind?

8 But what went ye out for to see? A man clothed in soft raiment? behold, they that wear soft *clothing* are in kings' houses.

9 But what went ye out for to see? A prophet? yea, I say unto you, and more than a prophet.

10 For this is *he*, of whom it is written, Behold, I send my messenger before thy face, which shall prepare thy way before thee.

11 Verily I say unto you, Among them that are born of women there hath not risen a greater than John

Ver. 7. The *question* to arrest attention. *Irony* here, a reed as a contrast to the unbending strength of John.

8. Three times the question is put. Orators love the *triplet*. Cicero's speeches are full of it.

Irony again, a contrast to the rough hair garment of John.

A *general truth* hinting at the luxury of Herod's court.

9. The third time the question is put in earnest. 'A prophet? Yea, I say, much more than a prophet' (gradually building up the effect). 'He was the special messenger of the Messiah. He was the greatest of all the prophets, yet . . . (*paradox* again) the least in the kingdom of heaven is greater than even

the Baptist: notwithstanding he that is least in the kingdom of heaven is greater than he.

12 And from the days of John the Baptist until now the kingdom of heaven suffereth violence, and the violent take it by force.

13 For all the prophets and the law prophesied until John.

14 And if ye will receive *it*, this is Elias, which was for to come.

15 He that hath ears to hear, let him hear.

16 But whereunto shall I liken this generation? It is like unto children sitting in the markets, and calling unto their fellows,

17 And saying, We have piped unto you, and ye have not danced; we have mourned unto you, and ye have not lamented.

18 For John came neither eating nor drinking, and they say, He hath a devil.

19 The Son of man came eating and drinking, and they say, Behold a man gluttonous, and a winebibber, a friend of publicans and sinners. But wisdom is justified of her children.

John—', bringing into relief against the background of John's dispensation the greatness of the new Gospel. John's ended in repentance, that of Jesus began with the free grace of God.

12. 'the violent take it by force', almost 'pillage it', a strong *hyperbole* to show the enthusiasm roused by John for the new Gospel.

13. John was the culmination of the whole line of prophets, the second Elijah—no name made a greater appeal than Elias.

15. 'he that hath *ears*'. Cf. the striking effect of Shakespeare's

'Friends, Romans, Countrymen, lend me your *ears.*'

Contrast the weak effect of 'Listen to me', or 'Attend to these my words'.

16. Change of theme, the reception of John, introduced again in *question* form, and at once attention is secured by a *simile* from the common scene in the market, children playing at weddings and funerals, and some of them in a mood for neither, sulking. It is put in the tersest language,

'We piped, and you danced not, we mourned, and you lamented not.'

18, 19. Note the *vigour of the phrasing* here and its *simplicity*; 'neither eating nor drinking', an abstainer living on the simplest fare.

'He hath a devil.' 'A gluttonous man and a winebibber,' the enemy's exaggeration of eating and drinking.

The notable *conclusion*, as brief as weighty, to dismiss the subject.

The rest of the chapter is put by Luke in a different arrangement, and may not have been delivered on the same occasion.

Note especially the words 'in that hour' and 'at that time' used by Luke and Mark, though they put the passage in different places and assign them to different occasions.

The *balance and dignity* of the Hebrew style, with its majestic repetitions and parallelism, is best seen in the talk on the Last Judgment.[1] This balance is more in evidence in Matthew than in the other Gospels, as we have seen, but it is a marked feature of our Lord's addresses, whoever reports them.

It will be seen how closely the address to the 'Goats' answers that to the 'Sheep'. It is the close correspondence that makes the whole passage so impressive. It is shortened in the second part by using one verb 'minister' for the several verbs used before, but to have shortened it further would have reduced the impressiveness.

One more instance may be given to show how Jesus gave life and vigour to his addresses by the use of simile, analogy, and imagery: the talk on 'the last things'—

'As the lightning cometh from the east, and shineth unto the west, so also shall the coming of the Son of man be.'
Simile.

'For where the carcase is, there the eagles will be gathered together.'
Metaphor.

'Immediately after the tribulation of those days, shall the sun be darkened, and the moon shall not give her light, and the stars shall fall from heaven, and the powers of the heaven shall be shaken.'[2]
Imagery such as the prophets used.

Then there is a sudden 'apostrophe', as he turns to the audience, and gives a simile of a fig-tree:

'Now learn a parable of the fig tree . . .'
Apostrophe.

'When his branch is yet tender, ye know that summer is nigh;
Parable.

So likewise ye . . . know. . . .'

This is followed by a comparison from past history:

'As the days of Noah were, so shall also the coming of the Son of man be.'

[1] Matt. xxv. 31–46.          [2] Matt. xxiv. 27 ff.

This crisis is explained in balanced clauses    Parallelism.
cast in parallel form:

'Then shall two be in the field,
The one shall be taken, and the other left.
Two women shall be grinding at the mill,
The one shall be taken, and the other left.'

To keep interest from flagging, two *stories*    Parables.
follow, to show the need of watchfulness, the
second of which is introduced in *question* form.    Rhetorical ques-
The device of *refrains* is also not forgotten:    tion.

'So shall also the *coming* of the Son of man be'    Use of Refrain.
(three times).[1]
'Of that *day* and that *hour knoweth* no man.'[2]
'Ye *know* not what *hour* your Lord doth *come*.'[3]
'In such an *hour* as ye think not, the Son of
man *cometh*.'[4]
'The Lord shall *come* in a *day*, when he looketh
not for him.'[5]

For the *climax* of the address is fitly reserved
the punishment, and put in the strongest
terms:

'shall *cut him asunder* ... there shall be weeping and *gnashing of teeth*.'    Climax.

And with this piece of vigorous diction the
discourse probably ended.

All the oratorical methods of the old prophets, and in fact
of all good speakers, are here employed by Jesus. Like them,
he kept his hold upon his audience by the arts that are necessary
to retain their attention undivided, rousing them by questions
and dramatic changes from third person to second, enlivening
them by apt illustrations from life or nature or past history,
driving the warning home by effective repetition (though never
overdoing this), startling them by a hyperbole, charming them
by the choicest because the simplest and most forceful words,
never losing sight of his main point, and summing up with
some epigram or saying that rang out like a proverb, which the
audience could not help carrying away with them, reverberating
in their ears as they unwillingly melted away or followed him

---

[1] vv. 27, 37, 39.    [2] ver. 36.    [3] ver. 42.    [4] ver. 44.    [5] ver. 50.

to his lodging, because, as was said of a lesser orator, Pericles the Athenian, he had 'left his sting in his hearers'.

No wonder that a public speaker could say that he made a point of reading the Bible daily, not for its devotional side, primarily, but for the improvement of his style, especially alluding to the parables of Jesus.[1]

## The Art of Story-telling. Parables.

The literary genius of our Lord is, of course, felt most powerfully in his *parables*.

Take a short one first, from Matthew's version; Matthew seems to preserve it in its original form, and Luke to have adapted it to hearers not familiar with the conditions of Palestine.

The House built on the Rock:[2]

A man is prospecting for a site for his house, and comes to one of the valleys or ravines called 'wadys'. It looks sheltered and attractive, especially a flat piece of sandy ground nestling under the steep bank, with signs of a stream that will give him water part of the year. But he knows the country and chooses instead a site on the rocky bank overlooking the ravine, more bleak, but, as he knows, more permanent. For the rainy season is at hand, and the unwary prospector who chose the attractive sandy corner in the ravine itself finds the stream is a raging torrent when it comes, and it does come very suddenly with the rains.

Matthew preserves throughout the perfect balance and rhythm of sentence and phrase, on which the effect of contrast depends. He has one variation of construction and one of diction to avoid too much sameness.

A. 'Every one who heareth these sayings of mine, and doeth them, I will liken him to a wise man, who built his house upon the rock.
And down came the rain, (In the Greek the verb comes
and (along) came the floods, first with stronger force, which
and (fierce) blew the winds, one misses in the A.V. transla-
and *fell* upon that house: tion.)
and it fell not, for it was founded upon the rock.'

B. 'And every one that heareth these sayings of mine, and doeth them not,
shall be likened unto a foolish man, who built his house upon the sand.

[1] Riddell, *Things that matter*, p. 76.      [2] Matt. vii. 24 ff.

And down came the rain,
and (along) came the floods,
and (fierce) blew the winds,
   and smote upon that house:
and it fell, and the fall of it was great.'

The ending must be noticed for its restraint of diction, 'It fell, and the fall of it was great'.

In Luke the balance and rhythm are less perfect, and we miss the impressive arrangement of Matthew—

'and when the flood arose,
the stream beat vehemently
   upon that house . . .'[1]

The impressiveness is still further sacrificed in the second half (ver. 40). In recasting the parable Luke has also made it a question of deep foundations, going down to the rock, and of good building, not of a choice of site. He wrote for people less familiar with the geography of Palestine.[2] Jesus would deliver the parable in a form true to Jewish surroundings, and, as we may well believe, with the balance and strength that Matthew has preserved.

The Parables of Jesus have been so much the whole world's property for centuries that it may seem almost superfluous to point out any of their merits, even in a literary sense. But it may be worth while to lay stress on some special features of three of the most popular. The Good Samaritan illustrates their lifelike detail, and the completeness with which the main point of the parables is brought out in a few words. As for detail, the particular road from Jerusalem to Jericho was notorious for robberies, and Jesus thus, like all good teachers, introduces local interest into his story. Then, while the priest gives the body a wide berth, for fear of pollution, the Levite, a little less holy, as a lay priest, could afford to inspect the body. The distinction between the two is a fine point. The condemnation of both, or rather of the system that bound them and checked their humanity, is all the more effective because it is silent. The choice of a Samaritan for the hero shows that neighbour-

---

[1] vi. 47 ff.                    [2] Wright, *Synopsis of the Gospels.*

liness is no question of race. The completeness of the Good
Samaritan's treatment of the victim is the second notable
feature, the attention to the wounds, oil used to heal, wine
as a homely disinfectant; the lifting of the victim on to
his *own* beast, so that he himself had to walk, instead of
riding; the nursing of the patient at the inn ('took care
of him'); the instruction to the landlord to see the nursing
continued; the arrangement for the payment; the resolve to
look in again, and see the business through. That is how mercy
should be shown, Jesus suggests. That is the real neighbour.

In 'the Rich Man and Lazarus' an admirable feature is the
description of the two men in so few words, two or three powerful strokes to make a portrait: the rich man *in purple and fine
linen*—faring *sumptuously every day*—and the beggar *laid at his
gate* (he has to be carried to his pitch)—*anxious for morsels—full
of sores—the scavenger dogs lick his sores*. The extremes of
wealth and poverty could not be painted in fewer words, or more
graphically. Points to notice are that the beggar's 'dead' body
does not matter, but the rich man has a funeral·('the beggar
died . . .', 'the rich man died and *was buried*'). The beggar is
borne to Paradise, called by the Jews 'Abram's Bosom'.
Further, the request of the rich man is put with surprising
modesty, '*dip the tip* of his *finger* in water and cool my tongue'.
He does not ask for a drink. He has sunk very low. The answer
is made as gentle as possible, '*Son*, remember. . . .' That
dramatic 'gulf' forbids even this being granted.

The characters in these and other parables are common
types, not extreme cases. Their shortcomings are common
faults—selfishness, thoughtlessness, pride.

The censure is implied, not expressed. The rich man is blamed,
like the priest and Levite, only by implication, not in so many
words. The parables take for granted powers of judgment in
the audience. 'The rich man dies, and is buried. And in Hades
. . . being *in torments*. . . .' The parable does not waste time in
justifying the suffering, and in ver. 25 the principle of compensation is quietly assumed as known to the rich man.

The rich man has the grace to think of his brothers. Even
the prodigal son is only thoughtless, and 'comes to himself'

(his sound, normal self) and has the grace of humility. He blames himself, but his father cuts him short. These parables in fact take a high view of human nature. The tragedy of the Rich Fool (Luke xii. 16–21) also springs from thoughtlessness, and the rebuke is not without its tenderness, 'You senseless man (not the stronger term 'fool'), that soul which you call yours (cf. I will say to *my* soul, ver. 19) they are demanding back from you this night. Then to whom will your goods go?' In 'the Wedding Supper' the guests refuse through preoccupation, in 'the Foolish Virgins' the fault is again thoughtlessness. In fact Jesus held up the reddest light of danger not to criminals, but to the respectable for what they *don't* do. It is the man who did *not* use his talent, the virgins who did *not* take oil in their lamps, the rich man who did *not* notice Lazarus at his gate, the people who did *not* give the cup of water and visit the prisoner, who are held up as examples. Their punishment is to be left outside in the darkness, like children looking through the window-panes at the party inside, the music and dancing and good things, their desolation more terrible than physical pain, and even causing 'gnashing of teeth'.

To the question why the parables make such a universal appeal, the answer will be best seen from the longest of them, the Prodigal Son. We are dealing with its literary beauties; its other beauties have been the subject of thousands of addresses.

First, its *rapid movement* as a story keeps the interest at full pitch. The downfall of the young man is told in two phrases, 'he wasted his substance in riotous living, and when he had spent all . . .'; his return in one sentence, 'he arose and came to his Father', while the father's only reply to his son's confession is an order to his servants to do him honour.

Secondly, it is 'things' that make stories go well, not emotions and abstractions. One of the secrets of the story's appeal to all ages and intelligences is its *concreteness*. Everything in it is concrete and vigorous. Everything is described in solid terms.

It is a story of goods, and spending, of bread and husks, and hunger and swine, of journeys and hired servants, and a concrete welcome, with robes and rings and shoes, and fatted calf and music and dancing. The parables have been called earthly stories with heavenly meanings; as literature, they are concrete stories with an abstract meaning. Everything is tangible. The son's offence is described as 'wasting *goods*' or, as the elder brother puts it, 'devouring his *living*', and his lost, abandoned state described as a hunger that would 'fill itself with *husks*' contrasted with the '*bread* and to spare' of the servants—solid symbols every time.

The story is one of great moral issues, repentance, forgiveness, jealousy, but it is all expressed in incident and action. The younger son's feelings take concrete form: he 'comes to himself', he 'will go back and say "I have sinned".' The sin is not merely a personal disgrace; it goes out from him and hits against heaven itself, and hits his Father too ('sinned against heaven. . .'). The only phrases expressing feelings as feelings are 'he had compassion' used of the father, and 'he was angry' used of the brother. The brother's jealousy takes a concrete form: 'Thou gavest me no *kid*.' The father's welcome takes a concrete form, he 'falls on his neck and kisses him tenderly'.[1] So does his joy: 'Bring forth the best *robe*, a *ring*, and *shoes* (to show recovered sonship, for slaves went barefoot), and *kill, eat*, and be merry' (start *dancing* and *music*, ver. 25). His son's sin was a concrete thing to him, 'he was *dead*, and is *alive*'. The feelings and emotions are not analysed, they are instantly turned into action.

The vivid *dialogue*, as usual, and the use of direct speech, keep the story lively and quick. Even in such a small detail as the informing of the elder brother, the brother calls a servant and receives the news in direct speech.

The *diction* is simple in the extreme: 'when he had spent all, he began to be in want'; 'no man gave unto him'; 'when he was a great way off, his Father saw him'; 'thou art ever with me, and all that I have is thine'; and yet it is vigorous, 'there arose a mighty famine'; 'longing to fill himself with husks'; 'devoured thy living with harlots'; 'sinned against heaven and in thy sight'; a clear, forceful phrase, worth much abstract theology. All sin is sin against God.

[1] Gk. κατεφίλησεν.

As in the Old Testament stories, *repetition* is purposely used to bring out the main points of the story: e.g. in vv. 18 and 21: 'Father, I have sinned. . .'; and in vv. 24 and 32: 'for this my son was dead and is alive again. . . .'

The final phrasing of the close is specially beautiful in its balance, rhythm, and vowel-sounds:

'it was meet to make merry and be glad;
for this thy brother was dead, and is alive again;
    and was lost,              and is found.'

What a range of vowel-sounds, and what a happy close on the more resonant ones!

Some other delightful touches have been pointed out: The prodigal fails to finish his speech to his father. He had meant to say, 'Make me a hired servant'. His father's welcome chokes him. He sees he cannot be anything but a son.[1]

The change in the prodigal's attitude is simply expressed by 'give' and 'make'. The father is no longer 'the Governor', as a boy would say, who signs the cheque for the allowance, and whose company can be easily dispensed with. The prodigal wants now to be in any humble relationship so long as he can be with him.[2]

The brother's attitude is shown by the use of the pronoun, 'as soon as this *thy son* was come' (thy 'precious' son), and the father's gentle correction, 'this *thy brother*'.[3] In the elder brother's conduct 'the injured air of the complacent, hidebound moralist is drawn to the life'.

*Allegory.*

The writers of the Old Testament used allegory with a very happy effect, blending the figurative language with the literal facts, as in Psalm lxxx, a pathetic appeal to God to revive the Jewish nation, which he had *planted* in the country *like a vine*, 'which threw out its branches to river and sea, till the wild boar (Assyria) rooted it up and trampled it down'. Uninterrupted allegory would have been too artificial for such an intimate appeal, but the quick changes from people to vine

[1] Deane, *How to enjoy the Bible.*     [2] Fosdick, *Meaning of Prayer.*
[3] Deane, ibid.

and vine to people keep the reality always before one, and underneath the beauty of the allegory the hard case of the nation shows all the more effectively. It is like a sculptor's use of light drapery to express and set off the human form underneath. The fine mould of the limbs shows better veiled than when exposed—a paradox. In John x there is a talk of Jesus in allegorical form, introducing the figure of the Good Shepherd leading his sheep, as was common in the East, and the contrast of the hireling. As he recurs to the figure again and again—his voice known to the sheep and his readiness to risk his life for them—the real meaning of his own relationship to his own 'flock' is obvious, and is all the more effective for the veil of allegory.

Another form of allegory also occurs. The figure called personification is the basis of it. This is the account of the temptation in Luke and Matthew. In Genesis the first temptation of humanity is related as an allegory, with abstract turned into concrete, sin and temptation personified—the fruit, the serpent, and the disgrace—a story to last for all time. Jesus selected this vivid figure of personification to present his own temptation. The disciples must have had it from his own lips, and when he described the experiences he had passed through, he used his favourite form of parable to stamp it on their minds.

Not that Jesus discouraged the idea of a personal Satan. He always speaks of him as a person. 'I have seen Satan as lightning fall from Heaven', 'Simon, Satan hath desired to have you. . . .', 'The enemy that sowed them is the devil'. But in the account of the temptation he scarcely wished his disciples to understand that Satan appeared in bodily form and carried him to a mountain top. He knew that accounts of our own feelings are dull to others, and he makes his own doubts as vivid and interesting as he did the idea of repentance in the Prodigal Son.

The figures then of this allegory are simple, yet striking pictures, grand in conception:

'Command that these stones be made bread.'
'He set him on a pinnacle of the temple, . . . "Cast thyself down, and the angels shall bear thee up".'

'He took him to the top of a high mountain and shewed him all the kingdoms of the world in a moment of time. . . . All these will I give thee, if. . . .'

How simply the issues are expressed, and how easy to remember in that form!

## His Great Sayings.

The greatest sayings of Jesus are not merely moral maxims like those of the sages of antiquity: 'Know thyself', 'Do nothing in excess'; or philosophical reflections: 'A life without a feast is a long road without an inn', 'Speech is the shadow of action'. Jesus could coin proverbs too: 'Cast not your pearls before swine', 'let the dead bury their dead', but his greatest sayings were personal appeals and personal claims or manifestoes. Such appeals and manifestoes, never made before or since, no doubt helped to prompt the verdict of the officers, when they could not arrest him: 'Never man spake like this man.' They recognized a personal force that distinguished the sayings from empty bombast. But beauty as well as power distinguishes them. At the heart of them is usually some word that may be taken in two senses, or some image drawn from some common word of far reaching import: bread, water, light, door, vine, shepherd, yoke, a metaphor that all could understand. Through these images Jesus claims to be the very necessity of existence to all men.

Most of these sayings are in John's Gospel, and many think that they are not as Jesus uttered them but have been moulded by John. But take this one from Matthew, of equal power and of particular beauty, and with as marked a personal claim:

'Come unto me, all ye that labour and are heavily *burdened*, and I will give you *rest*.
Take my *yoke* upon you, and learn of me,
for I am gentle and lowly in heart,
    and ye shall find *rest* for your souls;
for my *yoke* is easy,
and my *burden* is light.' (Matt. xi. 28 f.)

The *strength* of the saying arises from the paradoxes, namely that one who offers a yoke as master, is at the same time gentle

and lowly; and that this yoke will bring rest. Its *beauty* arises
from the *simile*, prompted perhaps by the sight of loaded
baggage-animals passing by; from the *balance* of phrases, which
is obvious in lines 3 and 4, 6 and 7; from the *diction*, the rhythm
of the couplets 'labour' and 'heavy laden' or 'heavily burdened', 'gentle and lowly'; and from the slight degree of
*repetition* which emphasizes the main thought, 'ye shall find
rest' echoing 'I will rest you', 'yoke' answering 'yoke', and
'burden' echoing 'heavily burdened'.

This echoing of the main thought is seen in other sayings and
is a main feature of the longer talks in John's Gospel. There is
no doubt that the above is an unedited saying of Jesus; it has
the stamp of his genius upon it and the same ring as all his sayings in the Synoptists. Note how similar is the cast of the next
saying from John's Gospel, especially in the balance of the last
part of it, if we omit lines 3 and 4 from the passage in Matthew:

> 'He that eateth my flesh and drinketh my blood,
> hath eternal life;
> and I will raise him up at the last day.
> For my flesh is true meat
> and my blood is true drink.' (John vi. 54.)

Very powerful through its simple vigour and the terrible
shadow behind the words is:

> 'I, if I be lifted up, will draw all men unto me' (John xii. 32).

Perhaps the best instance of all of the special style of these
sayings is that in John xii. 35 f., with the favourite image of
light and darkness:

> 'Yet a little while, the light is with you.
> *Walk* while ye have light,
>     that the darkness may not overtake you,
>     and he that walketh in darkness, knows not where he is
>     going.
> While ye have light, *believe* in the light,
>     that ye may become *sons* of light.'

This comprises in the smallest space the true psychology of
*action*, followed by *belief*, and then a permanent state or
*relationship*, sonship. It also contains the usual contrast (light
and darkness), and the favourite structure of syntax, the usual

play upon the same words, and the arresting expression to close the syllogism, 'sons of light'.

The list cannot be closed without the rhythm of the couplet:

'In the world ye shall have tribulation:
but be of good cheer, I have overcome the world' (John xvi. 33),

which forms the fitting close to the last great address to the disciples.

# VII

## THE STORY OF THE PASSION

The four accounts, and their special features—selection of incidents—preferences and characteristics of each writer—the trial before Pilate in John.

JESUS himself was a climax. The Passion and the Resurrection are the climax of the Gospel history. Poetry and painting have tried to adorn them. The searchlight of criticism has played upon them. Year after year musical versions of them move great audiences. No story has ever been the cause of so much emotion. The word 'pathos' might be reserved exclusively to apply to it. It is the greatest of dramas, and the greatest of miracles. The people who recorded it were affected by the facts they relate in their whole life and conduct. Yet the narrative itself is plain and matter of fact. Never were witnesses more restrained in tone and style. There is no need, and apparently no desire, to embellish. The only comments are small explanations or parallels noted to prophecies in the Old Testament. When John with Peter saw the sight which was the deepest experience of his life, and which had brought him running posthaste to the tomb with a fearful excitement, and sent him away again in rapture, not a trace of his feelings appears in the sober record he left us: 'They saw and believed . . . and the disciples *went away again to their own home.*' Could sobriety and self-restraint go further?

The four Gospel records of these events could hardly be expected to cover the same ground. It was not a case of all having to give everything, but of selecting. The exhaustive and exhausting compilations of modern historians are made from a different standpoint. The account had to be kept short, if the writer wished to keep his matter within the limits of a 'roll', rolls being of a certain standard length, and also dear. It must be remembered that John, in the main, supplements Mark and Luke, and must have deliberately omitted much important matter that was known to him, but which already was before the Church. Take, for instance, the tribunals before which Jesus went.

Jesus was taken first before Annas, who questioned him; then before Caiaphas, the official High Priest, appointed by the Romans, who examined the witnesses before as many of the Council as could assemble at such short notice; then before the whole Council, which assembled at dawn, presided over by Caiaphas, on whose report the Council would condemn him.

Of these hearings John describes the first before Annas,[1] Mark the second before Caiaphas,[2] while Mark and Luke both record the formal verdict of the Council meeting held at dawn, which would be by a special summons.[3] From Caiaphas Jesus was led to Pilate. John gives much more space to this trial, and has to omit the trial before Herod, related by Luke, for which brief hearing there would be time enough, for 'it was early', says John, when they arrived before Pilate, and the verdict was not given till midday. Herod was in the city, and it would not take long to go to him and return to Pilate.

The pieces contributed to the whole record of the Passion by the various Gospels show the same preferences and characteristics as we have noted in their other matter.

### Mark.

The special contribution of Mark is the scene in the Garden of Gethsemane, once again in his graphic way bringing out the humanity of Jesus, the human agony and the divine calm which followed it. Mark has the strongest expressions for the depression of Jesus, 'he began to be appalled and agitated' (Moffat), 'sad even unto death', feeling the weight would kill him, and under this stress 'he fell upon the ground' (or, according to one reading, 'kept falling'), whereas Luke has modified this to 'knelt down'. By those three withdrawals and separate prayings, which Luke has shortened to one, Mark shows Jesus gradually mastering the crisis. How his humanity also comes out in the request to the disciples to watch with him and pray too, that their spirit might go out to support his own, and in his disappointment when he found them asleep: 'Couldst thou

---

[1] xviii. 13, 19–24.            [2] xiv. 53–65.

[3] Mark xv. 1, 'in the morning'; Luke xxii. 66, 'as soon as it was day'. Luke transfers the questioning by Caiaphas to the formal Council meeting, Mark gives it place at the preliminary hearing during the hours before dawn.

not watch one hour?' His calm is restored by prayer,[1] and this calm is just as significant. The noise of the approaching enemy does not ruffle it. 'Rise up; let us be going. My betrayer is here.' In his replies and silences it·is undisturbed to the end. It is the calm of one certain that the Son of Man will be seen 'sitting on the right hand of power'. The Son of Man in his power is Mark's special presentation of Jesus, and his account of the Passion is consistent with the rest of his Gospel. 'Truly this was a Son of God', says the centurion.[2]

### Matthew.

Matthew follows Mark closely. It reads as a Jew's account, similar in tone and colour. But it adds fresh incidents from another source, which are interesting in themselves, and useful in explaining and confirming the other accounts.[3] Several are dramatic: the message to Pilate from his wife, just before the verdict, 'Have thou nothing to do with that just man . . .' (had she seen Jesus in Jerusalem, and her attention been so aroused that she should dream about him?); Pilate's washing of hands before the crowd, and the terrible curse invoked by the Jews upon themselves, 'His blood be on us and on our children', unconscious, though the reader knows it, that within forty years those children would be suffering the horrors of the siege of Jerusalem, a good instance of what the Greeks called 'dramatic irony'; then, thirdly, the end of the traitor, satisfying poetic justice. Again, after the Crucifixion the mystery is heightened in Matthew by the appearances of spirits from the graves, while another addition is the Jews' deputation to Pilate and the watch of soldiers set by them over the tomb, the helpless dismay of these soldiers at the Resurrection, and the bribery of them by the Jews to hold their tongues.

Here and there Matthew has a fresh saying of great importance, 'They that take the sword shall perish by the sword',

---

[1] Cf. the changed phrasing of our Lord's petition in Matt. xxvi. 42, which suggests that Jesus now more calmly accepted the Divine will. (Rawlinson, *Mark*, p. 212.)

[2] Luke xxiii. 47: 'Truly this was a righteous man.'

[3] Some of them, especially Pilate's washing of hands, seem improbable, and the tradition is less well authenticated than the rest of the record.

'Thinkest thou that I cannot now pray to my Father and he shall even now send me more than twelve legions of angels?' This word from Jesus' own lips, when placed by Luke's statement that in his agony an angel appeared strengthening him,[1] explains how he had regained his self-possession and contact with the realities of his Father's kingdom. Once more his spirit moved in its proper sphere.

Some have admired the sentence, 'And sitting down they watched him there',[2] as full of tragic meaning, but as this refers to the soldiers sitting down to watch or guard the crosses, and should be rendered, 'sitting down they kept guard over him there', it is less significant.

### Luke.

In the account of the Passion Luke is still himself, that is, always dwelling on the note of hope, and he relieves the gloom by several streaks of light. It is true that all the accounts agree on one point, the note of certainty that Jesus sounded, before his suffering, of final triumph, 'after I am raised, I will go before you into Galilee', 'I will not drink of this fruit of the vine till I drink it new in my Father's kingdom' (Mark), 'let not your heart be troubled . . .' (John, at great length).[3] But the assurance of success is further brought out in Luke by the word spoken to Peter: 'Simon . . . I have prayed for thee that thy strength fail not. When thou art converted, strengthen thy brethren.'[4] The work, that is, was to go on. Again, by the saying to the disciples, 'I am appointing for you a kingdom that ye may eat and drink at my table in my kingdom and sit on thrones';[5] and the saying to the thief, 'To-day shalt thou be with me in Paradise', which has been the hope of millions; yet again by the prayer, 'Father, into thy hands I commend my spirit', the most composed words spoken from the cross, contrasting with the last saying that Mark preserves, a saying of despair, that was not the last word, however, 'My God, why hast thou forsaken me?'

---

[1] Luke xxii. 43, 44 are not in a number of manuscripts, and Luke's account without these verses omits the agony altogether.
[2] xxvii. 36.　　　[3] xiv and xvi.　　　[4] xxii. 32.　　　[5] xxii. 29, 30.

The watchful thoughtfulness of Jesus is nowhere shown so clearly as in his own hours of agony and suffering, when he thinks, for instance, of his mother during his worst moments, and commits her to the disciple who was closest to himself, 'Woman, behold thy son . . .' (John). But Luke's account shows that thoughtfulness of Jesus embracing all kinds and classes of people—the wounded servant, whose ear Jesus heals; the women following the procession,[1] 'Daughters of Jerusalem, weep not for me'; the Gentile executioners, 'Father, forgive them, for they know not what they do . . .'; the outcast suffering beside him, promised a place beside him in consolation. All these sayings are part of the tenderness which Luke loved so to illustrate, and without these gleanings of Luke the story of the Cross would have lost much of its richness. Nor ought one to forget that dramatic act at Peter's denial: 'The Lord turned and looked upon Peter.'

Luke's interest in the crowd embraces 'all the people that came together to *see the spectacle*', who smote their breasts, as well as the women from Galilee, whom Mark also mentions. Ever interested in officials and official procedure, Luke mentions the *Captains of the Temple* among the band that arrested Jesus, and also the jurisdiction of Herod recognized by Pilate. He also emphasizes Pilate's three attempts to save the prisoner (xxiii. 20, 22).

Lastly, in keeping with the literary beauty of his Gospel, we have that last elegy uttered by Jesus on his way to the cross. It is cast in the mould of Hebrew prophecy, beautiful in balance and form, and finished in the epigrammatic way that Jesus used:

'Women of Jerusalem, weep not for me,
but weep for yourselves and for your children.
For behold, the days are coming, in which they shall say,
Blessed are the barren, and the wombs that never bare . . .
Then shall they begin to say to the mountains, Fall on us,
and to the hills, Cover us.
For if they do these things in the green tree,
what shall be done in the dry?'

[1] See also p. 96, note 1.

*John.*

But it is to John that we Westerners turn for the most intimate account of the Passion and Resurrection, first for its convincing detail, the evidence of one who, as an acquaintance of the High Priest, obtained entry to the Palace and saw more even than Peter, and could glean his information more safely; secondly, because the Roman trial appeals to us more than the Jewish, and it is more fully given in John; thirdly, because of its dramatic incidents and situations. The scene in Gethsemane, it is true, is omitted, the other Gospels having it already, but other sayings of Jesus give the spirit of it, 'The cup which my Father hath given me, shall I not drink it?' (xviii. 11), and 'Now is my soul troubled. And what shall I say? Father, save me from this hour? But for this cause came I unto this hour' (xii. 27).

The parts of the drama which John fills out in so masterly a way are (i) the prelude to the arrest, (ii) the trial before Pilate, and (iii) the Resurrection. As usual, this writer turns his searchlight upon the *motives* of the actors, and on the thoughts of the Master, which engross him before everything else.

He has also preserved the dramatic order of the events; for instance, after tracing the growing hostility of the enemy, he narrates the raising of Lazarus not only as a climax of the 'works' of Jesus, but as the work that caused the enthusiasm of the Triumphal Entry and decided the Jewish council to take prompt action. He now turns to Jesus and shows him to us consciously preparing for the trial to come. In drama the audience is allowed to see something of the mind of the hero before the final act, and Hamlet ponders the question 'To be or not to be'. So John, while omitting the institution of the Last Supper as known already, has given us a full account of the thoughts of Jesus and his preparation of the disciples for the struggle.

How impressive is the opening of chapter xiii, with one of the longest sentences in the Gospel emphasizing the consciousness of Jesus as the crisis draws near:

'Now before the feast . . ., *when Jesus knew* that his hour was come . . ., *having loved* his own . . . *he loved them* unto the end, and supper *being ended* (*the devil having now put* into the heart of Judas Iscariot, Simon's son, to betray him), *knowing that* the Father had given all things into his hands, *and that* he came forth from God, and goeth unto God, *he riseth* from supper, and laid aside his garments, and he took a towel and girded himself.'

This long weighty sentence with elaborate structure, so rare in John, ushers in the final stage, and Jesus by a last symbolic act impresses on the disciples the need of unity.

Then follows the last intimate talk of Jesus. How it conveys the atmosphere of the closing scene! 'Let not your heart be troubled. . . . I go to prepare a place for you. . . . A little while and ye shall see me, and again a little while. . . .' The beauty of the words and the consolation they have always given makes us overlook their literary fitness. The tinge of sadness all through this talk prepares our minds as it prepared those of the disciples for the catastrophe that follows. We are being carried down a broad river to some great falls, over which the boat must plunge.

But before this intimate talk John describes the exit of the man whose presence must have spoilt it. The giving of the sop to Judas, not mentioned by the Synoptists, is a further dramatic feature, and the order 'That thou doest, do quickly', not understood by the disciples, adds mystery. 'He then . . . went immediately out. And *it was night*.' He went out into the dark to do the deed of darkness, night in his soul as well as outside—a much admired touch this, and it is John's own addition, and yet his style is apparently so artless. As soon as Judas has left, Jesus knows that the end is at hand, and breaks out, 'Now is the Son of Man glorified'. Jesus sees the cross, but beyond it the glory, and gives the flock he is leaving his final message: 'As I have loved you, love one another.'

And how even in this denouncing of the traitor John fills out Mark's brief outline into a vivid tableau! There is John himself *reclining up against* his Master, Peter *beckoning* to him to ask Jesus who it is to be, as the disciples look at one another in fear and amazement, and John *leaning back* still further to look up and put his inquiry. The giving of the sop is meant for

John's benefit alone, and to John it seems as if, with the sop, Satan enters into Judas and takes full possession.

The prayer of Jesus in chapter xvii is again dramatic. It is Jesus' declaration of all that he has lived and worked for—before he steps across the brook Kedron, his Rubicon, to his death—the unity of God, Father and Son, with mankind. 'And when he had spoken these words, he went forth . . . over the brook. . . . And *Judas knew the place.*'

Small points that John explains before the actual trial are:

i. The swords and staves of the arresting crowd in the Synoptists, the swords belonging to the *band* or cohort, the staves or clubs being the weapons carried by the priests' officers (xviii. 3, R.V.); the band was the cohort of Roman soldiers allowed for the authorities' use (cf. Matt. xxvii. 65);

ii. why Jesus went before both Annas and Caiaphas, and their relationship;

iii. how Peter got admission to the High Priest's house (xviii. 16 f.);

iv. reasons for two of Peter's denials, the natural curiosity of the maid opening the door, in the first case, and that of the relative of Malchus, whose ear Peter cut off in the garden, in the second case;

v. the reason for the fire of coals (ver. 18), less commonly wanted in that climate;

vi. how Judas could leave the supper-room without causing a sensation, and incidentally his position as treasurer.

He also quietly corrects Mark in an important point, by three times stating that the meal Jesus took was not the regular Passover but his own farewell Passover meal the day before the official one. 'Buy those things we have need of against the feast' spoken at the actual supper (xiii. 29) confirms xiii. 1, and xviii. 28. John is quite definite about it.

All the accounts refrain from actually describing the face or the bearing of Jesus, or commending his patience. They record the effects of them upon witnesses and leave them to be imagined. Thus Pilate is impressed by them, 'I find no fault in him', in spite of the refusal of Jesus to answer him. The thief is impressed, 'This man has done nothing amiss', and the

centurion, 'Truly this was the son of God'. Even the mere
sightseers, 'All who came together to that spectacle', were filled
with a sense of tragedy (Luke). One may compare the much-
quoted instance in Homer, who never describes the beauty of
Helen of Troy, but expresses its effect upon the old men who
see her pass by: 'No wonder', they say, 'the Greeks and
Trojans suffer such ills for such a being; strangely is she like
unto the immortal gods.' You could not describe it. It could
only be received with reverence. So there is no word to
describe what Jesus looked like, or his bearing. It must be
gleaned from the effects upon others. John even implies that
his majestic bearing so disconcerted the band who came to
arrest him that they fell down in fear,[1] which recalls the incident at Nazareth when his enemies were similarly overawed,
and Jesus, 'passing through the midst of them went his way'.[2]
We have to understand that Jesus assumed at times a look of
authority that was irresistible. Some spiritual force in his
face had an overpowering effect. This we should expect from
one who could still the storm, and clear the Temple of a crowd
of business people and bitter enemies in their own stronghold,
Jerusalem. Still more remarkable is the absence of emphasis
upon the physical sufferings of the Crucifixion. The pathos of
the story is conveyed without it.

The trial before Caiaphas with its atmosphere of bitter
hostility and foregone conclusion was quickly decided, and
John has left it to the synoptist gospels. He himself has done
much fuller justice to the trial before Pilate, and to Pilate himself, and his efforts for the prisoner. Only John shows us that
curious feature of the trial, the magistrate compelled to go in
and out, first to talk to the Jews outside, because their caste
system and fear of pollution forbade them to approach within
the bounds of the praetorium, then to question the prisoner

---

[1] John xviii. 6. One critic says the attitude of Jesus at his arrest is incon-
sistent with his agony in the garden, but this ignores the careful account in
Mark of his restoration through prayer. The incident John describes, when the
band 'went backward and fell to the ground', would follow the action of Judas
(whose presence John, of course, notes), and would precede the parley between
Jesus and the officers, parts of which are given in each Gospel, and the assault
of Peter on Malchus would follow the parley.

[2] Luke iv. 30.

within. Three times this Roman dignitary acts as go-between and passes to and fro. Only John has brought out fully the drama of this trial, the prolonged strain between contending forces, the fierce eagerness of the priests, who had the best reasons for haste and a quick verdict, and the obstinacy of the magistrate. John only has preserved those wonderful tableaux, when the Governor tried his appeals to pity and gave vent to his irony at the same time. 'Behold your King', 'Behold the Man', in its double sense, 'Behold the poor fellow', as Pilate meant it, 'Behold the ideal man', as it doubtless meant to John. How could we have spared them? And John only, by reporting those short dialogues between Pilate and Jesus, has really filled out the portrait of the Roman governor, merciless ordinarily to the Jews, but with some sense of decency roused in him by the person of the prisoner. In Pilate, as in Gallio of the Acts, we meet something more familiar and congenial to us as Europeans, the detached outlook and impartial justice which gained respect for the Roman rule in spite of its deficiencies. Pilate's position was that of an English Civil Servant protecting a native from native corruption. Very natural and true to life is his questioning of the prisoner. With the quiet innocence of the prisoner inside the Hall, and the rancorous noisy mob outside, he is instinctively on the side of justice. Yet his portrait is only too faithfully drawn, a weak loser saving his face by sarcasm, even to Jesus, whom he respects, 'Are you a king then?', 'Am I a Jew?', 'What is truth?', and by sarcasm avenging his defeat, when he puts up the title that mocks the Jews; obstinate again, as a weak man can be, when pushed too far, 'What I have written, I have written'. The crowd's preference for Barabbas furnishes another instance of John's dramatic brevity, 'Now Barabbas was a robber', a preference too tragic for comment. It reminds us of the exit of Judas from the supper, and the words 'And it was night'.

No scene could be more moving than this presented in the eighteenth and nineteenth chapters of the fourth Gospel, with the disciple watching it to the last, by the side of the Mother of our Lord.

## THE ACTS OF THE APOSTLES

THIS little book of twenty-eight chapters, the bridge between the Gospels and the Epistles, cannot be valued too highly. It is our chief description of Christianity in the first century A.D. Without it, however much we might infer from St. Paul's letters, we should have a very faint notion how Christianity came into action, what that action was, how it 'caught on', how it became European instead of merely Jewish, and how the Church came to be built up. This book, then, is of tremendous importance, and a very large part of its value is due to its literary method, and to the temperament and genius of the writer.

### Buoyant Tone of the Acts.

Think first of the tone of the book. Here we have a record of what it felt like to the ordinary man to be a Christian, to a man who had not been one of the disciples' band. The tone of the early Christians, their strange joy and its lasting effects, come out clearly in Luke's plain and happy narrative. We might have been incredulous of the raptures and mysticism of St. Paul's letters. But the Acts must carry weight. The glad tidings of the birth of Christ (Luke ii) are still the glad tidings of the gospel (Acts xiii. 32). 'The eunuch went on his way rejoicing.' There is no more solid fact to Luke than this, nor any more emphasized by him. 'It was the joyousness in the church that attracted Luke—not so much the teaching or the theology or the organization, but the new life of the Church. This fascinated him, the joy and gladness. . . . All through is the optimistic note of one who saw the spirit triumphing over

human frailties.'[1]  For Luke did see these frailties.  The buoyant
tone of the book is the more remarkable because Luke was a
quiet, steady observer, who did not conceal drawbacks—the
'murmuring',[2] the 'no small dissension',[3] the 'tribulation'[4]—or
exaggerate in his enthusiasm.  Paul was his hero and fell out
with Barnabas, and Luke notes it, and can still praise Barnabas.
Paul was continually engrossed and worried with the Gentile
question, as his letters show, yet Luke, though so much with
Paul, can give a very sober version of the struggle of the two
parties.  Paul had to blame Peter for his non-committal attitude, yet Luke can give Peter credit for his handling of the
question.[5]  Though aware of these troubles, he watched the
early Christians with the happiest confidence.

We can best gauge the buoyancy of the Acts if we imagine
what another writer might have made of it, a Christian Jew 'of
the circumcision', for instance, living in Jerusalem, and living
there always, with the temperament and graver outlook of a
Jew of Jerusalem.  We have seen the difference in tone of St.
Mark's Gospel and that of St. Luke.[6]  Such a difference might
have been noticed in the Acts.  The tale could easily have dwelt
upon the gloomier side, the sufferings of the persecutions after
Stephen's death, the complaints that resulted in the appointment of deacons, the poverty that succeeded the communal
sharing of property.  In a conservative and partisan spirit the
writer might have traced abuses in the Church, such as we find
in Corinthians, to St. Paul's admission of Gentiles, and have seen
in Paul's sufferings a judgment upon him for his hastiness and
heresy.  How Paul could have won over the Jews, he would
have said, but for his admission of Gentiles!  The whole account
could have been a rather melancholy story, dwelling on the
dangers of heresy, and only relieved by the faithfulness of the
poor handful of saints at headquarters.  The movement, he
might have said, should have been on narrower and more
cautious lines.

Instead of this the triumphant note of the Acts springs from
this 'door' to the western world of Gentiles or Europeans,

---

[1] Rackham, *Acts, Introd.*, p. xxxvi.    [2] vi. 1.    [3] xv. 2.
[4] xiv. 22.    [5] Acts xi. 1–18; Gal. ii. 11.    [6] See p. 35.

timidly pushed open by Peter with his hand on the handle, and then flung open by Paul and fastened back securely. Every push in from without is cause for joy, whether of the once hated Samaritan or of the busy folk of Antioch, the fickle folk of Lystra, the vain Athenian, or the curious medley of Corinth. Christianity to St. Luke was a plant of universal growth, one that will root anywhere, no shrub of Judaea with subdued foliage, but a rich-tinted tree that gladdens town and country from Jerusalem to Spain.

Only an early Christian historian could have produced such a history as the Acts, one who felt the atmosphere of that first generation. In the Acts there is the 'sense of big things being done in a quiet way'. The writer was struck by the power of the movement, shown in the 'signs and wonders' done. Stephen was 'full of power', 'with great power gave the Apostles witness'. This is reflected in the outsiders' view, 'the people magnified them', 'the officers feared being stoned by the people'. It is reflected in the Christian's attitude, too, 'fear was on all the church', only this fear was never free from gladness, singleness of heart, praising and rejoicing.[1] All emanates from certain outstanding personalities, and from two in particular, and this brings us to the second great feature of the Acts.

### The Acts—a Book of Personalities.

The Acts is a book of persons, not things; of personalities, not institutions and church organization. Some critics hold that great events in history are naturally grouped round great personalities. The history of Christianity in Luke's narrative centres in Peter and Paul. Luke has made them cover the early growth of the Church, as Peter fights its home battle, and Paul the battles abroad. The selection of these two, with Stephen as a link between, has given something of a unity to the book. Luke has not made the mistake of ranging too widely. The material at his disposal must have been bewildering. But as a Greek of Asia Minor[2] he gazes back eastwards

---

[1] v. 41.
[2] What Luke was exactly is not certain, see Rackham, *Acts*, Introd., pp. xxviii–xxxii.

to Jerusalem, where Paul was first active, and then faces west-ward to Rome, where Paul eventually arrived. That is his view of Christianity, as it moves under the impulse of Peter and Paul from Jerusalem to the capital of the world. This unity being secured, we may put aside the criticism of gaps which he has left—the growth of the Church in Egypt and farther east, and its origin in Rome itself—especially bearing in mind the narrow limits of a roll of parchment or papyrus, the book of those days. Critics point out that Luke does not mention Paul's stay in Arabia after his conversion. To these Luke would have held up his roll of material with a smile.

The Acts, then, has all the liveliness of a book of personalities. The very title strikes the personal note. This is fortunate. It is the only kind of book that could have been sufficiently readable, coming just after the peerless gospel memoirs. Suppose our only record of the Church had been written by a dull chronicler with a passion for names, lists of officials and their duties, who might have given us the genealogies of the seven deacons or the times and places at which they distributed relief, with no appreciation of the outstanding personality of Stephen! The impression might have been as flat and uniform as a bad photograph. On the contrary, how quickly Luke passes from the deacons as an institution to the spiritual work of Stephen, and to the tale of Philip and that interesting eunuch.

Think, too, if Luke had had a bent for constitutional history and left us an 'Organization of the early Church'. That conception of history was fortunately less known then. Some lament this lack. They would have welcomed more light on institutions, on bishops and presbyters and church government. They would say it was Luke's business to trace the course of church organization. But most will prefer Luke's artistic concentration upon his 'dramatis personae'. He has indeed stayed here and there to note organization and institution, but only the biggest matters have stayed his pen. As soon as he can pass from organization to personality, he does so. The religious routine of the Christians is covered by two verses—instruction by the Apostles, 'breaking of bread', and prayers,[1] with daily

[1] ii. 42.

worship in the Temple.[1] Quite as if by the way it is mentioned
that there was a definite hour for their Temple service, and that
the 'breaking of bread' took place at home.[2] The appointment
of deacons is told in six verses, but the doings of two of them in
nearly three chapters. The greatness of Stephen is as much
more to Luke than church finance, as 'the Word' was more to
the Apostles than 'the serving of tables'. If we did not know
Luke better, it would almost seem that the financial trouble
was mentioned just to introduce the figure of Stephen and
explain his prominence, but Luke's method of introducing
personalities in the process of describing the growth of the
Church is part of his artistic genius.[3] So the first dangers that
threatened the Church from within are not discussed; they are
illustrated instead by striking incidents, the story of Ananias
and Sapphira, and that of Simon Magus. The momentous
doctrinal question about the Gentiles is introduced by another
striking incident and another personality, Cornelius. The
ministry of women in the Church, a typical Christian feature,
is represented by the incident of Dorcas, and by the brief
account of Lydia. The system of collections by the daughter
churches for the mother church in Judaea is briefly mentioned,
but here again Luke directs our eyes to the great figures who
carry the alms, and are soon to absorb the story, Paul and
Barnabas.[4] In Paul's letters we find such collections frequent,
but Luke, in mentioning what was perhaps a regular piece of
organization, skilfully seizes the opportunity to bring these two
men before us, acting together for the first time. After he has
described Peter's arrest and retirement from the scene, Luke
returns to the subject of this collection, 'Barnabas and Saul
after their ministration returned from Jerusalem to Antioch'.[5]
Nothing could be neater or more economical of space than this
little insertion, which at once completes the subject of the
mission of help, and sets the stage afresh for these new actors
and their doings, especially for Paul who now replaces Peter.

[1] ii. 46.                          [2] iii. 1; ii. 46.
[3] See p. 108.                      [4] xi. 29.
[5] xii. 25. Or, 'Barnabas and Saul returned *to* Jerusalem *and* fulfilled
their ministration *and* took back with them to Antioch John' (Rackham, *Acts*,
pp. 183-4).

By this skilful manipulation of his 'dramatis personae' he also passes quietly from the doings of the church at home to the spread of the Gospel in Europe. Note, too, the quiet exodus of Peter (Peter 'went to another place'), typical of Luke's stage management. But the point is that while doing all this Luke has not overlooked an important item in church organization, such as collections.

### References to Organization.

For the Acts of the Apostles are not so isolated and spasmodic as the concentration upon particular persons would suggest. Though the references to organization seem so haphazard, they are fairly regular and opportune, for instance, to the systematic missions of the Apostles to confirm converts in new districts, as of Peter and John in Samaria,[1] the general tour of Peter,[2] the mission of Barnabas to Antioch,[3] of Judas and Silas,[4] and the second missionary journey of Barnabas and Paul, primarily to strengthen infant churches,[5] Barnabas confirming in Cyprus, and Paul in Syria and Cilicia. 'Confirm' is of course used in a broad sense here. The 'decrees of the Apostles and Elders' are 'delivered' to these churches 'to keep'. Besides mentioning these missions and, as we have seen, the religious routine after Pentecost, the appointment of the board of deacons, the collections for the mother church, and the provision for the government of new churches by instituting 'elders'—all referred to as unobtrusively as possible, because the main interest is in persons, not things—Luke pauses from time to time to give brief summaries of the Church's growth.[6] One summary is a picture of its harmony and generosity, another of its consolidation, another of the security it enjoyed after Paul's conversion, 'then had the churches rest . . . and were built up and multiplied'.[7] These summaries methodically draw the curtain on one act in readiness for the next advance. By some such phrase as 'in those days' Luke covers the lapse of uneventful

---

[1] viii. 14.　　　　　　　　　　[2] ix. 32.
[3] xi. 22.　　　　　　　　　　　[4] xv. 32.
[5] xv. 36. Cf. xx. 2, Paul took a year 'going over those parts'.
[6] Cf. ii. 41–7, v. 42, xii. 24.　　　　[7] ix. 31.

years, just as he abbreviates a debate by a précis, 'when there had been much disputing'.

*Introduction of Personalities.*

Luke has a characteristic way of introducing his big people. Space being limited, and the action pressing, the introductions are brief and rapid, and yet smoothly and quietly done. Notice how Peter is brought to the front. 'In those days Peter stood up *among the disciples* and said (their number was about 120)...' Yet the unanimity of the band acting with him is quietly stressed, 'But Peter standing up *with the eleven* . . .', 'they said to Peter *and to the rest of the Apostles*', 'then Peter *and the other Apostles answered*. . . .'[1] The introduction of Barnabas is a better illustration still.[2] He is going to be one of the great figures, so Luke gives us a glimpse of him in the first act of the drama, as giving all his property to the cause, before bringing him to the front of the stage in the second. This mention of him, which seems so casual, has much method behind it, serving a double purpose in Luke's scheme. For Barnabas, who gives all, serves as a contrast to Ananias, who pretended to but did not; Barnabas is the light in the picture, Ananias the shade. Secondly, Luke is able to bespeak our interest in him by a rapid preliminary sketch, 'Joses, a Levite of Cyprus', with a complimentary nickname, which he translates as if to make a special point of this 'consoling' or 'strengthening' power by which he will take in hand the new convert, the firebrand Saul, when no one else dare approach him,[3] and also consolidate the new church at Antioch.[4]

How quickly Stephen seizes the stage, and how quickly he seems to move to his fate! The deacons are barely mentioned, the success of the church briefly described, then 'Stephen, full of faith and power, did great wonders among the people. Then arose certain . . . disputing with Stephen. And they were not able to resist his wisdom. . . .' And his arrest follows immediately.[5]

[1] i. 15; ii. 14, 37; v. 29.
[2] iv. 36.
[3] ix. 25 and xi. 25.
[4] xi. 24.
[5] vi. 8.

*Saul.*

The hero of the Acts first appears as 'a young man whose name was Saul'. Rackham thinks this the best example of Luke's dramatic method. His past history we have to glean elsewhere—a pupil of Gamaliel, a strict Hebrew, born a Roman citizen at Tarsus. Luke lets his characters grow upon the reader, as the play unfolds, and loses no time in descriptions. So the next reference is, 'And *Saul* was giving his approval to *Stephen's* death'. Whether as an official or not, the word does ŋot imply. But the sentence brings the new great figure, as Luke intended, right up against the other. Some think he meant us to suppose that Stephen's death first goaded Saul's conscience (which 'kicked against the goads'), especially as Paul himself refers to his part in Stephen's death. Luke anyway saw drama here. He has taken pains to depict the intense spirituality and greatness of Stephen, his radiant face before the council ('as of an angel'), his vision of Jesus himself, his kneeling down, and his Master's prayer on his lips, 'Lay not this sin to their charge', and then this striking sentence comes, 'And Saul was approving . . .', to turn our eyes to Saul. This may well be Luke's silent way of recording actions and reactions. For he then mentions the persecutions following on this martyrdom, then Stephen's burial, and then Saul again. In a couple of vivid phrases Luke keys up our sense of Saul's importance as the leading actor. He 'did outrage to the Church, *haling* men and women . . .', and a little later, after a change of scenes, Saul 'yet *breathing threatening and slaughter*'.[1] How finely the zealot is expressed! Most skilful, by the way, is the introduction of Philip to occupy the interval between Paul's first activities and his conversion, and then of Peter's further acts to cover the time that Paul is in retirement. The change of the hero's name, too, is remarkably done, 'And Saul, who also is Paul', after which the 'Saul' fades out.[2]

---

[1] viii. 1–3 and ix. 1.

[2] The change comes curiously just after the mention of the Roman proconsul, Sergius *Paulus*, xiii. 7, 8. Luke evidently wanted to mention Apollos, who made such a name in Corinth ('I am of Paul, I of Apollos'). He neatly introduces him, therefore, along with the surviving sect of John the Baptist, which Paul came across in Ephesus, and of which Apollos was a member. Another example of Luke's clever editorship (xviii. 24–8; xix. 1–7).

You feel Luke would like to say why, but he may be thinking of the space allowed by the roll on which he writes. How quietly he brings Paul to the front by inverting the position of the names Barnabas and Paul! We start with this order, then have 'Paul and his company', and after that, with two exceptions, 'Paul and Barnabas'.[1]

But it is when Luke comes upon the scene himself that his brevity is most amazing. That 'we' changed from 'they', without a word of comment, is probably unparalleled in literature. Such an unobtrusive entrance. Out again, and in again once more, still without comment.[2]

*Graphic Scenes.*

We saw that in spite of his dominant interest in persons Luke does conceal much methodical attention to details of organization and the Church's growth. The framework is there, but artistically covered. One has only to make a brief synopsis of the Acts to see the clear and natural plan on which Luke proceeds. He follows the extension of the Church. In a nutshell the plan comprises:

The commission of the Apostles (i. 1–11).

The Church in Jerusalem (i. 11–viii. 3).

The Church in Judaea and Samaria (viii. 4–xi. 18).

The Church in Antioch (xi. 19–30, xii. 25–xiii. 3).

Paul's three missionary journeys (xiii. 4–xxi. 16).

Paul in Jerusalem (xxi. 17–xxvi).

Paul's journey to and arrival in Rome (xxvii, xxviii).

In the main, however, Luke believes in the 'living picture'. He has contrived to make his history a series of such pictures, in which his personalities figure. The pictures are not selected haphazard, they are usually typical of some special feature and never repeated.[3] The scene at Pentecost is typical of a mass conversion, the picture of the eunuch of an individual baptism. The eunuch, the treasurer of the Candace, 'was sitting in his chariot, reading. . . . He commanded the chariot to stand still,

---

[1] xiii. 13 and xiii. 43, 46, 50; xv. 2, 22, 35, Paul and Barnabas; xiv. 14, xv. 12, Barnabas and Paul, and also in the official letter, which Luke would not alter.

[2] xvi. 10, xvi. 40, xx. 5.          [3] Rackham, *Acts*, Introd., p. l.

and they both, Philip and the Eunuch, went down into the water, and Philip baptized him'. Martyrdoms were numerous in the first century, but the typical example was that first one, so graphically drawn: 'they cried out upon him . . . stopped their ears, and rushed upon him, . . . they laid their garments at the feet of . . . Saul. . . . He kneeled down, and cried, "Lord, lay not this sin to their charge", and saying this he fell asleep.' The Christian religious service had new features, but Luke does not give us a dull outline of one. He gives us instead an actual scene at a typical service, which was also a farewell service, 'in an upper chamber', where there were many lamps, and the sermon was long, and a youth sitting in the window was nodding with sleep, until he nodded over,[1] and fell from the third story. Yet even in this picture Luke includes some precise notes of historical exactness, of *time*, namely, the first day of the week, showing the change from the Sabbath to the Lord's day; of *place*, a room in a private house, high up (for quietness' sake), of *terminology*, 'breaking of bread' at a 'gathering together', the technical term for a service; of *custom*, the 'many lamps' being perhaps not only for lighting, but including those hung to mark the opening of the Sunday as a festival day.[2] Luke in fact combines the liveliness of the journalist or artistic writer with the fidelity of the historian. This is the third great feature of his book. It gives Luke's history that appeal which the best histories have, 'an appeal both to the general reader and to the student'.[3] The Acts is 'not only a good story, but one which can be trusted as a reliable record of events'.

The incidents at Philippi and Ephesus are good examples of Luke's appeal as artist and historian. The Church at Philippi was one of the most loyal, and Luke, left there by Paul, perhaps had much to do with the happy, generous spirit that seems to have prevailed. Luke no doubt could have dilated upon the work there, but he extracts one main incident, and that one the cause of Paul's departure. The account is rapid as usual,

---

[1] Luke conveys the suddenness of this by a skilful change of Greek participles.

[2] Rackham, *Acts*, p. 379. Jews and Gentiles had such illuminations.

[3] Trevelyan, *Blenheim*, preface, quoted by Archbishop Temple in the *York Quarterly*, January 1931.

and the turn in Paul's fortunes in this colony is dramatic, and
the language does justice to it: 'they *laid hold* on Paul and
Silas, and *dragged* them into the market . . . *the mob rose up* . . .
the magistrates had the men's garments *torn off* and the men
beaten. . . . The jailor cast them into the *inner prison*, and made
their feet fast *in the stocks*. . . . He called for lights and *sprang
in*, and *trembling with fear* fell down at the feet of Paul.'

But even in an account so vigorous and so lively Luke finds
time to be precise: about the *motive*, commercial loss and anti-
Jewish feeling in a Roman colony ('these being Jews, . . . for
us, being Romans') ; about the *court*, the 'rulers' or 'authorities'
of the town assembled, and the magistrates or 'duumvirs' of a
Roman colony presiding; about the *punishment*, beating with
rods or 'fasces', such as were carried before the Roman
magistrate by 'lictors', who are also mentioned by their correct official name in the Greek (xvi. 35).

So again at Ephesus, with the liveliness of the journalist he
paints the scene of riot, 'Filled with rage they *ran into the
street*,[1] . . . rushed *like one man* to the theatre . . . some were
shouting one thing, some another, but the majority did not
know what the meeting was for. . . . When they saw he was a
Jew, they all called out together *for two hours*, "Great Artemis
of Ephesus!"' But this liveliness is blended with the sure
touches of the historian, with his exact use of technical terms,
the 'Asiarchs', the 'town clerk' or 'secretary', 'proconsuls',
'ordinary meeting' (opposed to the sudden one which would
rouse suspicion of sedition), the title 'neocoros' or 'temple-
sweeper', which Ephesus enjoyed as the home of Diana's great
temple. 'Great Artemis' as the regular and distinctive epithet
of the goddess. 'Robbers of temples' is quite in place, for
temples served also as banks for the safe keeping of treasures.
The psychology is true, too, the guile of the Greek Demetrius,
the impetuous attempt of the unpopular Jew to transfer the
blame, the fanaticism of the Ephesian mob, the clever tact of
the town clerk, first pacifying, then rebuking and warning. The
clerk's sarcasm would appeal to Luke. He had seen much of
Eastern mobs, too much for even his kindly nature not to

[1] Bezan Text addition.

indulge in some irony: 'the greater part did not know what the meeting was about' (but called out for two hours all the same).

Luke's sense for pictures and scenes and drama is most evident of all in the last nine chapters. Memoirs have an advantage over history, in that the writer is freer to select from his material, develop a part which has dramatic possibilities, in which too he may have a personal interest, and, while observing proportion, not be a slave to it. The last chapters of the Acts may be disproportionately full of detail, but by allowing himself this amount of disproportion and confining his story to his hero Paul, Luke has given the Acts a dramatic close. One is always happy while the chief actor is on the stage, and in these chapters Luke has concentrated on what has been called 'the Passion of Paul'. If Luke did not know Greek drama, he at least knew the device of 'dramatic irony'. The end of the drama, Paul at Rome, is deftly prepared for by a verse in chapter xix, Paul's remark at Ephesus about his plans, 'After I have been there, I must also see Rome.' He was not thinking of going there in chains or that his seeing Rome would first entail more hairbreadth escapes than he had yet experienced. 'I must also see Rome.' How artless it seems in the narrative, but to Luke it meant drama, and he proceeds to work up this drama with unusual detail, the stages of the journey to Jerusalem, the farewells of the churches, the ominous predictions of danger on the way, everything that can intensify the feeling of an approaching crisis.

Three times Luke introduces warnings given to Paul, as he goes 'bound in spirit' to Jerusalem. The shadows gather as he draws nearer. We are reminded of our Lord, who '*set his face steadfastly* to go up to Jerusalem', and 'his disciples were afraid', for he also had three times warned them of what was in store. So in the Acts we have Paul's own foreboding in the pathetic scene near Miletus, when he tells the elders of Ephesus of the bonds and afflictions prophesied for him, and they 'grieved most of all for the saying that they should see his face no more'. At Tyre the disciples warn him '*through the spirit* that he should not go up to Jerusalem'. At Caesarea the prophet Agabus binds Paul with Paul's own girdle and says: 'So shall the Jews at Jerusalem bind the owner of this girdle and deliver him to the Gentiles.'

Again there is almost a counterpart to our Lord's triumphal entry amongst enthusiastic disciples, as Paul is escorted to the ship at Miletus, and again by those at Tyre, who 'all brought us on our way, with their wives and children till we were out of the city'. Something of the atmosphere of our Lord's last talk with his disciples is conveyed by Paul's address to the elders of Ephesus. 'I count not my life dear unto myself, if I may finish my course.' Like our Lord, he claims to have been among them 'as one that serveth', he warns them to watch, and he closes with the words of the Lord Jesus: 'It is more blessed to give than to receive.' And the enemy is the same. It is his own countrymen who want Paul's life, as they sought our Lord's, and it was the Gentiles who saved him, as Pilate tried to save Jesus.

In the graphic scenes following Paul's arrest we have Luke at his best, as he rapidly sketches the city in an uproar, the rush of the Eastern mob beating Paul to death, the soldiers running down, the fight for Paul between the crowd and soldiers, who literally carry him above their heads up the steps to safety, pursued by the mob yelling 'Away with him!' Then the deep hush, as Paul *beckons with the hand* for silence, and makes his first defence; the renewed uproar at the word 'Gentiles', clothes thrown off, dust tossed in the air, and the prisoner's removal to the castle. Luke seems to have remembered that crowd with wonder.

The trials all excite interest. You feel Paul straining to penetrate the prejudice against him, and yearning to reach the better feeling of his countrymen. But as the word 'Gentiles' wrecks him with the mob, so 'resurrection' cuts short the patience of the council. They are out for blood. It was just the time when the temper of the Jews was working up to make the Roman government impossible, the time of constant rebellions, of 'dagger-men', launched on a policy of assassination, and a small insignificant countryman like Paul might easily have been thrown to the wolves. Considering this the Roman rulers come out well in Luke's tale. Of each of them we get a clear and fair impression. Luke adds many an interesting touch from his own observation or inside information: 'the captain *took* the boy by the *hand*'—a kindly captain; 'Felix trembled'; the promptness of Festus and his pride in it, in contrast to the dilatoriness of Felix, is quietly expressed by facts.[1] Luke makes you feel as if you were listening yourself by giving you a gesture of the president, or a look of the speaker, as he stands on the rostrum: 'the governor *beckoned* to him to speak',[2] Paul '*looking earnestly* at the council';[3] and while abridging the speeches Luke always contrives to leave a first-hand impression of the speaker and the court. Very true to type is the professional orator Tertullus in that artificial exordium addressed to Felix, polite, fulsome, emphatic, 'Seeing that by thee we enjoy much peace . . . in *all* ways and in *all* places we accept it, *most excellent Felix*, with *all* thankfulness.' Yet Felix was a notoriously bad governor. The stylish plausibility with the vagueness of the charge ('a pestilent fellow, a mover of sedition'), epithets substituted for facts, evidently struck Luke, and he lets the rhetoric stand self-condemned.

### Paul before Agrippa.

The story of Paul before Agrippa is as stirring as that of Elijah on Mount Carmel. It is the old issue in a revised form: 'If the Lord be God, follow him.' 'If Jesus be the son of God, follow him.' Each plea is made before a king, with the people as witnesses. Luke has written up the tale with such care that he evidently felt it to be the climax of the history. His artistry consists in the fidelity with which, while making a précis, he preserves the salient facts of the scene and the spirit of the speeches and dialogue. The scene comes through to us as he saw it, and the actors speak for themselves. 'Hast thou appealed to Caesar? To Caesar shalt thou go.' Luke might have written, 'And Festus allowed the appeal.' When Luke allows those words to stand in their brevity (there are only five words

---

[1] Festus *the third day after* coming into his province went up to Jerusalem, xxv. 1. He stayed there not many days, and went down to Caesarea. And *on the next day* he took his seat, xxv. 6. '*I made no delay, but on the next day*,' xxv. 17.        [2] xxiv. 10.        [3] xxiii. 1. Cf. vi. 15.

in the Greek, two for the question, three for the statement),
and probably in their original order, he allows the feelings of
Festus to appear, his surprise, almost annoyance, at Paul's
sudden stroke, and his effort to appear unconcerned.

One would gather that Luke wrote out this scene just after
witnessing it, so real is the impression of Paul's speech and of
the dialogue, his tone more and more earnest, his delivery with
its own emphasis. The speech before Agrippa was occasioned
by a social event, the call upon Festus the Governor of the
province paid by Agrippa and Berenice. Agrippa had been
given the kingdom of Chalcis, and in A.D. 53 the Emperor
Claudius had given him part of North Palestine in exchange
for it, still with the title King, and also the charge of the
Temple in Jerusalem. He had just returned from Rome, where
he spent his youth, and had added Roman sympathies to his
Jewish.

*'As they tarried there many days'*, they used up the topics of
conversation, the gossip of the Roman court, and for a new
subject Festus mentions his prisoner. As Jews, Agrippa and
Berenice will be interested. *'I was wanting to hear the fellow'*,
said Agrippa. Festus had referred to him as 'man'; the less
complimentary 'fellow', which Luke preserves, shows the attitude of Agrippa well. *'To-morrow you shall hear him.'* The
reply suggests Festus eagerly accepting the chance of providing
a new interest for a guest, and he immediately sends round
invitations, as we gather from what follows. 'The man can
talk', you can almost hear Festus say. It is evidence of Paul's
powers and reputation that twice in the Acts he is given a 'full-
dress audience', with himself as sole orator, once before the
critical philosophers of Athens, and now before all the best
people of Caesarea.

Notice how the scene comes up out of Luke's concise description. It is graphic enough at the first reading, but when
each word is given its full meaning, it is like focusing a picture.
*'So on the morrow'* they assemble for a display of oratory, such
as Greeks and Romans loved. Agrippa and Berenice in court
dress and jewels and with their military escort (*'with great
pomp'*), enter the *auditorium* or great hall of the palace (*'place*

*of hearing').*[1] After them came the officers of the garrison and the civic authorities (*'chief captains and principal citizens'*). When they were entered in and seated expectant, 'on the order of Festus *was brought in—Paul'*. To the brilliant audience in military dress and colour entered a Jew of mean presence, a chained prisoner to provide sensation for the Governor's guest. Festus introduces the prisoner. *'You behold this man,* about whom *the whole multitude* of the Jews, *both at Jerusalem and here, beset* me, *shouting* that he ought not to live.' The vigorous language indicates the attitude of Festus to the violence of the Jews.

It shows the importance of the occasion that Luke, who does not repeat details, lets Festus repeat in public the explanation already given to Agrippa, and lets Paul repeat for the third time in the Acts the story of his conversion. Instead of shortening it, Luke leaves it with even fuller detail and its small discrepancies unaltered. He wishes this climax to have the utmost room he can afford.

'This speech marks the supreme effort both of the speaker and of his reporter. It is one of the most finished passages in the Acts, adorned with rare words and with an elaboration of style, not to say, grandiloquence.'[2] But here we are only concerned with Luke's skill as editor. What he has left out, we do not know. Paul must have spoken for a long time. Yet what we have would only have taken him four minutes to deliver. Festus would not invite a great audience to hear an orator and then cut him short so soon. Yet the speech is not disjointed or flat. What Luke has left in, shows Paul giving of his best. It was not the kind of best that Festus expected, but one full of personal experience and personal appeal. He starts with the orator's gesture, the hand stretched forth with the chain upon it, and he pays the usual polite compliment to the judge (he can match any Tertullus), but one that rings true, for Agrippa had the requisite knowledge. In unfolding the message of his

---

[1] Not the basilica or hall of justice. It is to be a public hearing, not a trial. That is impossible after Paul's appeal to Caesar.

[2] Rackham, who collects 13 words found here alone in the New Testament. See Rackham, *Acts*, p. 462, note.

Gospel Paul takes in not only Agrippa but his mixed audience, selecting from it a motive that will appeal to the majority, hope, a national hope, it is true, appealing more particularly to Agrippa, as a Jew, but as he soon shows, a universal hope, too, embracing the Gentiles, the whole assembly before him. Luke also preserves the flash of irony, 'About this (national) hope I am accused by *Jews*, O King!' and then the orator's sudden turn to the audience, as he identifies this hope with the Resurrection, and the orator's question, 'Why do you think it incredible that God doth raise the dead?' then once more the story of the vision, just as Paul brought out the words, as each detail came to memory,

'At midday—on the way—I saw, O King, from heaven—above the brightness of the sun—shining round me—a LIGHT—and (round) those that journeyed with me.'

and the matchless dialogue, with its tender repetition, 'Saul, Saul . . .', its question of remonstrance, 'Why persecutest thou me?', its proverbial idiom, 'hard to kick against the goads'— all so characteristic of the manner of Jesus himself in the Gospels (his Simon, Simon, . . . Martha, Martha. . . .' Why are ye so fearful?' . . . 'Why tempt ye me?' . . .).[1]

Even from this précis we can see Paul's growing emotion and enthusiasm, for on this occasion the mention of his commission to preach the gospel is not sufficient; he rushes on into a full statement of what that gospel means,[2] turning people 'from darkness to light', 'from the power of Satan to God', giving 'remission of sins' and 'an inheritance among the saints' by 'faith in Christ'. All through the speech the orator's emphasis rings out, 'in *all* the synagogues, *often* punishing them . . . being *exceedingly* mad against them . . .' 'in Damascus and Jerusalem and in *all* the land of Judaea, and then to the nations . . . I preached. . . .' '*For this* (!) Jews (!) arrested me in the temple and tried to dispatch me!' . . . 'witnessing *both to small and great* . . . *both to the people and to the nations*'.

Festus could stand it no longer. This was far too emotional

---

[1] Luke x. 41, xxii. 31. For the question of remonstrance see Matt. xiv. 31, xxvi. 50; Mark v. 39; John xviii. 23. Gore, *New Commentary*, p. 346, note.

[2] Contrast Acts xxii. 6–16 for greater brevity.

and personal for his audience, this talk about repentance. Afraid for his guest's feelings he broke out rudely, 'Paul, thou art mad. Much learning has driven you to madness.' But Paul for the fourth time turns to address Agrippa, and earnestly appeals to the Jewish side of him, 'Agrippa, you believe the prophets? I know you do.' It is Agrippa's turn to be uncomfortable. He fences with sarcasm: 'With but little persuasion you are for making me a Christian.' The remark is promptly but with Christian charity turned against himself, 'I would to God that *whether with little or much not only you but all* who listen to me this day might become such as I am, *except for these bonds.*' Paul's reply with its eager appeal, quick repartee, and humorous afterthought, must have impressed even that assembly.[1] Anyway, 'the King arose . . .' abruptly, it would seem, and the court withdrew to give its opinion quickly in the prisoner's favour.

Only a short space in the roll remains. How quickly Luke gets to business, 'And when it was determined that we should sail to Italy, they delivered Paul . . . and embarking in a ship . . . we put to sea . . ., and the next day we touched at Sidon.'

Once again we have the graphic pencil of the artist with the care of the historian.[2] 'The Augustan cohort' and the title 'First Man of the island'[3] are some of those many historical accuracies that research has shown to be the rule with Luke, while the 'corn ship' bound for Italy from Alexandria, and the stages of the voyage are according to known fact of ancient geography and history. But it is the account of the voyage itself that has contributed so much to Luke's reputation. 'The accuracy of his nautical observations is shown by the great help he has given to our understanding of ancient seamanship. From his description contained in a few sentences the scene of the wreck has been identified. Yet nautical critics tell us the accuracy is that of a landsman familiar, however, with the sea, and with a faculty of careful observation, who must have been

[1] Cf. Epistles for the same mixture of charity, wit, and irony.
[2] See note on p. 24.
[3] Cf. *C.I.L.* x, no. 7495, Mel(itensium) primus omni(um); *C.I.G.*, no. 5754, Prudens, a Roman knight, first of the Maltese, quoted by Rackham, *Acts*, p. 493, note.

himself on board.'[1] The fate of a ship and its company was never better written.

But even this careful scene-painting has not distracted Luke from his interest in personalities. The voyage only serves to show the ascendancy of Paul. He is the best man on the ship as he had been in the audience hall of Festus. When all had given up hope, his spiritual sense sees comfort, 'thou must stand before Caesar', and his common sense suggests the cure for depression, 'take some food: for this is for your safety'. His prayers were not only for himself but for the whole ship's company and even the prisoners. 'God hath granted thee all that sail with thee.' Luke seems to imply that Paul was depressed too, and prayed, and that the vision came in answer.[2]

So Luke shows peril after peril surmounted, and his hero's wish at last gratified, 'After that I must also see Rome.' Two bodies of Roman Christians came out of Rome thirty and forty miles to meet him, and 'he thanked God and took courage'. Luke as usual mentions the recovery of good spirits, and leaves the depression or nervousness to be inferred. At Rome Luke leaves him, till the curtain should rise for the last act, which unfortunately is wanting from our records.

### Diction and Style.

Something should be said about Luke's special vocabulary and style. The scenes he saw so vividly owe much of their vigour to his special vocabulary, such words as 'looking stead-fastly at'[3] of the speaker taking in his audience, 'shaking downwards with his hand' as he beckons for silence.[4] His most expressive words are often post-classical, that is, of the time when words took on metaphorical meanings, and are more highly coloured, than when they were first used. For instance converts in Athens '*glued themselves*' to Paul (A.V. 'clave to'), and Paul and his company '*tear themselves away*' from the

[1] Rackham, *Acts*, Introd., p. xlv., and pp. 476, 478.
[2] Rackham arguing from the 'we', ver. 20, and from 'God hath *granted thee*', ver. 24.
[3] A favourite word, also used of Peter looking at the cripple, iii. 4, of Paul, xiv. 9, and in i. 10, ii. 12, vi. 15, vii. 55, x. 4, xi. 6.
[4] xxi. 41.

elders of Ephesus, but as Luke uses the same word of Jesus *'removing himself'* about a stone's throw (A.V.) in the Garden, it is not certain how much force he intended to put into the word in the former passage. Then Apollos was *'boiling'* in spirit or 'fervent', the audience at Pentecost were *'pricked* in their heart', and Stephen's hearers were *'cut to the heart'* (lit. sawn asunder), Paul *'makes havoc of'* (lit. 'sacks') those who believed. Sometimes a medical metaphor lends colour, as when between Paul and Barnabas there came a *'paroxysm'* (A.V. 'sharp dissension') so that they separated, the word meaning a sharp attack in an illness. The same word is used of Paul 'exasperated' or 'sharply stirred' by the idolatry in Athens. Luke treasures up anything vigorous or expressive that he finds in his sources: 'What will this *seed-picker*[1] say?' the Athenian slang word for the superficial trifler who picks up scraps of knowledge like a bird picking up seed. *'See ye to it'*, says Gallio, or 'look to it yourselves', the very Roman phrase Pilate uses in Matthew. 'This thing was not *done in a corner'* is Paul's expressive idiom before Agrippa. 'Paul *shook out his lap*, and said . . .' preserves another gesture, and 'knower-of-hearts' is Peter's favourite word twice reported for us.[2] Luke's use of rare compound words, which he employs, or perhaps coins, as freely as Paul in his letters, is more interesting to those who know Greek.[3]

When we come to phrase-making, Luke's simplest phrases give a fine pictorial effect, like the *'rushing mighty wind'* of Pentecost, or as when 'the crowd of believers *had one heart and soul'*, or 'the lame man *jumping up stood and walked round*, and went with them into the Temple, *walking round and jumping* and praising God', exactly what he would do, feeling the new life in his joints, first standing, then trying a walk round, then walking and jumping in turn. Again, how could the unimaginative common sense of the Roman and his indifference

---

[1] A.V. 'babbler', xvii. 18.

[2]. And perhaps the proverbial phrase 'serving tables' was Peter's, vi. 2.

[3] They include: 'fighting-in-spirit-against' (θυμομαχῶν, xii. 20); 'worm-eaten' (σκωληκόβρωτος, xii. 23) of Herod; 'suffered-their-manners' (ἐτροποφόρησεν, xiii. 18) of God in reference to the Israelites; 'straight-running' (εὐθυδρομήσαντες, xxi. 1) of a course at sea.

to unpractical questions be better expressed than by the famous phrase, 'And Gallio *cared for none of those things*'. 'If it had been a legal question, reason would that I should *bear with you*' (they were troublesome and required patience at all times, but unbearable in their fanaticism). 'And he *drave* them from the judgment seat.'

Consciously or unconsciously Luke collected words to give *atmosphere*. Impressed by the greatness of Ephesus, but equally impressed by Paul's progress there, a great victory over a great stronghold, Luke punctuates his account with words expressing the greatness and power of the Christian forces. Apollos '*powerful*' in the scriptures . . . '*keenly and thoroughly confuted*' . . . Paul 'spoke with *great power*' and 'exercised no *common powers*'. The man with the spirit '*mastered and prevailed over* them both'. 'So *mightily* grew the word of God and *prevailed*.' [1]

Necessity drove Luke to economize in words, and of all economies none infuses more vigour into style than 'direct speech'. 'Men and brethren, what shall we do?' 'Stand up, I myself also am a man.' Even the crowd at Pentecost is allowed to express its own wonder, 'How hear we every man in his own tongue, in which we were born?' followed by the list of peoples, 'Parthians and Medes and Elamites . . . we hear them speak. . . .' It is wonderful how this sentence sustains itself and keeps its pitch, and in spite of the long list of names is able to be read with great effect. Then by his skilful use of Greek syntax Luke packs important matter into relative clauses [2] and prepositional phrases, but more striking are his short cuts, as for instance from indirect to direct speech, 'he commanded them to wait for the promise of the Father, which *ye heard from me*' (A.V. supplies 'he said' after 'which').[3] 'Paul and Barnabas urged them to stand by the faith, *and that* through much tribulation *we must* enter the kingdom.'[4] Paul alleged that Christ 'had to suffer and rise from the dead, and that this Jesus, whom *I*

---

[1] xix. 20.
[2] A relative runs the preface straight into the narrative, i. 3. Cf. i. 3. For prepositional phrases cf. i. 14, where a preposition brings in additional information of much importance.
[3] i. 4, 5.      [4] xiv. 23.

preach unto *you* is Christ'.[1] 'Saul, who is also Paul'[2] (Greek, 'the also Paul'), as a notice of a change of name without further comment is unique.[3]

Luke compresses a whole journey of Paul into one verse,[4] and glances over two years' work in another, and the speed of his narrative can be illustrated from the story of Lystra, where Paul is first worshipped as a God, and two verses later is stoned and left for dead, the text reflecting the sudden reversal of favour.[5]

## *The Promise of St. Luke's Preface.*

So in this vivid and realistic way[6] Luke has fulfilled the promise of the preface of his Gospel, 'it seemed good to me also . . . having followed everything from the beginning *accurately* . . . to write to you *in order*. . . .' As already mentioned Luke is accurate to a degree.[7] What are we to say of a writer who has to mention at different times twenty or more officials of all kinds, such as captain, politarch, secretary, proconsul, procurator, Asiarch, 'First Man', each in respect of certain towns or provinces, to which only they apply, and that too only during certain periods, and is always correct about them, even though these official names changed with changing political arrangements during this period, as when provinces like Cyprus and

---

[1] xvii. 3.                                                    [2] xiii. 9.

[3] Another peculiarity of Luke is interesting, the use for brevity's sake of an aorist participle *following* a finite verb, and standing instead of another finite verb: e.g. 'Agrippa and Berenice arrived at Caesarea, and saluted Festus' (Greek '*having saluted* Festus'), xxv. 13. Cf. xxii. 24, xxiii. 23–5, xxiv. 22–3.

[4] xx. 2.                                                    [5] xiv. 18, 20.

[6] Owing to Luke's habit of letting his authorities speak for themselves, we get a Hebrew style uppermost in some of the earlier sections. A typical one is that about Philip; 'an angel of the Lord spake unto Philip,' 'the Spirit of the Lord caught away Philip' (like Elijah). Another is ix. 31–xi. 18 with its Hebraisms 'it came to pass' (ix. 32, 37, 43, x. 25); 'alms' (ix. 36, x. 22, 31); 'had in remembrance', cf. the Jews' constant prayer 'remember me, God', x. 31. Hebraisms also naturally occur in the speeches of Peter and James. Paul was Hellenist as well as Jew, and his speeches show a marked difference of style. In James' speech notice 'Symeon', the Hebrew form of Peter's name, 'God did *visit*' 'a people' 'for his name' 'from the beginning of the world', 'generations of old' 'turn to God', and other phrases reminding us of the Hebrew canticles in Luke's Gospel, ch. 1 (Rackham).

[7] For full evidence see Rackham, *Acts*, Introd., p. xlv. See also note on p. 40 *supra*.

Achaia were exchanged between the emperor and the senate, and the style of their governors altered accordingly?

Even the speeches are selected with care and evidently based on originals heard by Luke or trustworthy witnesses. Luke has not followed the custom of ancient historians of inventing speeches to suit the occasion. The only dull thing in the Acts, the long speech of Stephen, with its purely Jewish argument, would never have been invented by Luke. As he has left it, with its drift difficult to follow and its abrupt breaking-off, it is a proof of his faithful reporting and editing. The speech, however, is important as a manifesto to the Jewish world, protesting against the same narrowness that was going to attack Paul. James's speech to the Council has the authentic Hebraic stamp upon it, and Peter's speeches, as already noted, preserve his Hebraisms of thought and phrase. Paul's speeches reflect Paul, especially his ability to adapt himself to his audiences, and Luke had the best means of getting an outline when he did not hear them himself. Nothing is more characteristic of Paul's versatility than his attempt to explain the Cross to the Athenians, when he uses an Athenian altar as a text, and quotes one of their own Greek poets.

Luke is also accurate in his 'atmosphere'. One of the greatest issues for Europe began with the impact of the Apostles upon the Roman government, and Roman officers and officials. Luke's account of the attitude of these to the new sect tallies with historical accounts such as Pliny's or the Acts of the Scillitan martyrs.[1] Finding what the trouble is about is the chief care of the Roman governors. Luke's account of Pilate, Gallio, Claudius Lysias, Felix, Festus, gives the legal Roman mind exactly, hunting for the legal point in the Jewish charges against the prisoner, and not deceived in the motives of the accusers.

Luke has also written 'in order'. We have seen the plan on which he works, based upon the Church's growth. A great problem like the Gentile question he brings in twice, first as it occurred to Peter, just before the new move at Antioch, then as it came to a head through Paul. Things which he might often

[1] Gwatkin, *Early Christian Writers*, p. 79.

have harped upon, like the sufferings of Paul, his chronic anxieties and continual burdens, apart from abnormal persecutions, he reserves for the most suitable occasion, that of Paul's farewell charge to the Ephesian elders. Historic order under Luke's pen becomes dramatic order too.

Let us sum up then what Luke has done in the Acts. He has given us the essentials of the Church's birth and growth, its biggest personalities, its biggest problems, but subordinating the problems to the persons. He has presented these in graphic scenes with the liveliness of a journalist and the fidelity of a historian. He has given the history of a great religious conquest the interest of a novel. At the end he has concentrated on Paul's arrest and its sequel, in which he himself shared, the last act of a drama that began with the stoning of Stephen. The 'passion' of Paul brings a dramatic unity into the story. Paul has carried Christianity to Asia Minor and to Greece. He 'must also see Rome'. In the 'passion' at Jerusalem followed by Paul's imprisonment at Rome Luke finds his natural climax and close. The epilogue he had yet to write, but he seems not to have done so.

Luke has thus supplied us with the historical background of Paul's letters, and shown us a personality second only to Jesus in the world's history. Those who would set aside the Gospels as the dream of deluded enthusiasts, the disciples, cannot set aside the realism of Paul's story, as he moves along the Roman highways, in contact at every point with Roman, that is European things. The story being real, how is Paul's experience to be weighed? Think on the one hand of the vision near Damascus three times told in the Acts, the impulse that moved him. Think on the other hand of all that might have deterred and restrained him, the things he went through. Then ask what we are to think of that vision, whether it could be anything but a genuine experience.

This is the problem that Luke has illuminated in the Acts. He has made the spiritual concrete and historical. Paul cannot be explained away, nor his vision. His churches remained all over Europe in their Roman setting. Then come the letters of Paul, all of a piece with the Acts.

Luke has shown Paul to be a necessity. Unless Christianity had been transferred to European vessels from Jewish, it would have dried up. How many Europeans would have turned Jew in order to become Christian? Jesus had not abolished circumcision in so many words, but he had accepted 'publicani' and Samaritans. Peter, however, as we know from another source,[1] even after his vision in Acts x, gave way weakly to Judaisers, and as the disciples through their prejudices were going to fail, Jesus showed himself specially to Paul to make Christianity safe for humanity. Paul was 'a chosen vessel indeed', Jew, Roman, and Greek in one. His Master's name had been written on the Cross in Hebrew, Latin, and Greek. The religious zeal and intuition of the Jew, the respect for order of the Roman, which helped Paul to prescribe good citizenship to his followers, the breadth of Greek philosophy and the expressiveness of the Greek tongue were all his, and so constituted he penetrated everywhere. 'To the Jew I became a Jew, to the Greek I became a Greek . . .' All this Luke has vividly sketched in these few chapters, and he lays down his pen with the happy record, 'And Paul lived in his own hired house, and received all that went in unto him, preaching the kingdom of God . . . none forbidding him.' It is not possible, says Streeter,[2] to render in English 'the strong, rolling rhythm of the Greek' of the last four words of the Acts, *with absolute freedom, and without restraint*'. They recall the dignity of the preface to Luke's Gospel, a finale worthy of the exordium.

[1] Gal. ii. 11, 12.    [2] Streeter, *The Four Gospels*, p. 539.

# IX

# THE EPISTLES OF ST. PAUL [1]

Features common to private letters—outline of a letter of St. Paul—oratory of St. Paul's letters:, 'elevation', imagery, questions, exclamations, repetition, a passage from Plato compared, balance and antithesis, epigram, quotations, protestations, diction, concentration, personal appeal, irony, tactfulness—difficulties for modern readers, in (*a*) matter, (*b*) style—staccato style—perorations—summary.

ALL Paul's letters have a personal tone. He was too warm-hearted for official writing, even to converts he had not seen, like the Colossians. As he dictates, he seems to feel his correspondents in the room. His letters therefore follow, in the main, an outline common to personal or private letters. At the same time he was a natural orator, perhaps a trained one, and always pleading a cause, so that his letters are filled out by argument and appeal—argument about doctrine, appeals in respect of conduct. The quick changes from keen, impassioned argument to close personal appeal, such as we find in the letters, are just what one would expect from the man who spoke as he did before Agrippa.

Personal or private letters have features in common, and may run something like this:

| | |
|---|---|
| i. Dear . . . | Salutation. |
| ii. I am glad to hear you are well . . . | The health and |
| I congratulate you on . . . | interests of the person written to. |
| iii. I have been not too well myself . . . | Ditto of the |
| I have been very well since I saw you . . . | writer. |
| iv. I want to explain . . . | Information or |
| They tell me you have . . . | criticism. |
| v. My advice is . . . | Advice. |
| vi. I shall be seeing you soon . . . | The next meeting. |
| vii. Keep well. . . . Do your best to . . . | Closing injunctions. |
| viii. Remember me to . . . | Greetings sent. |
| ix. Yours affectionately . . . | Signature. |

We may follow out the above scheme in St. Paul's letters.

[1] The authenticity of the three Pastoral Epistles has been long disputed, but until the evidence for rejecting Paul's authorship is more unanimously approved by scholars, it may be excusable to retain the few references to the Pastoral Epistles which occur in this chapter.

## SALUTATION

i. The salutations of St. Paul's letters have been compared to the ornamental capital letter at the head of an old manuscript. In their simplest form they run:

'Paul, an apostle of Jesus Christ, to . . .'

and he usually adds, 'by the will of God', because he was sensitive about the denial of his apostleship and commission. But in happy mood he expands this to three verses, as in writing to Titus, or even to six (Romans), for in his enthusiasm he cannot mention Jesus Christ even in a salutation without a word about the promise or hope which Christ offered. The expansion is by his favourite prepositional phrase and relative clause:

'Paul, a servant of God, and an apostle of Jesus Christ,
*according to the faith* of God's elect and the knowledge of the
truth . . .
*in hope of* eternal life, *which* God, that cannot lie, promised
before the world began,
but hath in due times manifested his word through
preaching
*which* is committed unto me, *according* to the commandment
of God our Saviour;
to Titus, mine own son . . .'

In the greeting to the Romans these two prepositional phrases and two relative sentences become four and three respectively, so that the greeting develops into a creed of the Christian faith, in a long parenthesis.

In these salutations there is a subtle touch which may easily be missed, showing Paul's literary care and quickness of anticipation, namely the delicate variation by which he makes the greeting anticipate and harmonize with the main tone of the letter. For instance, the letter to the Galatians answers the doubts thrown upon his apostleship, and so we find straightway in the greeting:

'Paul, an apostle, *not from men, neither through a man,* but by Jesus Christ, and God the Father . . .

On the other hand, in greeting Philemon, he begins:

'Paul, *a prisoner of* Jesus Christ . . .'

again anticipating the line of appeal which he is going to use, when he pleads as 'Paul the *prisoner*' for his son whom he 'has begotten *in prison*', and would have liked to keep to 'minister to him *in prison*'.

ii. 'I am glad to hear you are well . . .'
    'I congratulate you on . . .'

After the greeting Paul's first thought is to give some praise to his correspondents, and almost without exception we find in some form or other:

'I thank my God for your faith,' or (if they have endured persecution) 'for your patience'.

Paul is generous with praise, and its omission is significant, for he is always sincere. He could not praise the faith of the Galatians who had changed so childishly, and in this case the thanks are omitted. On the contrary he exclaims:

'I marvel that you have swung round so soon. . . . O foolish Galatians. . . .'

As the Galatians are in one extreme, the Philippians are in the other, and Paul thanks God for their actual partnership with him. They had made him accept help more than once. In the Corinthians there is a subtle change and less personal congratulation. Their fidelity was uncertain and they had 'swelled heads', and Paul substitutes 'thanks for their *knowledge and gift of intellect*' (though it had caused conceit) and for 'God's grace to them'. In the second letter he is still restrained, and gives thanks 'for the comfort of God'. Again, writing to Timothy, Paul remembers the faith of Timothy's grandmother and mother, and he 'is sure that Timothy has it too'. 'Stir it up— this gift you have', he goes on. The omission of praise is perhaps significant again here, for where Paul could see good points, he loved to dwell upon them and give encouragement.

iii. 'I have been not too well myself . . .'

Paul cannot help sharing his own news with his correspondents, usually of sufferings and persecutions, but not with any self-pity. He at once lifts them on to a higher plane. By a paradox they are a cause for rejoicing, his badge and privilege, and an encouragement to the converts.

'I overflow with joy in all our affliction. For . . . we were
troubled on every side. Without were fightings, within were
fears. But God . . . comforted us by the coming of Titus, and . . .
by the consolation with which he was comforted in you.'

'I sent Tychicus to tell you my news and to comfort you.'

'I would like you to know that my imprisonment is helping to
spread the gospel' (then follow personal confidences at some
length).

'I rejoice in my sufferings for you.'[1]

Then comes the main business of the letter.

iv. 'I want to explain . . .'

'They tell me you . . .'

The people addressed are at fault, perhaps, in ideas or conduct. These wrong ideas Paul corrects, testing them always by
his Gospel and, where possible, by the 'spirit of Christ'. It may
be the relation of Jew and Gentile, as in Romans and Galatians.
It may be sectarianism or behaviour at the services, or the
question of woman's headdress in church, or the difficulties of
those who have pagan friends, or even disloyalty to himself, as
at Corinth. At Colosse it seems to have been a tendency to
worship angels. These topics do not always interest our generation, but Paul's treatment of them, though sometimes Jewish
in its appeal, invariably leads to some great or broad conclusions that hold good for all time.

v. 'My advice is . . .'

Practice follows hard on theory. After argument and teaching, which the converts' mistakes have called for, comes his
practical application. His 'therefore' is as persistent as in a
theorem of Euclid:

'I beseech you *therefore*, brethren, present yourselves a living
sacrifice . . .' (Romans).

'*Therefore*, my beloved brethren, be ye steadfast . . .' (1 Corinthians).

'Stand fast *therefore* in the liberty with which Christ has made
us free . . .' (Galatians).

and so also in Ephesians, Philippians, and the rest.

vi. 'I hope to see you soon.'

The reference to future meeting is as common as in our

[1] 2 Cor. vii. 4-7; Eph. iii. 13, vi. 21, 22; Phil. i. 12-14; Col. i. 24.

letters. 'I was hindered from coming to you, but now . . . I I hope to see you on my journey . . .', says Paul to the Romans. 'Now I will come to you when I pass through Macedonia. I may stay the winter with you . . .' he says to the Corinthians, and again in the second letter, 'This is the third time I am coming to you'. So in Philippians, ii. 24. Where he cannot hope to come himself, he announces the sending of a messenger, to give them news about himself. His yearning for them makes him confident that they in turn want news of him.[1] 'Taken from you, brethren, for a short time, in presence, not in heart, we tried the more to see your face . . . we would have come to you more than once, but Satan hindered us.'[2]

vii. 'Keep well . . . Do your best to . . . Remember me to . . .' The last wishes and injunctions consist mainly of greetings to various friends, or commendations of certain converts, or such requests as: 'bring the cloak and parchments' (Timothy), 'prepare me a lodging' (Philemon), 'pray for us' and 'have this letter read to all' (1 Thessalonians).

viii. Last of all the signature coupled with the sending of his love: 'The salutation of me Paul, with my own hand. . . . My love be with you all in Christ Jesus' (1 Corinthians). 'The salutation of Paul with my own hand, which is the token in every epistle' (2 Thessalonians, cf. Colossians). Some form of the 'grace' is often added: 'Peace be to the brethren and love with faith. . . . Grace be with all. . . .' (Ephesians, cf. Colossians, Thessalonians, &c.).

Such is the outline in general of Paul's letters. We have become used to the fact, but it is striking all the same, that our religious 'manual', 'vade mecum', text-book, or guide to life, should consist, after the Gospels and the Acts, almost entirely of a set of intimate personal letters. We might have had a book of Paul's sermons, or of Peter's. But the fatherly tone of these letters preserves better the tradition of our Lord, and his '*Children*, have ye any meat?' 'Fear not, *little flock*, it is your Father's good pleasure to give you the kingdom.'

---

[1] Rom. xv. 22; 1 Cor. xvi. 5; 2 Cor. xiii. 1; Eph. vi. 21; Phil. ii. 19, 25, 28; Col. iv. 17; 1 Thess. iii. 1 (and cf. Heb. xiii. 23).
[2] 1 Thess. ii. 17.

*The Main Topics of the Letters. Oratory of Paul.*

Paul was an orator. Oratory is only pleading, and in his letters Paul sees his correspondents present before him, and pleads with them. Then he is never dull. When he embarks upon the main topics of his letter, even if it is a purely Jewish argument, he has soon done to it what every good orator is supposed to do, 'elevated it', lifted it up, raised it above the particular or the commonplace, given it a wider significance. He also gives it point with quotations from many sources. He enriches it with illustrations, and coins many a fine saying on his way.

*Elevation of His Theme.*

Take some instances of the way in which Paul lifts questions of conduct on to a higher plane.

He is dealing with good citizenship and the payment of taxes. The arguments and excuses which men make for treating governments less fairly than individuals are not for Paul's church. He supplies a broad principle and high motive. For civil power has the highest sanction and the broadest base:

'There is no power but of God. Rebels rebel against the ordinance of God. Rulers are the ministers of God to you for good, not a terror to good works but to evil.' [1]

So pay your taxes, and treat the problem with the breadth that belongs to it: 'Render to all their dues, tribute to whom tribute is due, custom to whom custom, fear to whom fear, honour to whom honour.' It is an expansion of the high and broad conception of citizenship with which Christ surprised the Herodians, 'Render to Caesar the things that are Caesar's, and unto God the things that are God's'.

Or he is appealing for tactfulness in the matter of diet, the question arising whether a Christian was contaminated by eating meats offered to idols. It was a temporary problem, but Paul's solution of it makes it apply to us and to men of all time. 'Will those who see no harm in eating such meats respect the scruples of those who do?' He gives the highest of reasons:

'For the kingdom of God is not meat and drink, but righteousness and *peace* and joy in the Holy Spirit. For he who serves

[1] Rom. xiii. 1-7.

Christ in these, pleases God and is approved by men. Let us follow after the things that make for *peace*, and by which we may build one another up.'[1]

The question of particular foods is not vital in the kingdom of God. So Paul raises the tone of the argument. Ceremonial wranglings are to be hushed in the peace of the kingdom.

Again, he is dealing with impurity. The Corinthian standard was lower than that of the worldliest man of to-day, who says 'it is natural to live uncleanly'. The Corinthians said, 'It is legal', 'lawful'. 'All things are lawful unto me.' Paul raises the argument at once by an apt comparison:

'Do you not know that your body is a *Temple* of the Holy Spirit that is in you, which you have from God. And you are not your own, for you *were bought* with a price? So glorify God in your body.'[2]

The Corinthians would appreciate the legal rights over slaves. Since 'redemption', they had lost the legal ownership of their bodies, and with it 'licence'.

It is often an epigram that gives the higher turn to the argument, and ends it at the same time. For instance the long talk about speaking with tongues and its tendency to disturb a regular service in church, is crowned by the remark:

'God is not a God of confusion but of peace.'[3]

It is sometimes a striking simile, giving distinction to commonplace advice:

'Do everything without murmuring and disputings, that you may be blameless and innocent, children of God in the midst of a crooked and perverse generation, among whom you *shine as beacons* in the world, *holding up the word of life*.'[4]

Sometimes it is a rapturous conviction:

'Be humble, as Jesus was.'

Then he describes the act of humility in dying on the cross, the sublime reward of which strikes him, and he goes on rapturously:

'Therefore God highly exalted him, and gave him a name that is above every name, that in the name of Jesus *every knee* should bow, and *every tongue* confess that Jesus Christ is Lord, *to the glory of God* the Father.'[5]

[1] Rom. xiv. 17–20.    [2] 1 Cor. v, vi.    [3] 1 Cor. xiv. 33.
[4] Phil. ii. 14–16.    [5] Ibid. ii. 5–11.

*The Art of Oratory.*

In ways like these Paul lifts his subject on to a higher plane and adorns the commonplace, and in his letters the fluency of the natural orator, as he dictated, must have taxed his secretary's speed. Yet what he dictates shows all the studied devices of trained oratory too: the *simile* that makes the meaning clearer, the *metaphor* that does this more concisely; the *question* that arrests attention, the *exclamation* that invites the hearer to sympathize or admire; *repetition* to bring out salient points and help the hearer to keep the thread of the argument; *balance*, above all, of thought and phrase, since the human mind and ear love contrasts of feeling and sound; *exaggeration* and *paradox* to surprise and startle him into thinking; *epigrams*, or sentences with the ring of a proverb, that he can easily carry away with him; *perorations*, or powerful conclusions of extra pathos or vigour to round off the appeal.

The orator in his pleading has recourse also to *prayers, wishes,* and *adjurations or oaths,* to strengthen his case. His sentence constructions vary with his mood, a longer period and more measured style for quieter argument, staccato style in hurried or passionate appeals. His diction is often picturesque, often forcible.

Paul's style may be called 'rich' in virtue of the wealth of words at his command, the abundance of illustration, the wealth of apt quotation, the flow of ideas, and rapid suggestion of one topic by another. His speed, and perhaps the checks suffered in dictating, cause omissions in syntax, and faults of construction, and verbs are sometimes left to be supplied by the sense, but on the whole the style is well controlled and balanced. So is his main argument well developed, and if he leaves it for a space, he inevitably returns, and ends it with a suitable conclusion, or works up to a peroration.

Above all, the strong feelings of Paul, his enthusiasm for his cause, his affection for the people addressed, and all that constitutes the orator's personality, are the most persuasive things in his letters. He has the irony of the Hebrew, and can use it effectively, but he reins it in, and converts it the next moment into affectionate apologies for his sarcasm.

Let us take some examples of his pleading, to illustrate the different qualities above mentioned.

*Imagery.*

The first example depends on the use of imagery. Metaphors from warfare were natural to one so often in contact with Roman soldiers. Timothy is to be 'a good *soldier*',[1] and 'serve the good *campaign*',[2] and the Romans are to 'put on the *armour* of light'. In Ephesians [3] there is a fine peroration, closing the rapid series of instructions in Christian conduct:

'Finally, my brothers, be strong in the Lord, and in the power of his might. Put on the whole *armour* of God, that ye may be able to stand against the wiles of the devil. For we wrestle . . . against spiritual wickedness in the heavenly places. . . . Stand therefore having your *loins girt about* with truth, and having put on the *breastplate* of righteousness; your *feet shod* with the preparation of the gospel of peace; above all taking the *shield* of faith, with which you will be able to quench all the fiery darts of the evil one. And take the *helmet* of salvation, and the *sword* of the spirit, which is the word of God.'

Paul, steeped in the Old Testament, borrows the simile. Isaiah has the 'helmet of salvation' (lix. 17) and 'righteousness as a girdle' (xi. 5). The Wisdom of Solomon has 'righteousness as a breastplate, judgment as a helmet, and holiness as a shield' (v. 18). Paul follows out the analogy more completely, and in order, and produces in metaphor the full panoply of the Roman soldier—belt, breastplate, sandals, shield, helmet, sword—as a fine conclusion to the general part of his letter. We are further indebted to him for suggesting to Bunyan the picture of Christian meeting the fiery darts of Apollyon.

The foot-races and boxing matches at the Corinthian Games supply him with another striking analogy, very apt for the converts at Corinth: 'the men in the games go into *training* for a *garland* that fades, but our self-restraint wins us one that will not fade. . . . *Run* with conviction, then, and *fight* with a sure aim, not *beating the air*'. . . ., 'I *bruise* my body (i.e. beat it black and blue).'[4]

It is interesting to watch Paul developing one of his metaphors. In a well-known passage he quotes a proverb: 'a little *leaven* leaveneth the whole lump'. This suggests to him the

---

[1] 1 Tim. i. 18.  
[3] Eph. vi. 10–17.  
[2] 2 Tim. ii. 3.  
[4] 1 Cor. ix. 24–7.

metaphor, 'purge out then the old leaven, that you may be a new lump'. His quick mind then glances from 'leaven' to the Passover feast, and its 'unleavened bread' ('put away leaven out of your houses'). So he develops his metaphor, 'For our Passover has also been sacrificed, that is, Christ; therefore let us keep the feast, not with the *old leaven*, . . . but with the *unleavened bread* of sincerity and truth'.[1] By this happy metaphor he has perpetuated for us the relation of the new feast of Easter to the old Passover feast.

Paul's use of analogy in argument was naturally frequent. By the *body* and the *members* he illustrates co-operation in the Church,[2] by *grafting and planting olive trees*[3] he illustrates the inclusion of the Gentiles in the Christian community, by the *grain of wheat*[4] the truth of the Resurrection. The analogy of the *potter and clay*[5] he borrows from Isaiah. *Slavery, sonship, adoption*,[6] illustrate the position of the Jews at various stages, and as the son is under *tutors* and guardians,[7] so the Jews were under the Law, till Christ came and they received full sonship instead of being like servants.

Paul passes rapidly from one metaphor to another. The Corinthians have been '*fed on milk*', when they should have been ready for '*meat*' (1 Cor. iii. 2), they have been '*planted* by Paul, and *watered* by Apollos' (ver. 6). This planting and this watering, he says, were equally important, for Paul and Apollos were '*labourers*' together with God, and the Corinthians were God's husbandry or '*garden*', and God's '*building*'. And at once Paul goes on to develop the idea of himself as a *builder laying the foundation* of the churches, while other men *built upon them*. And so in ver. 16 the Corinthians are the *Temple* of God.

## Oratorical Questions.

The oratorical question is a marked feature of the letters. For a strong appeal the question is often more effective than command. 'Are we downhearted?' has more challenge in it

[1] 1 Cor. v. 6–8.
[2] Rom. xii. 14; 1 Cor. xii, xiv.
[3] Rom. xi. 17–24.
[4] 1 Cor. xv.
[5] Rom. ix. 20.
[6] Rom. viii. 15; Gal. iv.
[7] Gal. iv. 1.

than 'Don't be downhearted'. Again and again the question comes as Paul grows warmer in protest or admonition. In one chapter of Corinthians (vi) there are fourteen questions in twenty verses, and six of them begin, 'What, know ye not . . .' The sequence of questions is specially rapid when his feelings have been wounded or his indignation roused. In 1 Cor. ix there are four questions in the first verse, and twelve in the next twenty-four. It is part of the 'torrential' quality of Paul's eloquence. Judge it by comparing such passages with the measured and leisurely arguments of the writer to the Hebrews. Though in deeper arguments, like that of his theme in Romans, Paul has to feel his way more carefully, even there this lively use of the question is to be seen, in chapter vi. 1, 3, 15, 21, and in vii. 1, 7, 13, and these questions lead up eventually to the finest peroration in all Paul's writings. As a passage of beauty, it has been considered second only to the passage on love (1 Cor. xiii).

Nine[1] successive questions throw out the challenge to the audience:

'What shall we say then to these things? If God be for us, who can be against us? He that spared not his own Son, but delivered him up for us all: how shall he not with him freely give us all things? Who shall lay anything to the charge of God's elect? Shall God who justifieth? Who is he that condemneth? Shall Christ Jesus, who died, yea rather, was raised from the dead, who is even at the right hand of God, who also maketh intercession for us? Who shall separate us from the love of Christ? Shall tribulation, or anguish, or persecution, or famine, or nakedness, or peril, or sword? Even as it is written, "For thy sake are we killed all the day long; we are accounted as sheep for the slaughter".'

Then he answers the questions himself in the strongest possible terms:

'Nay, in all these things we are more than conquerors through him that loved us. For I am persuaded that neither death nor life, nor angels, nor principalities, nor powers, nor things present nor things to come, nor height nor depth, nor any other creature, shall be able to separate us from the love of God, which is in Christ Jesus our Lord.'

[1] Following the R.V. (margin) Rom. viii. 31–9.

Notice his choice of all the biggest things that there are, and his balancing of them in pairs (but all unpremeditated, we feel, thrown out in the heat of the moment), and passing in a crescendo from *death* and *life* to *powers natural* and *supernatural*, then to the limits of time itself, then, as if this were not big enough, to the dimensions of the Universe, height and depth. None of these nor anything else will 'separate us from the love of God which is in Christ Jesus our Lord'. Notice, too, the change from 'the love of Christ', in the question, to the longer and weightier phrase for the close, 'the love of God which is in Christ Jesus our Lord'. Paul has a genius for building up his sentence and his argument to a climax.

There are other points that give distinction to the passage: the striking saying, 'in all these things we are *more than conquerors* (one word in the Greek), through him that loved us'; the way in which that last phrase, 'through him that *loved* us', picks up the word 'love' in ver. 35, and links it up with the same word in ver. 39, so giving a unity to the passage; the quotation with its striking phrase 'we are *done to death all day long*'; the wealth of words that pour out to denote the sufferings of Christians in ver. 35. But the power of the passage in the main proceeds from the rapid questions, growing in intensity and enabling the answer to come with double force and emphasis.

*Exclamations.*

A whole series of exclamations would have an artificial effect, but some of the most famous passages in literature are best remembered for some striking exclamation:

'How are the mighty fallen, and the weapons of war perished!'

is the most memorable line in a poem memorable throughout.

'How beautiful upon the mountains are the feet of him that bringeth good tidings!'

recalls one of the great appeals of Isaiah.

'Oh, what a fall was there, my countrymen!'

calls up Antony's great speech over the body of Caesar. The

exclamation is often the greatest moment in a great speech, when the orator has made his point, and turns from the audience and the argument in rapture or anguish and makes the audience turn with him to admire the grand result of what he has been saying. It is the orator's Hallelujah note. This Hallelujah note often breaks out in Paul's letters.

An alteration in his travelling arrangements makes him think of the happy results of his bringing the gospel to the churches, 'Thanks be to God who always leadeth us in triumph in Christ, diffusing the perfume of his knowledge everywhere by me!' [1] A prayer for the Ephesians makes him break into a doxology, before resuming the practical advice of his letter, 'To him that is able to do exceeding abundantly above all that we ask or think . . . to him be glory in the church and in Christ Jesus unto all generations for ever and ever. Amen.' [2] The long argument to the Romans about the law and the inclusion of the Gentiles in mercy, when at last brought to an end after many chapters, prompts one of the greatest of his exclamations, 'O the depth of the riches of the wisdom and knowledge of God! How unsearchable are his judgments, and his ways past tracing out! For who hath known the mind of the Lord, or who hath been his counsellor? . . .' [3]

But the best known instance of the Hallelujah note of exclamation in Paul's letters is at the close of his Resurrection 'paean': [4]

'Now this I say, brethren, that flesh and blood cannot inherit the Kingdom of God, neither doth corruption inherit incorruption.

Behold, I shew you a mystery: we shall not all sleep, but we shall be changed, in a moment, in the twinkling of an eye, at the last trump: for the trumpet shall sound, and the dead shall be raised incorruptible, and we shall be changed.

For this corruptible must put on incorruption,
and this mortal must put on immortality.
So when this corruptible shall have put on incorruption,
and this mortal shall have put on immortality,
then shall be brought to pass the saying that is written,
"Death is swallowed up in victory".

---

[1] 2 Cor. ii. 14. R.V. has 'maketh manifest the savour of his knowledge'.
[2] Eph. iii.          [3] Rom. xi. 33 ff.          [4] 1 Cor. xv.

O death, where is thy sting?
O death, where is thy victory?
The sting of death is sin,
and the strength of sin is the law.
But thanks be to God, who giveth us the victory
through Jesus Christ our Lord.
Therefore, my beloved brethren, be ye steadfast, immovable,
abounding in the work of the Lord always, knowing that your
labour is not in vain in the Lord.'

The merits of the English version of this great passage Quiller-
Couch has dwelt upon in his *Art of Writing*. In passing we may
notice the fine effect of the parallelism, as Paul lifts his argument into poetry, and his emotion is quickened,

'flesh . . . blood', 'corruption . . . incorruption',
'corruptible . . . incorruption', 'mortal . . . immortălĭtў',
'sting of death . . . sin', 'the strength of sin . . . law',

and also in the English version the effect of the sound of the
two nouns, one syncopated, the other running on lightly,
'incorruption', 'immortălĭtў'—more easily felt than explained.
Notice too Paul's practical 'therefore', which never fails to
follow close upon his rhapsodies, and his fervour still lingering
on in the fine triad 'steadfast, immovable, abounding . . .', all
strong words, each stronger than the one before, and as if that
were not emphatic enough, the absolute 'always' weighing in
at the end; lastly, the assonance at the close, 'not in vain *in
the Lord*', corresponding to 'the work *of the Lord*'.

But it is by that exclamation we know the passage best: 'O
Death, where is thy victory?' That is the highest moment in a
passage of great moment. And what is this exclamation?
Paul found something like it in Hosea:

'O death, I will be thy plagues,
O grave, I will be thy destruction.'

The 'apostrophe' and the balance are there already, but Paul
has remade the lines. He has put his exclamation in the form
of a question with increased effect, and he has improved upon
the diction. He has brought in the word 'victory', catching it
up from his quotation from Isaiah in the previous verse,
'Death is swallowed up in *victory*', and introducing it again in
his final doxology, 'Thanks be to God, which giveth us the

*victory*', so that this fine, strong word gives unity to the whole passage.

*Repetition.*

The next passage, from 1 Corinthians xiii, illustrates the effect of repetition along with balance or 'antithesis'. Balance or antithesis by itself is stately but cold, repetition by itself is emphatic and warm; this passage is a blend of the two.

It is remarkable that this unruffled and majestic passage, the 'praise of love', should come in a letter dealing with so many questions of behaviour, some humdrum, some irritating; that Paul should be able to write in this strain after spending so much force in clearing up the misconceptions of the converts. It is the most philosophical passage in his writings. Its tone is almost Platonic, and Plato has a passage very like it (see p. 145). Yet this passage on 'love' fits into the rest of the letter most naturally.

In chapter ix Paul is somewhat ruffled, as the rapid questions show. 'Am I not an Apostle? am I not free? have I not seen Jesus Christ our Lord? Are you not my work in the Lord?' Then, leaving the personal question, always a little ruffling to a saint, he falls into a quieter strain of instruction, 'I would like you to know, brothers' (ch. x), 'Therefore, my beloved . . .' (ver. 14), 'And I want you to know . . .' (about the place of women in the church, ch. xi), 'And about spiritual gifts, brethren, I want you to know' (ch. xii). Then comes the long analogy of the body and members, then a list of different works for members to do. A typical series of rhetorical questions follows to show 'We can't all do everything', but we must 'try to cultivate the best gifts'. Yes, and 'I will show you a superlative way', better than all the rest.

And then the man who wrote 'You have many instructors, but not many *fathers*', 'I am your *father*', 'I have sent my beloved *son*, Timothy', 'my *son*, Onesimus, whom I begot in my bonds', goes on to dictate what is by universal consent 'the pearl of the letters', and the greatest passage in the New Testament after the talks of Jesus. Paul settles down, as far as he can, to a slower rhythm. For once he does not hurry.

His balance of phrase is undisturbed by rhetorical question or rapture, his theme mastering him, the praise of love, but himself the master of his theme, because of his intense experience of what it deals with, 'love suffereth long'. While the sentences roll off so easily, he is thinking steadily of what he has seen in the church at Corinth. Each phrase describing love corresponds to some weakness in his converts. Tongues, prophecy, knowledge were at present their all in all: envy, conceit, censoriousness, divisions, were some of their faults. So the gist of the passage is this, that while absence of love spoils all the best religious work, the presence of it ensures perfect balance of temper and spirit, a spirit that is kind, rejoices, hopes, endures. Moreover, love lasts on ; prophecies, tongues, knowledge do not ; they are temporary and partial, and when perfection comes, are put away, as childish things are put away by the grown man. Faith, hope, and love all last on, but the greatest of these is love.

The music of the passage will be found to depend mainly on balance strengthened by repetition:

1. *If I* speak with the tongues of men and of angels,
   *and have not love,*
   I am become sounding brass, or a clanging cymbal.
2. *And if I* have prophecy, and know *all* mysteries and *all* knowledge,
   *and if I* have *all* faith, so as to remove mountains,
   *and have not love,*
   I am *nothing.*
3. *And if I* bestow all my goods to feed the poor,
   *and if I* give my body to be burned,
   *and have not love,*
   it profiteth me *nothing.*
4. *Love* suffereth long, is kind ;
   *Love* envieth not ;
5. *Love* vaunteth not itself, is not puffed up ;
   Doth not behave itself unseemly, seeketh not her own,
   Is not easily provoked, taketh not account of evil,

Note (i) the favourite triplet arrangement of this section, vv. 1–3; (ii) the couplet, sounding brass or clanging cymbal; (iii) the emphatic repetition of 'all ... all ... all'.

Note again the triplet here,

6. *Rejoiceth* not in iniquity, but *rejoiceth* with the truth.

7. Beareth *all things*, believeth *all things*, Hopeth *all things*, endureth *all things*.

8. Love never faileth;
   but *whether* (there be) prophecies, *they shall be done away*;
   *whether* (there be) tongues, they shall cease;
   *whether* (there be) knowledge, *it shall be done away*.

9. For we know *in part*, and we prophesy *in part*;

10. But when that which is perfect is come, then that which is *in part shall be done away*.

11. When I was *a child*, I spake *as a child*, I felt *as a child*, I thought *as a child*. But when I became a man, I put away *childish* things.

12. For *now* we see in a mirror, darkly, *but then* face to face:
    *now* I know *in part*, but *then* shall I know even as also I am known.

13. And now faith, hope, love last on, these three, but the greatest of these is love.

*the couplet, and here the quartet.*

*Here again the triplet,*

*and here the couplet,*

*and again the triad.*
*In all these the balance makes for stateliness, the repetition brings vigour and force.*

One has only to look at the words italicized to see what the passage owes to repetition both in rhythm and force. There are other merits, of course. It is all about the abstract quality of love, and yet it is all concrete—what things love does, and how it wears better than any other gift, better than all those partial things, which will fade in the light of the perfection to come. The brevity, again, in the Greek is wonderful, especially in ver. 8, where twelve words only represent all the English. The whole of vv. 4–11 in Greek looks like a mass of verbs, which do more work than any other part of speech. Then there is the epigram to close, with its compactness and pleasant rhythm, ending aptly on the word 'love', the theme of the whole.

*A Passage from Plato compared.*

We find Plato and Paul writing in the same vein on much

the same theme. Plato [1] does his best with the highest kind of love that the pagan world knew, the happy, gay, eager love 'charming the minds of all'.

For his effect Plato relies most on antithesis or balance, but this becomes rather artificial, as will be seen; Paul relies on repetition as well. Plato's personification of Love as a guide and father is poetical, but less real than Paul's concrete phrases about what love does *within* the man, 'suffers long . . . is kind . . . hopes all things'.

Here then is the praise of love, passionate love (ἔρως), not Christian love (ἀγάπη):

'This is my feeling, Phaedrus. Love first is himself fairest and best, and then is the cause of such qualities to all others. And I may quote a line of verse, this is he who makes
  'Peace among men and quiet in the air,
  Calm on the ocean, rest and sleep mid care.'
It is he who *empties* us of strangeness          Couplet.
      and *fills* us with friendliness,
ordaining all our social gatherings,
our guide in festivals, in dances, in sacrifices;
  *compelling* gentleness, *expelling* cruelty,
  *bountiful* of kindness, *niggardly* of hate,
gracious to the good,                              Triplet.
  admired by the wise,
  revered by the gods;
  coveted by the portionless,
  desirable to the rich,
the father of daintiness, softness, delicacy,
graces, longing, desire;
  careful of the good,
  careless of the bad;
in labour, in fear, in desire, in speech,          Quartet.
pilot, mariner, ally, and saviour the best,
  the ornament of all, Gods and men;
  the fairest and best of guides, whom every
  one ought to follow,
  making fair melody, sharing in the fair
  song,
which *he* sings, charming the mind of all,
both Gods and men.'

[1] *Symposium*, 19.

*Balance and Antithesis.*

We are always balancing one thing with another for comparison or contrast. Greek writers and orators were almost too fond of doing so. It suited their special temperament, and they had special particles to mark balance and antithesis. As a fervid Hebrew, Paul's oratory is less restrained, often, in fact, 'torrential'. He then has not time for particles, though even on these occasions he controls his speech with balance and antithesis:

> 'We are pressed on every side, yet not straitened,
>     perplexed, but not despairing,
>     persecuted, but not abandoned,
>     struck down, but not destroyed,
> always bearing about the *dying* of Jesus in my body,
> that the *living* also of Jesus may be shewn in my body.' [1]

The rush of thought that pours out four antitheses in quick succession does not prevent him from rounding off the whole with a still more complete one. One section of the letter to the Romans shows the use of balance and antithesis successively in argument (xi. 10–24), in rhapsody (xi. 33–5), and in exhortation (xii. 3–16). The last portion illustrates it best, where in the Greek participles are poured forth, main verbs omitted, or when inserted, promptly changed in construction, and everything seems to show Paul dictating at full speed. Yet the orator in him still balances his participles and other constructions in pairs, or for a change, in threes.

As with participles, so with adjectives and nouns. They come out with a rush, but some small word is repeated to check the rush and preserve balance:

> '*Whatever* things are true, *whatever* things reverend, *whatever* just, *whatever* pure, . . . *if* (there is) any virtue, and *if* any praise, think on these things.'
> '*If* there is any consolation in Christ, *if* any comfort of love, *if* any fellowship of the spirit, *if* any compassions and mercies, fill up my joy.' [2]

So we get the hammerlike emphasis of the enthusiastic pleader.

----

[1] 2 Cor. iv. 8–12.                    [2] Phil. iv. 8 ff.

The next passage, from 2 Corinthians, is perhaps the best instance of Paul's torrential style, because his personal feelings have been wounded and issue in a natural outburst. He has suppressed these feelings all through the letter, but at last they will find vent. He holds himself in at first by frequent apologies (chaps. xi. 1, 16, 21, 23; xii. 1, 11), characteristic of his affection ('bear with me, foolish as I am'); then comes a passage which in spite of its speed will be seen to preserve balance and antithesis, in every part of it, from the opening questions, through all the prepositional phrases, down to the closing questions of the peroration.

He is stirred by the ungraciousness of the Corinthians. After all he has gone through for them, to be lightly put aside as not a real apostle!

'Are they Hebrews? So (am) I:
Are they Israelites? So (am) I.
Are they the seed of Abraham? So (am) I.
Are they ministers of Christ? (It is foolish of me to talk like this) I (am) more so:
in labours more abundantly,[1]
in prisons more abundantly,
in stripes above measure,
in deaths often.

[1] Notice the hammer-like emphasis here and the similar effect of the numbers, 'five times', 'thrice', 'once'.

Of the Jews *five times* received I forty (stripes) save one;
  *thrice* I was beaten with rods;
  *once* I was stoned;
*Thrice* I suffered shipwreck;
A night and a day I have been in the deep;
(in) journeyings often,[2]
(in) perils of rivers,
(in) perils of robbers,
(in) perils from countrymen,
(in) perils from the Gentiles,
(in) perils in the city,
(in) perils in the wilderness,
(in) perils in the sea,
(in) perils among false brethren;
in labour and travail,[3]
 in watchings *often*,
in hunger and thirst,
 in fastings *often*,
in cold and nakedness.

[2] The prepositions are omitted here, the grammar sacrificed in the hurry, but the balance is always retained.

[3] As a relief from the repetition, threatening to become monotonous, there is a change of rhythm, and the balance of this quintet arrange-

Besides the things from without, (there is) that which presseth upon me daily, the care of all the churches.[4]
Who is weak, and I am not weak? Who is made to stumble, and I burn not?
If I must needs boast, I will boast of the things of my weakness. The God and Father of the Lord Jesus knoweth, who is blessed for evermore, that I lie not.[1]

ment should be particularly noticed.
[4] The biggest thing of all saved for the peroration.

There the passage properly ends, but an afterthought occurs to him, the memory of his escape from Damascus, natural enough in a letter, though out of place after the climax of vv. 29–31, the indignant questions and the oath to his sincerity. It is a remarkable piece of oratory, because it looks so spontaneous. It looks like, and probably was, an indignant outpouring dictated at one sitting, too full of feeling for Paul to trouble much about form. Yet the oratorical form is there, with its quick and subtle changes of emphasis and rhythm, its groupings of phrases, its delicate changes of diction even in the matter of adverbs (ver. 23). The A.V. here preserves the effect of the Greek excellently, its vigour and brevity, as well as the qualities just mentioned. More modern versions tend to spoil it.[2]

### Epigram.

An instance of *paradox* has just been given, and the emphasis of *hyperbole* can only be illustrated by isolated quotations, but *epigrams* are continually coming in the letters, to add force to an argument or close it summarily. Paul has a genius for coining a phrase, and giving it the ring of a proverb, and the truth of an axiom. They are another source of the richness and exuberance of Paul's style. In the Greek these epigrams are still more compact than in English, for Paul often omits the verb 'to be' and whatever else can be understood without saying.

'*None of us lives unto himself*'[3] is a great enough saying, of wide bearing on life, simple and compact—yet it only comes out of a discussion about eating particular foods and keeping

[1] 2 Cor. xi. 22–31.
[2] For another famous passage, on the great paradox of the Christian life, see 2 Cor. vi. 1–10.    [3] Rom. xiv. 7.

certain days. 'If we live, we live unto the Lord', like slaves
who lived only for their masters and owners. '*God is not* (a God)
*of confusion, but of peace,*' rounds off the instructions about
order in the churches, and the danger of uncontrolled talking.[1]
'*For the wages of sin is death*' will be found a particularly
interesting case of the forceful epigram concluding the argument, when you look at its setting:

> 'When ye were servants of *sin*, ye were free from righteousness.
> What fruit had ye then in those things, of which ye are now
>     ashamed?
> *for the end of those things is death.*
> But now being made free from *sin*, and having become servants
> of God, ye have fruit unto holiness, and the *end* eternal life.
> For *the wages of sin is death*,
>     but the gift of God is eternal life,
>         through Jesus Christ our Lord.'[2]

Here you see an epigram in the making. Paul did not think of
it all at once. Sin merely 'ended' in death. But '*servants*' suggests '*wages*' (or 'rations'), and, in contrast, God, as a master,
*gives* more than is earned, gives a gift beyond mere wages. So
in the epigram that comes in so easily and aptly to crown the
argument, 'wages' is introduced as a contrast to 'gift'. The
other delicate verbal antitheses in this passage must not detain
us here.

'*The love of money is the root of all evil*'[3] ends a few remarks
upon riches. In fact Paul rarely leaves an argument without
saying something better than all that has gone before it. Even
the passage on 'Love' is greatest in the close,

> 'And now abide faith, hope, love, these three, but the greatest
> of these is love,'

where 'abide', though a fine English word, does not give all the
force of the Greek word, and Moffatt has substituted 'last on';
'faith, hope, love last on. . . .' 'These three', an artless little
phrase, provides the slight pause required between the two big
propositions, with a delightful bit of rhythm in the Greek
original, and effective even in the English. The three Christian

----

[1] I Cor. xiv. 33.                    [2] Rom. vi. 20–3.
                    [3] I Tim. vi. 10.

qualities, which Paul selects and combines in a moment, have been accepted for all time.

Even in familiar talk, as with his great friends the Philippians, about whether he will be released to see them, he coins the memorable epigram that sums up his outlook on life and death,

'To me to live is Christ, and to die is gain.'[1]

Here as often the epigram is the kernel of the talk, the great saying that slips out all unpremeditated, a polished coin ready for currency, and on he goes with his argument. Some such sayings were no doubt proverbs which Paul is quoting, for he quotes abundantly as we shall see, but he can improve upon his original.

As for Christian mottoes, Paul is full of thumbnail expressions of the Christian way of life. Among them few say so much in little space as:

'Rejoice evermore; pray without ceasing; in everything give thanks,'[2]

or again the orders to Christians as soldiers:

'Watch, stand, play-the-man, be strong,'[3]

four strong words abruptly introduced in the closing messages to the Corinthians. Then there is the bracing tonic effect of:

'The night is far spent,
the day is at hand;
   let us cast off the works of darkness,
and let us put on the armour of light.'[4]

This has balance and striking images, 'the dawn' and 'putting on armour', and it paves the way for a shorter, bolder motto still, a hyperbole, 'put on the Lord Jesus Christ'. In the following one Paul's optimism cannot express itself emphatically enough, with its double contrast and very strong adverbial phrase:

'Our *light* affliction which is *for a moment*
produces more and more exceedingly for us
an *everlasting weight* of glory.'[5]

[1] Phil. i. 21.    [2] 1 Thess. v. 16.    [3] 1 Cor. xvi. 13.
[4] Rom. xiii. 12.         [5] 2 Cor. iv. 17.

Several times Paul epitomizes Christianity most happily in a
verse or two, as in the letter to Titus (ii. 11–15). It is done in
his stride among miscellaneous recommendations.

*Quotations.*

Paul's capacious memory has the Old Testament within call
from end to end, but he can quote freely too from pagan literature, a proverb perhaps, 'a little leaven leaveneth the whole
lump',[1] a Greek poet, in a talk to Greeks, 'for we also are his
offspring',[2] a saying again about the Cretans, also in verse, 'the
Cretans are always liars, evil beasts, idle gluttons'.[3] When
pressing an argument, his quotations come thick and fast. In
one chapter of Romans [4] he quotes eleven times, in the next
eight times, and in the next five times, in rapid succession from
Genesis, Exodus, Jeremiah, Malachi, Isaiah, Hosea, Deuteronomy, Joel, Kings, Psalms. His consciousness of this may
have suggested to him the maxim at the end of his letter, that
'all things written aforetime were written for our learning'. In
Galatians iii we have Genesis in ver. 8, Deuteronomy in 10,
Habakkuk in 11, Leviticus in 12, and Deuteronomy again in 13.
This rapid use of quotation in support of his argument is often
too Jewish for us. More attractive to our ears is his 'Death is
swallowed up in victory',[5] aptly quoted from Isaiah (xxv. 8)
as the climax of his talk on the Resurrection, or the promise
'Thou shalt heap coals of fire on his head' from Proverbs.[6]

*Titles of God.*

There are many other things that make Paul's style rich.
In his stride he will treat us to great descriptions of God.
Timothy is to keep the commandment blameless, until the
appearing of our Lord Jesus Christ, which in his own good time
*he* shall show, 'who is the blessed and only Potentate, the King
of Kings, and Lord of Lords, who only hath immortality,
dwelling in the light, which no man can approach unto, whom
no man hath seen or can see, to whom be honour and power
everlasting. Amen.'[7] When he interjects a prayer for the *peace*

[1] Gal. v. 9; 1 Cor. v. 6.       [2] Acts xvii. 28.       [3] Tit. i. 12.
[4] Ch. ix.      [5] 1 Cor. xv. 54.      [6] Rom. xii. 20.      [7] Tim. vi. 15.

of mind of the Thessalonians, it is 'the *Lord of peace*' himself who is to give them peace.[1] In one chapter of Romans [2] three times he gives God the title that fits the thing prayed for:

'We that are strong ought to bear the infirmities of the weak. . . . Things written aforetime were written for our learning that through *patience* and *comfort* of the scriptures we might have hope. Now *the God of patience and comfort* grant you . . .'

From a literary point of view how the title harmonizes with what has gone before! These titles have also made some contribution to our religious thought. Paul goes on to speak of the promises to the Gentiles, and quotes four times from the Old Testament about the joy and trust of the Gentiles. So his second prayer on the same note also has its suitable title for God:

'Now *the God of hope* fill you with all *joy and peace in believing*, that ye may abound in *hope*.'

So the prayer exactly corresponds in thought and sound to the reasoning that precedes it, for peace in believing is the same as 'trust'. Yet one cannot think that Paul while dictating had much time to think out such correspondences and elaborate his sentences so carefully. They have a spontaneous look. The third prayer and title ends the chapter:

'Now the *God of peace* be with you all.'

In 2 Thessalonians ii. 16 we find these titles expanded by a relative sentence:

'Now our Lord Jesus Christ and God our Father, who loved us and gave us eternal comfort and good hope through grace, comfort your hearts, and stablish them in every good work and word.'

These perfect little prayers, thrown out with such apparent ease all ready for use through the ages, beautifully rounded in phrase, and full of theology, show Paul at his best in thought and expression. Sometimes they give a finish to the whole letter like the beautiful one at the close of the first letter to the Thessalonians:

'The God of peace sanctify you wholly, and may your whole

[1] 2 Thess. iii. 16.    [2] Ch. xv.

spirit and soul and body be preserved blameless until the coming of our Lord Jesus Christ.'

Or he can afford to close a mere paragraph with such a finale as this:

'Now unto the King, eternal, immortal, invisible, the only God, be honour and glory for evermore. Amen.'[1]

*Orator's Protestations.*

Like all orators Paul has also to give emphasis by oaths and adjurations. One of the most celebrated passages of Demosthenes the Athenian is famous for the oath 'by those who risked their lives at Marathon I swear it. . . .' Paul, too, makes effective use of this additional appeal,

'I beseech you, *by the mercies of God* . . .'[2]
'I beseech you, *by the meekness and gentleness of Christ* . . .'[3]
'Every day I am at death's door; I swear it, *by my pride in you.*'[4]

Even in these oaths Paul's fine literary sense is seen in the aptness with which the oath fits the rest of what he is saying. The first of those quoted springs naturally out of the last point made, 'God hath shut up all unto disobedience that he might *have mercy upon all.*' The second fits his prayer that he may be able to rebuke them as gently as possible (x. 2). The third corresponds with his chief feeling towards the Corinthians expressed in the opening of the letter (i. 4–6).

*Diction.*

The diction of Paul is as striking as his force of epigram. It is continually enlivened by metaphor, '*glueing* yourselves to the good',[5] '*boiling* with the spirit',[6] '*buying up* the opportunity',[7] 'let the love of Christ *make its home* in you',[8] 'let the peace of Christ *be umpire* in your hearts',[9] obviously the diction of an enthusiast using the strongest and liveliest expressions, and still more so, when he uses doublets: 'I *maul and master* my body' (to keep it in subjection),[10] '*rooted and founded* (A.V.,

[1] 1 Tim. i. 17.    [2] Rom. xii. 1.    [3] 1 Cor. x. 1.
[4] 1 Cor. xv. 30.    [5] Rom. xii. 10.    [6] Ibid. 11.
[7] Eph. v. 16.    [8] Col. iii. 15.    [9] Ibid. 16.    [10] 1 Cor. ix. 27.

grounded) in love', or, as in the striking phrase about waverers, 'tossed-to-and-fro and carried-round-and-round by every *wind* of doctrine',[1] like cockle shells on stormy water, the two Greek words giving both motions of the storm. Nor must the great triad of adjectives already quoted as the corollary of the passage on the Resurrection be held superior to the original Greek words, 'Be ye *steadfast, immovable, abounding* in the work of the Lord.'[2] Even superlative phrases and absolute terms seem insufficient at times for his enthusiasm, 'the grace of our Lord abounded *exceedingly*' (lit. 'over and above'), and again, 'more and more exceedingly' (lit. 'from excess unto excess'), and again, 'God is able to make *all* grace abound toward you, that you may be *all*-sufficient in *all* things on *all* occasions, and abound in *all* good works'.[3] In his Greek you can hear the pulsations of Paul's energy.

As often in a vigorous, impetuous style, one word suggests the next idea, as in Rom. xii. 13, '*pursuing hospitality*' suggests 'Bless those who pursue (persecute) you', and a mild expression a stronger one for the same idea: 'These things, which I used to count gain, I count as *loss*, yes, I count them as *dung*.'[4]

He is Shakespearian in his bold creation of words, 'I *wild-beast-fought* at Ephesus', 'not with *eye-service* as *men-pleasers*', '*person-respecting*' (respect of persons), 'will-worship' (or 'self-imposed devotions', Moffat).[5] And the following sentence shows like many others his skilful use of compound verbs in Greek,

'Let every soul be *subordinated* to (lit. '*ordered* under') the higher powers, for there is no power except from God, and those that exist are *ordered* by God. So that he who opposes (lit. '*orders—himself—against*') authority, stands against the *ordinance* of God.'[6]

For the full vigour of Paul's diction take a passage in Colossians, (chaps. i and ii) with its '*thrones, dominations, principalities, and powers*', '*holy, blameless, irreproachable* before him', '*founded and steadfast* in the faith', 'walk in Christ, *rooted and*

[1] Eph. iii. 17, iv. 14.                              [2] 1 Cor. xv. 58.
[3] 1 Tim. i. 14; 2 Cor. iv. 17, ix. 8.               [4] Phil. iii. 8.
[5] 1 Cor. xv. 32; Col. iii. 25; Eph. vi. 6; Col. ii. 23.   [6] Rom. xiii. 1.

*built-up* in him, and *confirmed* by the faith'. 'See that no one', he goes on, '*leads-you-off-as-spoil*' . . . 'in Him dwells all *the fullness of the Godhead* bodily, and you are *complete* in him . . . *buried-with* him in baptism, you were *raised-with* Him through faith.' '(Christ) *blotted-out the* handwriting of ordinances, which was against us, . . . *nailing it to his cross.*' Chapter iii is equally exuberant with its array of nouns in vv. 5, 8, 12, Christian qualities and the reverse, and 'love, the *bond of perfection*' to crown them, and again the picture of 'musical' Christians in ver. 16, where the syntax is at fault but the diction full and free:

> 'Let the word of Christ *dwell* in you *richly* in all wisdom, *teaching and admonishing* one another with *psalms and hymns and spiritual songs, singing* with grace in your hearts to the Lord.'

Proceeding to sketch his own task, as preacher, he cannot help expressing himself too, his own force and driving power, in the very diction:

> 'Whom we preach admonishing *every man* and teaching *every man* in *every* wisdom that we may present *every man perfect* in Christ, to which end I labour, *struggling* according to the divine *energy* that is a *power* within me (Moffatt, lit. according to his *energy* that *energises* in me in *power*).'

This is the diction of one who '*pressed forward* to the *goal* unto the *prize* of the high calling of God in Christ Jesus', one who would be emphatic with his last breath when speaking of his cause. 'The style is the man.' Repetition, absolute terms, and strong significant words are his means of expressing it.

### Concentration upon a single idea.

The force of some well-known passages is due to a play on certain words in concentration upon a single idea to drive it home. Take the passage which contains Paul's great paradox. 'The Gospel of Christ', he says to the Corinthians, 'is a foolish thing, as the world counts wisdom, but it is the wisdom of God.' He will not try therefore to attach it to Greek ideas and wisdom as he did at Athens (Acts xvii). On this paradox, that the clever man must forget his cleverness to understand the

Gospel, he plays with skilful variations until he has driven it home to them triumphantly.

> 'For Christ sent me not to baptize, but to preach the Gospel; not in *wisdom* of words, lest the cross of Christ should be made of no effect.
> For the preaching of the cross is to those who are perishing *foolishness,*
> but unto us who are being saved, it is the *power* of God.
> For it is written, I will destroy the *wisdom* of the wise
> and will reject the prudence of the prudent.
> Where is the *wise?* where is the scribe? where is the disputer of this *world?*
> Hath not God *made foolish* the *wisdom* of this *world?*
> For since, in the *wisdom* of God, the *world* by *wisdom* knew not God,
> it pleased God by the *foolishness* of preaching to save them that believe.
> For the Jews require a sign, and the Greeks seek after *wisdom,*
> but we preach
> Christ crucified,
> unto the Jews a stumblingblock, and unto the Greeks *foolishness,*
> but unto those who are called, both Jews and Greeks,
> Christ the *power* of God and the *wisdom* of God.
> For the *foolishness* of God is *wiser* than men,
> and the *weakness* of God is *stronger* than men.'[1]

Almost every kind of literary device is in this short passage, contrast, balance, triad arrangement, quotation, epigram, dramatic question, crescendo, climax, but the main point to notice is the play upon the main ideas 'wisdom' and 'foolishness', 'weakness' and 'power', 'the world' and 'God', to illustrate his great paradox. They are the pattern running through, or like the main motive in a musical composition, striking the ear again and again. The arrangement of one sentence in particular (ver. 21) seems too perfect to be spontaneous, but it is doubtful if Paul made a rough draft of these letters. The faults of syntax are against that. Scott the novelist has been described as one who 'drew his characters at breakneck speed with strokes that challenge the microscope'. So Paul dictated his letters, framed his arguments, and struck off his epigrams. And notice that as soon as the oratory is in

---

[1] 1 Cor. i. 17–25.

danger of becoming too sententious and clever, removed from practical life and the case in hand, 'the weakness of God is stronger than men', he immediately strikes a personal note, 'Look at your own ranks, brothers.' They were no doubt a strange mixture, the Corinthian converts. Religious movements do not begin high in the social scale, and the greatest obstacle is the fear of degrading oneself and of contempt. So Paul again applies his paradox to them, to encourage them, 'God picks out the *weak* things to confound the strong.' Their particular case is only an example of the glorious general rule of providence.

So, he says (ch. ii), 'I came not to you with cleverness and *wisdom* but in *weakness* and fear and trembling, not in persuasive words of *wisdom*, but in a display of the Spirit and of *power*, that your trust might not be in the *wisdom of men*, but in the *power of God*', a practical end as usual. Even then he has much to say about pride in wisdom, for it was the Corinthians' chief fault (chaps. ii, iii).

### Personal Appeal.

The orator, if he wishes to be convincing, must also throw into his argument *himself*, his whole personality, whatever he has of it. It is this personal side of Paul's letters that keeps them fresh and living. His heart was large enough to hold all the churches of Europe, even those he had not seen. 'I would like you to know how greatly I am concerned for you and those at Laodicea, for *all who have never seen me.* . . . I am with you in spirit. . . . It is a joy to note your steadiness.' 'We were gentle among you, as a nursing mother cherishes her own children . . . in our yearning affection for you eager to give you not only the Gospel but our own souls as well, you had so won our love. . . . We have been longing for you. . . . You are our glory and joy.' 'I will very gladly spend and be spent for you, though the more I love you, the less I be loved.' [1] The tenderest of all is the letter to the Philippians.

His letters vary in buoyancy and happiness. When he wrote to the Thessalonians, the problems there were not so disturbing to his personal affection as the divisions and carping at

[1] Col. ii. 1; 1 Thess. ii. 7; 2 Cor. xii. 15.

Corinth, but even when disappointed, he does not scold; he uses personal appeal instead. Take, for instance, the very bad case of ingratitude and vanity, when the precocious but shallow Corinthians wished to throw off Paul's direction (1 Cor. iv. 8–16). Instead of heavy scolding notice the fineness of his reply. He would not hurt their feelings, but he reminds them of the contrast between the pupils, comfortable and complacent, and the minister, to whom they owed their happy faith, going into the depths, between their 'reign' as critics, and his (the Apostle's) hard life. This is an appeal to their sense of decency. Then follows a picture of the depths to which the Christian leader had to sink (vv. 11–13). But it strikes him as a wrong sort of appeal, and he pulls himself up. He can hardly bear to write three lines of censure or suggested censure without some expression of personal affection to take the sharp edge off it. So he makes the appeal more personal, first to his affection and their sonship (vv. 14, 15), then to their loyalty (ver. 16), then more sternly, when he thinks of the worst offenders, to his authority:

'(vv. 7–10) What do you possess that has not been given you? And if it was given you, why do you boast as if it had not been given you?

(vv. 11–13). You are now satisfied; you have heaven's rich bliss already, you have come into your kingdom without us. I wish indeed you had come into your kingdom, so that we might reign with you. For it seems to me that God means us apostles to come in at the very end, as doomed men (in the arena). For we are made a spectacle to the world, to angels and to men!

We for Christ's sake are fools, you in Christ are sensible. We are weak, you are strong; you have glory, we are dishonoured. To this very hour we hunger and thirst, we are ill-clad and knocked about, we are waifs, we work hard for our living; when reviled, we bless; when persecuted, we put up with it; when defamed, we try to conciliate. We are treated as the scum of the earth, the very refuse of the world to this day!

(vv. 14, 15) I do not write these things to shame you, but to warn you as beloved sons. You may have ten thousand instructors in Christ, but you have not many fathers. For it was I who became your father in Christ Jesus through the Gospel.

(ver. 16) Imitate me then, I *beg* you. To ensure this, I am sending Timothy . . . who will remind you of those ways in Christ, which I teach everywhere in every church.

(vv. 17, 18) But some are puffed up, as if I were not coming myself. I will come to you before long, if the Lord will, and then I will find out from these puffed up persons not what their talk but what their power amounts to. . . . Which is it to be? Am I to come with a rod of discipline, or with love and a spirit of gentleness?'[1]

The irony in ver. 8, and the pathos of vv. 9–13 are equally fine. In the letter to the Galatians, who had foolishly gone over to the Judaising party, the appeal again is very personal and human. After an impatient outburst showing almost desperate anxiety, 'O foolish Galatians, who has bewitched you . . . you who had Christ the crucified placarded before your very eyes. . .', he feels that all argument will fail and personal appeal only is left. Few pleadings could be stronger or more touching:

'Do take the line I take, brothers, as I once took yours. . . . My dear children, with whom I am in travail over again, till Christ be formed in you, would I could be with you . . . for I am at my wits' end about you.'

For the last illustration of personal appeal one naturally turns to the only purely personal letter, to Philemon. In it he makes a personal request, and the delicacy with which he makes it has been universally praised. We are not concerned here with the happy mood which can play upon the word 'Profitable', Onesimus, the slave who had run away and become a Christian and known to Paul in Rome, but with the skilful way in which Paul introduces his request, and masses so many pleas in its support in one short paragraph that its appeal is overwhelming. He links his request to his praise of Philemon, the Greek words in ver. 8 exactly corresponding to those in ver. 7: he has heard of Philemon's *love* to the saints and felt much joy and *encouragement* from it, and so

'though I feel bold enough in Christ to order you what is befitting, I *encourage* you rather on the ground of *love*, (1) thinking of myself as an *old man*, and a *prisoner* (2) . . . I encourage you about *my son*, (3) whom I *begot* in my *imprisonment* . . . whom I have sent back to you, that is, *my very heart* (3) . . . whom I wished to keep by me, that he might serve me *in my imprisonment* for

---

[1] The close personal touch is best brought out in Moffatt's more modern English (slightly altered above).

the gospel *in your stead* (4). But without your consent I would do
nothing, so that your goodness to me might come with no con-
straint, but of your free-will. For perhaps for this reason he was
separated for a season that you might receive him back for ever,
no longer as a slave, but more than a slave, a brother beloved,
to me especially so, but how much more to you, both as a man
and as a Christian. If then you count me a *partner*, (5) receive him
as you would me, and if he has robbed you of anything, or owes
you anything, put it down to my account (6). I, Paul, write it with
my own hand, "I will repay it"—not to mention that you *owe
me even your own self* (7). Yes, brother, let me *make some profit*[1]
from you in the Lord! Refresh my heart in Christ (8). I write
relying on your obedience, and knowing that you will do even
beyond what I say. . . .'

He puts off his authority and asks it:

(1) for the sake of the love shown by Philemon (vv. 7, 9);
(2) as a boon to an old man and a prisoner (ver. 9);
(3) for the love Paul has for Onesimus, a son, the fruits of
    his preaching while in prison (ver. 10);
(4) for his usefulness to Paul, doing for him what Philemon
    would like to do ('in thy stead' (ver. 13));
(5) as one partner of another (ver. 17);
(6) as himself ready to make good any loss (ver. 18);
(7) as the creditor of Philemon (ver. 19);
(8) as an encouragement to himself.

'I put in all these pleas,' he adds, 'but I know they are not
needed. You would do this and much more.'

### Blend of Modesty and Egoism.

Another charming personal element in the letters is the blend
of modesty and egoism, the first constantly correcting the
second. He had to assert himself, for he was the only man living
who could win the Gentiles their rights, and he was conscious
of it. He knew he had outshone even the chiefest apostles,
though his modesty only claims to have done so by hard work
and the special grace of God.[2] He does not mention his
superiority in learning and intellect, which was just as marked.
But he is always correcting any apparent assertiveness by the

---

[1] Again the play on words, Onesimus, 'profitable'.    [2] 1 Cor. xv. 10.

phrase with which Wesley schooled himself, when he saw the
drunkard, 'There, but for the grace of God, goes John Wesley.'
When he gives a ruling, it is always 'I say, *through the grace
given unto me,* to every man among you, "Do not think too
highly of yourselves"'. To the Romans he excuses his boldness
in advice,[1] he only 'reminds them of what they are quite quali-
fied to admonish one another, because of the grace given him to
be the special minister to the Gentiles'. His consciousness of
his title to lead, when he says, 'Be followers of me', is based
only on his deeper experience of Christ.[2] He hurries invariably
from egoism either to the grace of God or to the thought of
others, 'a crown laid up for me, *and for all who love his appearing.*'[3] Even in his private letter to Timothy he modestly pronounces himself a typical instance of 'Christ's utter patience'.[4]
He has a detached wonder at and admiration for the results of
the gospel he carries. He claims to be fit to carry it, because
sincere, but he wonders at himself, as a modest surgeon may
at the operation he has performed, always with the feeling, 'the
grace of God did that'. As a 'vessel' he began, and as a 'vessel'
he always remained to himself. He takes no credit for his work.[5]
His only satisfaction and boast is that he works for nothing,
and can give his services. When he talks about this, he is
really defending his non-official, unpaid servant's attitude, and
implies that they would have perhaps respected more a salaried
'bishop'.

How careful he is to distinguish between his own suggestions of conduct and those which he drew from Christ's own
teaching:

'I speak this by way of concession, not as a command'
(1 Cor. vii. 6);
'To the married I command (not I, but the Lord)' (ibid. 10);
'To the rest speak I, not the Lord' (ibid. 12);
'Concerning unmarried women I have no commandment from
the Lord, yet I give my judgment *as one whom you can trust after
all the Lord's mercy to him*' (ibid. 25, Moffatt's excellent rendering).

---

[1] Rom. xv. 14 ff.  [2] 1 Cor. iii. 10, and elsewhere.
[3] 2 Tim. iv. 8 (assuming Paul's authorship).
[4] 1 Tim. i. 12–17.  [5] 1 Cor. ix. 16–19.

Delightful modesty, to be commended to dogmatic theologians and party leaders to-day! [1]

*Irony.*

Very rarely, as in Galatians, quite a fierce ejaculation is wrung from him, 'I wish those who trouble you would cut themselves off', which reminds one of his impatient 'God shall smite thee, thou whited wall', in the court at Jerusalem. But usually his impatience is kept well in hand, and the Hebrew irony is the commoner vent for his very human sensitiveness. Every orator has recourse to it at times, and Paul is like the Hebrew prophets of his race. 'Busybodies instead of being busy' reminds us of their play on words. Even the chief apostles provoked his irony by their weak-kneed attitude over the Gentile question, 'those who were *reputed to be somewhat*' (what they actually were, makes no difference to me, God respects no man's person), 'those who were reputed to be pillars'. This is the passage where Paul shows more distress than in any other part of his letters, except perhaps in the second part of 2 Corinthians, where irony is again the vent for his disappointment with the converts. 'Did I commit a sin . . . because I preached the gospel to you without payment? . . . In what were you made inferior to the other churches except that I myself was not a burden to you? *Forgive me this wrong.*' 'You put up with fools so readily, you who know so much. You put up with a man who assumes control of your souls, with a man who spends your money, with a man who dupes you, with a man who gives himself airs, with a man who flies in your face. *I am quite ashamed to say, I was not equal to that sort of thing.*' Moffatt brings out the spirit of it more strongly than the A.V. and the R.V., almost too strongly, for Paul always stops short of a sneer, and the irony of a man so affectionate must not be given too violent a twist. As it is, he falls into frequent apologies for it.[2] The kindest of men will indulge their irony more freely when writing to personal friends, and

[1] For this modesty cancelling out what might seem boastful see also 2 Cor. ii. 17, iii. 1 and 5; xi. 16–18, 21; xii. 1, 5.
[2] xi. 1, 16, 21, 23; xii. 1, 11.

writing to Timothy more confidentially, Paul can be severe.
On wranglers and mere talkers for instance:

> 'Doctors of the Law is what they want to be, but they have no
> idea of the words they use, or of the themes on which they harp.
> I know the Law is admirable, provided one uses it *lawfully*
> (legally), but they must remember the Law is not made for
> honest people but for the lawless',

or again on young insincere widows:

> 'they learn to be idle, gadding about from house to house',
> 'the widow who lives in pleasure *is dead before ever she dies*'.

*Tactfulness.*

For real tactfulness in personal appeal few passages can excel
that in which Paul applies himself to extract donations from
the business men of the Corinthian church, playing first, but
not too obviously, upon the competitive instinct, as he instances
the generosity of the Macedonians, and touching upon the
generosity of Christ, on a fair sharing of burdens, and on his
pride in their liberality, which he hopes they will not disappoint.
To get the full flavour of the delicacy of the appeal, here again
the chapters should be read in a modern version, such as
Moffatt's (2 Cor. viii, ix).

*Difficulties for Modern Readers.*

We now come to the drawbacks of Paul's letters for modern
readers, their peculiarities of subject-matter and of style.

a. *Subject-matter.*

Christianity had to pay at first for its advantage of being
launched through the Jews. The Jewish obstinacy for ceremonial purity threatened the spirit of Christianity, as the
Jewish earnestness for religion was its strength. So in several
letters of Paul the question of circumcision and of the Jewish
Law take up more space than we should like. Paul has to fight
the battle wherever Jews were numerous, the battle of the
grace of Christ against the Jewish Law. In Romans is a long
argument on justification by the Law or by faith, and on the
Jews' rejection of Christianity because of their Law. The

Galatians' letter is full of it, and in Ephesians and Colossians [1] there are references to the party of the circumcision. The writer of the letter to the Hebrews spends most of his labour contrasting the old Law with the new Covenant of Christ, and naturally argues on Jewish lines. We may vote these arguments dull, but it was a fight for the very existence of Christianity, that is, the Christian spirit. Circumcision was really a question of caste. Hence Paul's tremendous anxiety, absorbing interest and space in the letters that might have been spent on more complete instruction in Christian morality and mysteries. The instruction at the end of each letter is therefore 'delivered' in a hurry in the short space left by the main contention, which even then bursts in from time to time.[2]

Another thing which repels the modern reader is the amount of quotation from the Old Testament. Paul's use of his reading is one of his strong points, but it has its defect for us, when he applies it in the Jewish manner, to us often fanciful and far-fetched.[3] It has been said that, whereas our Lord 'appeals to the deeper sense of Scripture' and 'never interprets it unnaturally, but takes it in its obvious sense, and criticizes it freely', Paul 'shows an exaggerated reverence for everything written and treats it as of equal value'. Still it must be admitted that just when Paul is in danger of upsetting the Christian boat by too much Jewish cargo, his spiritual gifts and loving mind right it and keep the boat on even keel, and in those parts of his letters which seem to us so Jewish and remote from our needs, when he indulges in narrow and far-fetched applications of the Old Testament, he immediately frees himself from the harmful results of such application by 'the mind of Christ'. From the lower levels of his argument Paul's spirituality soars constantly and lifts us with him, as for instance at the end of the eleventh chapter of Romans.

b. *Style.*

Then there are the difficulties of his style. Paul is quite

---

[1] Eph. i. 11; Col. ii. 20–3.
[2] Rom. xv. 31, xvi. 17; Gal. vi. 12–15.
[3] Cf. 1 Cor. i. 19, ix. 3, 10, xiv. 21; 1 Tim. ii. 13 ff.

capable of constructing good 'classical' periods,[1] but in his rush
he makes some very loose sentences, too, overloading them
with prepositional phrases, relative clauses, and participial
clauses, till the main idea is obscured and the sentence proper
uncompleted. Look at the skeleton of the sentence in Eph.
iii. 1–7:

> 'For this reason I, Paul, the prisoner of Jesus Christ on behalf
> of you Gentiles,—*if* you have heard of . . . *how that* the mystery
> was made known to me . . . (*just as* I wrote before . . . *by which*
> you can perceive . . . ) *which* (mystery) in other ages was not
> made known . . . *as it* is now revealed to his holy apostles . . .
> *namely that* the Gentiles should be fellow-heirs . . . through the
> gospel, *of which* I became a minister . . . according to the working
> of his power.'

So the sentence is left 'in the air', and the parenthesis is expanded and made to contain another parenthesis, so that a
return to the original subject is out of the question. The next
sentence (vv. 8–12) is similarly expanded by loosely tacking on
a final sentence (ver. 10), a prepositional phrase (ver. 11), and a
relative clause (ver. 12). This style is neither good classical
Greek style nor good Hebrew; it is the impetuous rush of a
Jewish orator using Greek connecting words in a non-classical
and non-Jewish manner. His chief fault is the stringing together of prepositional phrases as in the following:

> 'in order that *from* many persons the gift *to* us may be an
> object of thanksgiving *by* many *for* us.'[2]

It is hard to grasp, especially when he condenses as well:

> 'So also *through* Him is the Amen *unto* the glory of God',[3]

which is almost unintelligible without the additions of Moffatt:

> 'Hence it is through Him *that we affirm our* Amen *in worship*
> to the glory of God.'

Similarly in the last three verses of Romans six successive prepositional phrases, three of them alike, obscure the meaning for
the English reader, and even as Greek are not good writing.
    But the most remarkable instance is the first chapter of

---

[1] As in Rom. ii. 14, 15; xi. 24; 2 Cor. i. 3, 4; iii. 7, 8.
[2] 2 Cor. i. 11.                              [3] Ibid. v. 20.

Ephesians. Taken as a whole it is a fine lyric with its chief motive the phrase, 'redemption in Christ according to the rich grace of God to the praise of his glory'. When analysed in its syntax, however, it discloses considerable tautology, and the loosest connexions, one word suggesting the next thought, and relative piled on relative. It will be noticed that 'unto the praise of his glory' comes three times, 'according to his pleasure (or counsel)' four times, and 'in Christ' or 'in him' ('in whom') nine times, and the prepositions are 'legion', while several ideas are repeated in slightly altered form.

Besides his loose connexions Paul is apt to leave a sentence unfinished, through breaking it by a parenthesis or switching off on to another thought. Emotion upsets his syntax in Galatians (ii. 4) so that he does not finish his sentence about the circumcising of Titus, but hurries on to the thought of the false brethren and his contest with them (ver. 5), and then twice starts his next sentence (vv. 6, 7), altering his construction, and further omitting a verb of requesting (ver. 10). Ellipses are also common: 'If I boast, I shall not be ashamed (*but I will not*) in order that I may not seem . . .', 'If a chance comer preaches . . . you put up with it. (*Why not put up with me*) for I am not a whit behind.[1] . . .' So emotion accounts for the constant repetitions of 'folly' and 'weakness' in his remonstrances to the Corinthians.[2] Sometimes he starts with a prayer or doxology and pauses to give information so that the prayer is apt to become a statement. All this is the outcome of a sensitive and impetuous nature, very unlike the temperament that produced the stately letter to the Hebrews, so orderly from start to finish.

## '*Staccato*' Style.

The style of the end of his letters is simple enough. The argument is followed by a rapid *ex tempore* pouring out of moral injunctions, and the style at the close is 'staccato'. 'Rejoice evermore, pray without ceasing, in everything give thanks.' 'Be perfected, be comforted, be of the same mind,

[1] 2 Cor. x. 8, 9; xi. 4, 5.
[2] 2 Cor. xi. 1, 16, 19, 21, 30; xii. 5, 6, 9, 10, 11.

live in peace.' 'Watch, stand fast in the faith, play-the-man, be strong.' 'Preach the word, be instant in season, out of season, reprove, rebuke, exhort.' [1]

But rapid and miscellaneous as these injunctions are, they are not so isolated and disjointed as one might expect from one who was anxious to say so much in a small space and in haste. It is this practical part of the letters that keeps them so popular to-day as an expansion of the Sermon on the Mount, and usually it is presented in convenient paragraphs, like those on family relationships, or the duty of masters to servants, or the Christian's attitude to the outside world, or to the state and authority, or to marriage. The paragraphs are not designed, they grow naturally out of a single thought, which he develops to a climax. 'Walk worthily,' he says, 'trying to keep the *oneness* of the Spirit in the bond of peace', and that 'oneness' immediately gives him his paragraph for 'there is *one* body and *one* spirit, as you were called in *one* hope of your calling, *one* Lord, *one* faith, *one* baptism, *one* God and Father of all, who is *above all and through all and in all.*' [2] Even so far it is a fine little paragraph with its climax, expressing the unity of the Christian faith and ideal in a nutshell, but he goes on to mention that 'to every one is given a different gift for the work of the ministry . . . till we all attain to the *oneness* of the faith'. Sometimes he does not expand the idea at once, but recurs to it after a verse or two: '*Render to no man evil for evil.* Provide things honest . . . live peaceably. *Avenge not yourselves,* beloved. . . .', [3] and the rest of the paragraph commends the opposite of vengeance.

Paul gives some sort of unity to all the different pieces of advice by using some recurrent phrase. In Ephesians we have in iv. 1: '*walk* worthy of (your) vocation'; in ver. 17, '*Walk* not as others *walk* . . .'; in v. 1, 'be followers of God and *walk* in love . . .'; in ver. 15, 'see then that ye *walk* circumspectly'. When some particular need or weakness is uppermost in his

---

[1] 1 Thess. v. 16–18; 2 Cor. xiii. 11; 1 Cor. xvi. 13; 2 Tim. iv. 2.
[2] Eph. iv. 2–6, cf. Col. ii. 14, where 'ordinances' leads to a paragraph of warning against slavish observance of ordinances.
[3] Rom. xii. 17–21.

mind, he recurs to it again and again. Timothy, for instance, is warned repeatedly against the danger of losing the simple Gospel truth in arguments with 'talkers', 'Avoid old wives' fables, strifes of words, perverse disputings, vain babblings, oppositions of science, falsely so-called' (1 Tim. iv. 1, vi. 5, 20); 'hold fast the form of sound words' (2 Tim. i. 13), 'the things thou hast heard of me' (ii. 2), 'remember the Resurrection (ii. 8) and remind your hearers of it and avoid useless words (ii. 14) and vain babblings (ii. 16) and foolish and ignorant questions (ii. 23). Stick to my doctrine, which you know (iii. 10, 14) and let others go after fables (iv. 4).'

Throughout one letter, namely that to the Galatians, Paul concentrates on one main idea, the freedom of the Spirit, and brings his moral injunctions into harmony with it. If his syntax is sometimes loose, his thought is not; he may leave a sentence unfinished, but never an argument, and he is at more pains to keep his connexion clear than his translators have been. '*Covet earnestly* the greater gifts', he says, before his digression on 'love' in 1 Cor. xiii, and when he has finished his panegyric, he resumes, 'Follow after love, and *covet earnestly* spiritual gifts' (as I was saying and as I am about to describe them), where the A.V. alters the Greek word the second time and does not preserve the connexion, as Paul meant to do.

### Perorations.

Paul is also keeping his connexion clear when he crowns sections of his argument with those masterly perorations, which sum up and lift up at the same time. In the first three chapters of 1 Corinthians the first theme is their divisions (i. 10) and the second arising out of it is the simplicity of the Gospel, and how little man's wisdom has to do with it (i. 18). Both these are kept before us (notice 'Paul' and 'Apollos', i. 12, iii. 5), and both rounded off together in the vigorous peroration (iii. 18–23):

'Let no man deceive himself. If any man thinketh that he is wise among you in this world, let him become a fool that he may be wise. For the wisdom of this world is foolishness with God, for it is written, "He taketh the wise in their own craftiness...." Therefore let no man glory in men, for all things are yours.

Whether *Paul, or Apollos, or Cephas*, or the world, or life, or death, or things present, or things to come, ALL ARE YOURS, AND YE ARE CHRIST'S, AND CHRIST IS GOD'S.'

## Paul a Practical Mystic.

This triumphant little peroration can be matched by many others at the end of paragraphs and chapters, summing up and lifting up his theme. At these moments Paul seems to let himself be lifted up to the heavens. But the next moment he is back on earth, thinking of very practical details. 'O death, where is thy sting? . . . Thanks be to God for giving us the victory . . .'—triumphant peroration. 'Now about those (*church*) *collections* . . .' Paul must often have felt like his Master coming down from the mount of transfiguration to the epileptic boy.

## Summary.

So these letters have been a gold mine. With their 'love, joy, peace, longsuffering, goodness' they have given us our code. With their 'knowledge of the mystery of Christ' they have given us our vision. With their grand indifference to life and death, 'whether we live or die, we are the Lord's', they present us with a philosophy. With their certainty of the future they guarantee our hope, 'Henceforth there is laid up for me a crown of righteousness . . . not for me only but for all that love his appearing.' 'I reckon that the sufferings are not to be compared with the glory that will be revealed in us.' Fosdick speaks of the 'sense of spiritual wealth in which the first Christians rejoiced. They found an Eldorado in the gospel that God had loved every son of man'. This 'wealth' is the burden of the letters, 'riches towards God', 'the unsearchable riches of Christ', 'heirs of God', 'the riches of his grace'. So 'joy' in Paul's list of Christian qualities comes second to 'love', 'love, joy, peace', and the Philippians, in spite of the memory of the rods and prison stocks, receive from him a letter in which 'joy' and 'rejoicing' occur eighteen times. This 'joy' is always '*in Christ*', his motto and real watchword, the commonest phrase of the letters.

But the point that concerns us here is that all this rich content of thought and religious ethic is presented to us with all the resources of oratory, the art of the trained orator, and the vigour and freshness of the natural orator. Yet it comes in the guise of a frank, personal, warm-hearted letter, the least formal type of literature.

# X

## THE EPISTLES TO THE HEBREWS, AND OF ST. JAMES, ST. PETER (1), ST. JOHN, ST. PETER (2), AND ST. JUDE

*The Epistle to the Hebrews.*

The letter to the Hebrews appeals less strongly to modern readers than those of St. Paul. It is a thesis of which the main purpose is to set forth the finality of Christianity, and stately as it is, almost poetical in places, it aims at removing Hebrew objections to Christianity by an argument on Jewish lines about Jewish ceremonial. The two main Jewish objections met are: firstly, the stumbling-block of the Cross, and secondly, the superseding of the famous Holy of Holies, the High Priesthood, and the system of purification by sacrifice, as old as Aaron.

These objections are met in a masterly way from the point of view of a Jew. Two quotations are made from a Psalm which the Jews themselves held to refer to the Messiah: (1) 'Thou are a priest for ever after the order of Melchisedek'; (2) 'Thou art my son, this day have I begotten thee.' The combination of these is used to the full. For Jesus is the new High Priest, of a higher and earlier order than Aaron's high priesthood, for Melchisedek blessed even Abraham; and Jesus offered himself as the one complete sacrifice. The Law was only a shadow of the greater things to come. The veil in the Holy of Holies stood for the flesh. The Holy of Holies stood for Heaven. The new High Priest entered into Heaven after his crowning sacrifice, as the old High Priest entered the Holy of Holies. By this act of sacrifice and obedience, Son as he was, he brought a *perfect cleansing from sin*, which the old sacrifices could not bring (else they would not have had to go on and on yearly).

Here is skilfully brought in the Christian hope. It is by looking to this High Priest, Jesus the Son, that Christians may hope to reach *perfection*, and enter into the rest, which is ordained for the people of God. He is 'the author and the *perfecter* of our faith'.

The Cross then need not be a stumbling-block. It was a

sacrifice that brought to an end a long series of sacrifices that could never make the worshipper perfect. Nor need the Jews be offended because Aaron's line is superseded. This had been foretold (x. 1–14). A new covenant or agreement had been promised by their own prophets. Unlike Aaron's order Melchisedek's was to be eternal, 'for ever' (five times quoted[1]), as their own Messianic Psalms foretold.

The argument must have gone far to convince Jews, but the law and ceremonial of the Jews does not stir modern interest. When the writer turns his thesis to practical teaching, which he does five times, a rather severe tone of warning, recalling the Hebrew prophets, replaces the warm-hearted, optimistic encouragement of Paul. Remove from the Hebrews these Hebraic arguments and warnings, and not much is left. But that residue is of permanent interest. There is firstly the emphasis on the sonship of Jesus, his humanity, and his relation to the angels; secondly, what we might call the hymn to 'faith', with its fine conclusion; and thirdly, some really great sayings, which, like the whole epistle, are in the grand manner. There is a dignity and composure about the whole thesis, and the majestic rhythm of these special passages still wins admiration for the letter to the Hebrews.

What could better serve as a summary of the faith of the complete Bible than the stately opening period, best rendered in a slightly modified form of the A.V.:

'God, who in many degrees and in many ways spoke unto our fathers by the prophets, has in these last days spoken unto us by his Son,
whom he appointed heir of all things, through whom also he made the worlds,
who, being the radiance of his glory, and the image of his substance, and upholding all things by his word of power,
when he had made a purification from sins,
sat down on the right hand of the majesty on high.'

There we have an epitome of the Old and New Testaments from the Creation of Genesis to the vision of Revelation, expressing in one orderly sentence all the deep truths about Jesus Christ, a sentence with splendid poise, two shorter relative sentences

[1] v. 6, 10, vi. 20, vii. 17, 21.

nicely balanced, and the third with a powerful movement
carrying the rich diction easily to the conclusion.

Then there are some equally fine practical corollaries to
the argument:

> 'Seeing then that we have a great High Priest, who has passed
> through the heavens, Jesus the Son of God, let us hold fast our
> confession. For we have not a high priest who cannot sympathize
> with our infirmities, but one tempted in all points as we are, yet
> without sin. Let us therefore come boldly unto the throne of
> grace, that we may obtain mercy and find grace to help in time
> of need.'[1]

These sentences are as balanced and majestic in the original
Greek. Not even Paul himself expresses spiritual optimism
with more conviction, and the well-turned phrases are excellently matched in the A.V.:

> 'This hope we have as an anchor of the soul both sure and
> steadfast.'
> 'There remaineth therefore a rest for the people of God.'
> 'He looked for a city which hath foundations, whose builder
> and maker is God.'[2]

What a solid way of expressing the hope of the homeless wan-
derer Abraham! 'Entertained angels unawares' is a phrase one
could not spare, nor again the watchword, though it may be a
quotation,

> 'Jesus Christ, the same yesterday, to-day, and for ever.'

All through the letter, with the persistency of the old prophets,
he has his refrains, one repeating his ideal of perfection through
Christ,[3] the other on 'hope', 'hold fast the confidence and rejoicing of our hope' (iii. 6), 'keen to fulfil your hope' (vi. 11),
'lay hold upon the hope set before us' (vi. 18, cf. x. 23, 35). But
undoubtedly the 'purple patch' of the letter for us to-day is the
peroration of the passage on faith. 'The righteous man', he
says, 'shall live by faith. We are not of those that shrink back,
but of those that have faith.' Then with the touch of a philosopher he defines faith as 'the assurance of things hoped for, the
conviction of things not seen'. Without it you cannot please

---

[1] Cf. also x. 19–23, xii. 1, 2.          [2] vi. 19, iv. 9, xi. 12.
[3] ii. 10, v. 9, vi. 1, vii. 11, x. 1, 14, xi. 40, xii. 2, xiii. 21.

God, for 'the man who comes to God must believe that God *is*, and that he rewards those who seek him'. And he illustrates faith by the action of all the heroes of Jewish history from Abel and Enoch down to Rahab, instances not all of equal interest to us. Then he sums up:

'And what shall I say more? for time would fail me to tell of Gideon, and of Barak, and of Samson, and of Jephthah, of David also and Samuel and of the prophets: who through faith subdued kingdoms, wrought righteousness, obtained promises, stopped the mouths of lions, quenched the power of fire, escaped the edge of the sword, from weakness were made strong, waxed valiant in fight, turned to flight the armies of the aliens.'

The A.V. has surpassed itself in the last phrases, 'waxed valiant' . . ., 'the armies of the aliens' . . . , the diction of the one and the rhythm of the other both being spoilt in the R.V., even if that is slightly more accurate.

'They were stoned, sawn asunder, tempted, slain with the sword, they wandered about in sheepskins, in goatskins,
    being destitute, afflicted, tormented.
Of whom the world was not worthy.
    They wandered in deserts and in mountains and in dens and in caves of the earth.
    And these all, having obtained a good report through faith, received not the promise, God having provided some better thing for us, that they without us should not be made perfect.'

Then follows another of his practical corollaries in a fine full period:

'Therefore, seeing we are compassed about with so great a cloud of witnesses, having laid aside every weight, and the sin which so easily besets us, let us run with patience the race that is set before us, looking unto Jesus, the author and perfecter of our faith; who, for the joy that was set before him, endured the cross, despising the shame, and has sat down at the right hand of the throne of God.'

Few passages are so well worth committing to memory, and those who do so commit them will wonder more and more at their architectural beauty, which even seems to grow with familiarity.

The style of the Hebrews no doubt reflects the writer.[1] In

[1] Hastings, vol. ii, p. 336.

reading the epistles of St. Paul 'we feel in every page', says
Bruce, 'that the man who wrote them has passed through a
great religious experience. In reading Hebrews we have no
such feeling. Instead of a tragic experience there has been a
smooth quiet studious life, whose passage into Christian faith
has resembled the dawn of day rather than the sudden flash
of light from heaven, which smote Saul of Tarsus to earth on his
way to Damascus.'

### Epistle of St. James.

The epistle to the Hebrews is more like a thesis than a letter.
The general epistle of James is less like a letter than a collection
of practical vigorous sayings after the style of the Sermon on
the Mount. There is no argument. The practical advice starts
with the second verse and goes on to the end. The sayings are
very loosely connected. The writer passes abruptly from the
topic of snobbery towards the rich ('respect of persons') to that
of keeping the whole law,[1] from a warning against evil speaking
to the advice to make no plans without adding D.V.[2] The letter
savours of the Old Testament, and appeals to the Old Testament for support, to Abraham and Elijah, and to the patience
of Job rather than the patience of Christ. Its tone, as distinct
from that of Paul's letters, is grave throughout, and should be
considered along with this absence of reference to Christ, who
is mentioned only twice. To the rich it is severe,[3] and to those
who plead 'faith without works' ironical and full of satire. It
is no use, says the writer, telling the destitute amiably to 'go
and get warmed and filled'[4] without supplying the means.

The analogies remind us of Christ's sayings, 'Does a fountain
send forth at once fresh water and salt?'[5] Some of the sayings
are striking additions to the stock of the New Testament, but
really as Christ's thought in a new form:

'The wrath of man does not work the righteousness of God,'[6]
or as Christ said, 'He that is angry without a cause . . .'

'A doubleminded man is unstable in all his ways',[7] reminding
us of 'if the eye be *single*, the whole body is full of light'.

---

[1] ii. 1–13.     [2] iv. 11–17.     [3] v. 1–6.     [4] ii. 16.
[5] iii. 11.     [6] i. 20.     [7] i. 8.

'Draw nigh to God and he will draw nigh to you.'[1] 'Knock and it shall be opened', says the Sermon on the Mount, and 'his Father saw him afar off', says the parable.

The most original paragraph and the longest is about the tongue,[2] that small member that is to the body what a bit is in a horse's mouth, or a rudder in a ship. It is 'kindled by hell and kindles great fires of mischief', 'an unruly evil, full of poison, with which we bless God and curse men made in God's image. A tongue that never offends marks the perfect man.' But this comparison is superficial compared with Christ's, for 'out of the heart', as Christ says, 'come evil thoughts', and the tongue does not control thought or action, as a bit controls the horse or a rudder the ship.

One specially vigorous and simple verse would serve as a text for the League of Nations:

'Whence come wars? . . . You lust and have not; you kill and covet and cannot obtain. You fight and war, yet you have not, because you ask not.'[3]

Another defines religion, in a way which will always be needed, as practical charity, or outward love and inward purity:

'Pure religion and undefiled before God and the Father is this, to care for orphans and widows in their trouble, and to keep oneself unspotted from the world.'[4]

## The Epistle of St. Peter (I).[5]

Of all the letters in the New Testament excepting perhaps the first to the Corinthians the plain man would probably choose the first letter in the name of St. Peter as his 'vade mecum' or guide in his attempts to live up to Christian standards. From first to last it applies to the plain man's case, a letter of encouragement and advice, like St. Paul's, covering the range of family, social, and political duties, but undisturbed by argument. It is just such a letter as we should expect from Peter, simple, practical, bracing. The diction and quotations

[1] iv. 8.     [2] iii.     [3] iv. 1.     [4] i. 27.

[5] Whether this letter can be ascribed to St. Peter is disputed. One reason alleged against it is the delicacy and idiomatic style of the Greek. Some think that Peter told the writer what he wished to say, and left him some freedom of composition. Moffatt, *Introd. to the Literature of the N.T.*, pp. 332 f.

from the prophets remind us of his speeches in the Acts.[1] Its
tone is less Jewish than that of James, more gentle and more
buoyant, and its outlook is more that of Paul. The kernel of
the letter, and evidently the chief inspiration of the writer, is
the memory of that scene in the High Priest's palace, part of
which he himself witnessed:

> 'Christ also suffered for us, leaving us an example that we
> should follow in his steps; who did no sin, nor was any guile
> found in his mouth; who, when he was reviled, reviled not again,
> but committed himself to him that doeth righteously; who him-
> self bare our sins in his own body on the tree, that being dead
> to sins, we might live unto righteousness. For you were as sheep
> going astray, but have now returned unto the shepherd and
> bishop of your souls.'[2]

With this memory uppermost ('I was a witness of the sufferings
of Christ'), he can show slaves the real nobility of service, even
when struck by a surly master, and he can show wives and
husbands how consideration and courtesy transform their
mutual relations as 'joint heirs of the grace of life'.

If we think when the letter was probably composed, just
before the first official Roman persecution under Nero, A.D. 64,
its frequent references to suffering will come with more force.
Even now they suffer as servants of pagan masters, suffer even
for well-doing, and without retaliation like their Master, but
the storm has not yet burst. Suffering will have to seem to them
a happiness.

The writer is speaking to the churches generally, and once
for all. How much is he to say? and in what order? The letter
is a model one in order and compass. Tonic is given first, for
it is needed, the Christian hope, the hope of the resurrection
and of salvation, to tide them over 'temporary sufferings'.[3]
'Redeemed, reborn, brace yourselves up to a holy life. . . .'[4]
Then more tonic—a little idealism. This of course needs
imagery, perhaps hyperbole, and the writer is capable of it,
and uses 'glowing titles' to express the high idea of the Christian's position. 'Think what Christ has made you, *living stones*

---

[1] Cf. the Cross called 'the tree', God as no 'respecter of persons', &c.
[2] ii. 21-5. Cf. also iii. 18, iv. 1, 13, v. 1.
[3] i. 3-9.     [4] i. 13, ii. 2, 3.

in his church, . . . a *royal priesthood*, a *holy nation*, a people for his possession.'[1]

But the common difficulties of life have to be met. They have social relations, and Christianity brings complications. They must show that Christians are good citizens. This section reminds one of Paul's style, especially the vigorous staccato at the close:

> 'Have your behaviour seemly among the Gentiles, that, whereas they speak against you as evil-doers, they may by your good works, which they behold, glorify God in the day of visitation.
>
> Submit yourselves to every ordinance of man for the Lord's sake; whether it be to the king as supreme; or unto governors, as sent by him for the punishment of evil-doers, and for the praise of them that do well. For so is the will of God, that with well-doing you may put to silence the ignorance of foolish men. . . .
>
> Honour all men. Love the brotherhood. Fear God. Honour the king.'[2]

Then too they are servants, with perhaps awkward masters, husbands with pagan wives, or wives with pagan husbands. Their hands are tied as Christians when wronged. The way out of all complications will be by sympathy, humility, love and service according to the example of Christ.[3]

'Always be ready to give a reason for the hope you cherish, but answer gently and with reverence' is a striking item in the general advice that follows.[4] As things are critical, a whole chapter urges them to see it through, again according to Christ's example. The last section is on the same note, with an arresting personification of sin:

> 'Keep cool and watchful, for your enemy, *the devil, prowls round like a roaring lion, looking for someone to devour.* Resist him, standing fast in the faith.'[5]

It is very much what St. Paul says to the Ephesians, but the fresh touches are welcome, and the passage quoted above on Christ's example is as good a summary of the New Testament story, as the opening verses of Hebrews are of the whole Bible truth.

[1] ii. 4–10.          [2] ii. 11–17.          [3] ii. 18–iii. 7.
[4] iii. 15.            [5] v. 8.

*Epistles of St. John.*

The style of these epistles is that of the fourth Gospel, especially of the talks in the fourth Gospel. It is very difficult to analyse, because of the curious progression of thought. John seems to think in sentences or small sections rather than in paragraphs; these sections he links together very loosely, a word in one, not a key-word, casually suggesting the thought in the next; and he often recurs later to the same thought (e.g. 'sin' in i. 7 suggests the next section, i. 8–10, and ii. 3–11 is a recurrence to the main thought of i. 5–10).

The thoughts uppermost in his mind when writing the first letter were two heresies, one of which was that Christ united himself with the human Jesus at baptism, and left him before the crucifixion. In three or four places in this letter John strongly rebuts this (ii. 22–3, iv. 3, vi. 1, 5 f.). Jesus was the Christ, one person throughout, not two, and 'he that does not admit this, is not of God'. The other heresy was that flesh and spirit are hostile to each other, and that sin lives only in the flesh; that the most important thing therefore is knowledge, not moral practice; sin, it followed, did not matter, and the flesh could be gratified, so long as one knew the mysteries of Christianity. To this he gives an equally emphatic denial, but in his usual way, not in one argument, but spasmodically, a section here and a section there, coming back several times to the charge (ii. 4, iii. 1–10, v. 16–20). He also warns them against false teachers, who must be judged by their fruits.

Later in the letter (iii. 11 ff.) he passes on to 'love' in theory and practice, love in its essence, love identical with God. The thoughts here again are more or less detached, but often connected in short sections. Paul as orator delivered his praise of love in one steady progressive effort, but the remarks of John in this part of the letter suggest a man thinking in an armchair, and putting down his thoughts discursively in a collection of notes on love from different points of view, and with constant recurrences to ideas previously stated. To love is to know God (iv. 8), to love one's brother is the test of knowing God is in us (iv. 12), love was first shown by God (iv. 10, 19), love is free from fear (iv. 18), and is bound up with love of men (iv. 21). Love of God is bound up with obedience (v. 3).

Love, life, walking in light, abiding in God, overcoming sin and the world, these are the ideas he dwells on and links together in the way described already, much as the talks of Jesus do in the Gospel of St. John.

Perhaps the chief literary feature of the letter is the way in which it lends itself to quotation precisely because of this method of John's of developing his ideas. In fact, as we try to get the impression of a whole chapter, the isolated sayings distract us by their excellence:

'If any man sin, we have an advocate with the Father, Jesus Christ the righteous.'

This is one of six consecutive verses upon sin, but each verse is quotable by itself as a distinct maxim.

'Perfect love casteth out fear.'
'The world passeth away, and the lusts thereof, but he that doeth the will of God abideth for ever.'
'He that loveth not, knoweth not God, for God is love.'

Though John shows continually [1] that he is writing a letter and not composing a homily, as Jude, it is the kind of letter one would expect from a man advanced in years, who has spent his life teaching again and again truths from within a definite circle of ideas. This circle of ideas has been drawn around the character and teaching of the Master. The ideas have become a second nature to him, and he draws on them with the ease and experience of age. They are all high truths of equal importance, and he does not trouble to arrange them as for a thesis or argument. They are like a collection of good things, which he keeps in heaps, and from which he selects two or three things at a time. The truths are simple, yet profound, and one feels consolation was more congenial to him than warning. Boanerges, the son of thunder,[2] in his old age became the son of consolation, and even now, when we want words of comfort, we 'hear also what St. John saith'.

[1] i. 4, ii. 7, 12, 13, 14, 21, v. 13.
[2] See Mark iii. 17.

*The Epistles of St. Peter (2) and St. Jude.*

The letter called the second of Peter and the letter of Jude will not detain us long on the ground of literary qualities either of matter or style, however interesting to the expositor. The letter of Jude is not really a letter, but a stern homily against false teachers, and in style and tone reminds us of what a Presbyterian minister two or three hundred years ago might have delivered in the pulpit against heretical sects. The heretic seems more hateful than the heresy, and denunciation more congenial than reasoning. The tone and thought are those of the Old Testament, and even the style and vocabulary of Jude and 2 Peter lack the freedom and spaciousness of Paul. They harp upon the old 'Prophets'. They were the Calvinists and Covenanters of their day. Paul and Peter (1) can be stern, but tenderness is uppermost. James does not relax his gravity, almost severity. Jude and 2 Peter are almost fierce.

What was a Christian leader to do with wilful opponents who distracted and spoilt the faith and morals of his churches? We know Paul's attitude well from 1 and 2 Corinthians, how stern he could be when necessary. But Paul thinks all the time of the wrongness of the opinion, and tries to change it by reasoning, only in the last instance ejaculating impatiently against the false teachers themselves, as in Galatians (v. 12). Where a man was past reasoning, 'The Lord reward him', he says, 'according to his works', and he turns away to something more cheerful.[1] His letters never become a tirade. Even in an extreme case in a private letter,[2] where he warns against a long list of various types of people (2 Tim. iii. 1–8), he is content with naming the actual types. He does not waste rhetoric on them or call them 'waterless clouds'. Only the better things inspire his oratory.

The spirit of the letter of Jude is different. Against false teachers that alarm him he piles up the evil examples of the Old Testament, the fallen angels, Sodom and Gomorrah, and

---

[1] 2 Tim. iv. 14, cf. 2 Tim. i. 15, ii. 17; Phil. i. 15.
[2] See note on p. 128 for a reference to its authenticity.

Cain, and hammers away at the similar vices of the false teachers:

ver. 8: '*these* filthy dreamers'.
10: '*these* speak evil . . . *these*, as brute beasts, corrupt themselves . . .'
12: '*these* are spots in your feasts'.
16: '*these* are murmurers'.
19: 'these set up divisions, are sensual . . .'

Then he indulges in rhetoric; they are

'Clouds without water, swept along by the winds, trees withering fruitless, twice dead, and so uprooted. . . . Raging waves of the sea, foaming out their own shame, wandering stars, for whom is reserved the blackness of darkness for ever.'

Contrast Paul's[1] realistic description of

'poor weak women, burdened with their sins, led by changing impulses, trying to learn and never able to grasp the knowledge of the truth' (2 Tim. iii, of which the A.V. gives a rendering too severe for the Greek).

2 Peter ii is another version of Jude, and this writer too is delivering a sermon thinly disguised as a letter. It is a different kind of literature from the letters of St. Paul. This letter is now almost unanimously judged by scholars to have been written by a Christian in the second century, a Christian who assumed the character of Peter to win attention to his message by a literary fiction which we should regard as fraudulent, but which was not uncommon in those days, when copyright was unimportant. There was no idea of fraud when a man publishing a collection of proverbs put Solomon's name at the head and wrote in the person of Solomon. 2 Peter's sermon is couched in an artificial and rhetorical kind of Greek, almost fantastic.[2] The first chapter recalls the experiences of Peter (vv. 14, 17, 18, cf. iii. 1) to give colour to the claim of Peter's authorship. The second is based on Jude, and the third is apocalyptic, anticipating the end of the world, and it has an interesting reference to Paul's letters (vv. 15, 16).

The doxologies and greetings at any rate are Christian, the closing doxology in Jude particularly fine, though it may have

---

[1] See note on p. 128.　　　　　[2] Peake, *Commentary*, p. 592.

been coined originally by some one like Paul, and by then have been current in the churches.

The style and tone of these letters is due not only to the Jewish temperament of the writers, less transformed than Paul's by the softer side of Christianity. Other influences have affected them. The first of these is the changed relations of Rome and Christianity. The letters of Paul and that attributed to Peter were written before the Roman attitude to the movement changed. The first official persecution by Nero using the Christians as scapegoats brought them into unhappy prominence, and when the courts even under good emperors tested their loyalty by requiring homage to the emperor as god, the Christians were unable to comply. Domitian's attempt[1] to press emperor worship upon them, coupled with the vices of Roman society, made the fiercer Jewish Christians regard Rome as a wicked Babylon, which must inevitably merit heaven-sent doom. The terrible destruction of Jerusalem in A.D. 71 had inflamed this feeling. Fear moreover of attacks from without begets nervousness of unfaithfulness within, and the Christians dreaded heresy. False teachers could be more dangerous Antichrists than the Roman emperors.

It is in the light of these facts that Jude and 2 Peter must be read. They were written under stress of a greater fear than existed in Paul's time or in later times. While they have not edified Christian readers by matter or style, they have at least supplied a record of Christian thought and outlook in the generation after the apostles.

The other influence which affects the study of Jude and 2 Peter is that of Apocalyptic literature. This type of literature succeeded prophecy, and was produced from 200 B.C. to A.D. 130. One example of it, Daniel, was included in the Old Testament. Other notable books are the book of Enoch, the book of Jubilees, the Testament of the Twelve Patriarchs, the Psalms of Solomon, the Assumption of Moses, 2 Baruch, and 2 Ezra.

The earliest of these books were written during the persecution of the Jews by Syria, in order to encourage and comfort the faithful. Sufferings and a sense of injustice drove the writers to look forward to God's intervention, some day of the Lord as already mentioned by the prophets, when innocent worshippers of a persecuted religion would come into their own, and they drew upon their imagination for a suitable doom for the enemy. Christian preachers later borrowed this doom for *their* enemy. The imagery used includes the darkness of the pit,[1] and destruction along with the world itself by fire and water.[2] The Stoic belief that the world would perish by fire no doubt influenced these apocalyptic writers, as Stoic philosophy was the popular one of the Roman world in that period. The influence of the thought and diction of these books has been traced also in the Gospels, and even in the discourses of Christ himself,[3] but their main interest is connected with the book of Revelation, which will be discussed in the next chapter.

[1] Jude 13.    [2] 2 Peter iii. 7, 12.    [3] See pp. 186–7.

# XI

## THE BOOK OF REVELATION

Apocalyptic literature—debt of Revelation to this literature—new features in
Revelation—descriptions of God—the letters to the churches—original
genius of the writer—the New Jerusalem—struggle between good and evil—
influence of the book.

ONE cannot discuss the literary genius of Revelation without
understanding its relation to the series of Apocalyptic books
mentioned in the last chapter. Even when we read that the
Vision of Revelation is ascribed to John, we must remember
that the writers of these books of revelation never wrote in
their own names but in those of past saints and heroes, as
Enoch, Daniel, Moses. So, although John the Apostle may be
meant, it is not implied that he wrote it. The style is certainly not
that of the Fourth Gospel. It is that of a writer who translates
Jewish ideas and phrases into ungrammatical Greek. When
again we hear that most of the symbolism of Revelation is not
original, but that its 404 verses contain 518 quotations from
the Old Testament, 88 from Daniel alone, we have also to
remember that these writers developed a traditional language
of their own, and that the same figures and symbols reappear
in writer after writer. Though the book of Revelation is unique
as a book of Christian apocalyptic, it is still one of a series, and
in much of its substance not unique at all.

### Former Books of Revelation.

The substance of this series of books dealt with questions
which the prophets had left almost untouched, but which
through the Gospels, St. Paul, and Revelation became associated in a purified form with Christian hopes, Satan as the
cause of evil, God's final triumph over Satan through the
coming Son of man, a day of reckoning, and a reign of the
righteous. Some writers still looked for an earthly Messiah,
and Israel supreme among the nations. Others turned their
thoughts to different speculations. Where the nation failed,
what was to happen to individuals? Would there be no reward

for a good life or compensation for sufferings? Their thoughts turned more and more upon death and life after death, upon a new kingdom raised above the level of earthly kingdoms, a new world perhaps, who knew? with evil and pain abolished for all good Israelites. The individual saint could rely upon a share in it. They were still hazy about this future. They could not as yet get material rewards out of their thoughts.

It may come as a shock to some of us to hear what scholars have known for some time, that not only the idea of the Messiah but that the teaching concerning the future life were pre-Christian, and that even the title of 'Son of man'[1] which Christ assumed is in the book of Enoch, written over 100 years before. At first Christ himself may seem to lose some of his originality till we remember how even Christian ideas had to obey the usual laws of evolution. Otherwise they would have fallen uselessly on shocked and confused minds. Between the prophets of the Old Testament and the prophets of the New there is a gap both in time and in thought. How was this gap filled? Jewish religious thought developed fast after Malachi. It was these books of revelation that express that development and fill the gap, preparing the Jews for those tremendous truths which Christ was to emphasize, especially the Kingdom of God and the Resurrection. We know how foolish the second of these seemed to the Greeks, when Paul broached it at Athens. But the Jews were not shocked by it. They might have been but for the Apocalyptists. The idea comes but rarely in the Old Testament, but it was one of the chief assurances of these visionaries, though reserved for the elect. Judas is commended in 2 Macc. xii. 44 ff. for offering sacrifices and prayers for the dead.

> 'For if he were not expecting that the fallen would rise again, it would have been useless to pray for the dead. And if in doing this he was looking for the gracious reward laid up for them that have fallen asleep in godliness, holy and pious was the thought.'

In the same way, when Jesus took the titles of the Son of man,

---

[1] In Dan. vii. 13 'a son of man' (not 'the son of man', as in the A.V.) does not refer to the Messiah.

the Christ, or was called the Elect One,[1] the Righteous One,[2] his nature was revealed to the people in a way they understood, and the necessary point of contact was established with the Jews. It was new to them, however, that the Messiah should be identified with 'the suffering servant of Jehovah' mentioned in Isaiah lii and liii.

These books had been so popular as to be translated into several languages of the ancient world, Greek, Latin, Ethiopic, Syriac, Slavonic, but by the second century A.D. they had lost favour with the Jews, perhaps because the Christians had adopted them. For the best part of these books was absorbed in Christian thought, both through Christ himself, who knew them and gave a new direction to their message, and by direct literary influence, as we see in Jude, 2 Peter, and Revelation. That best part amounts to this:

i. The idea that history moves by a great divine purpose, and is not a series of accidents leading to chaos.

ii. That Utopia is realized by God's will and man's efforts together. (The Jews thought a catastrophe or cataclysm necessary first, while the Greeks believed in unaided evolution through human effort.)

iii. The habit of looking away to a new unseen world, 'called in to redress the balance of the Old'.[3]

It is only fitting then that Revelation as the embodiment of these ideas of the future should close the New Testament as it does in so unique a manner. 'The final note is from the trumpets of Heaven.' The Gospel deals with the history of our redemption, the book of the Acts shows this at work in the life of the Church, the Epistles apply the faith to the practical needs of the community and the individual. Revelation proceeds to unveil the mysteries of God and the hereafter, 'the Lamb "as it had been slain" but now set in the midst of the throne for all to adore', and instead of the Church at worship in the upper room the redeemed at worship in the Presence.[4]

---

[1] Luke ix. 35, xxiii. 35.    [2] Acts iii. 14, vii. 52, xxii. 14.

[3] Peake's *Commentary*, pp. 431–5.

[4] *New Commentary*, pp. 678 ff. Cf. also *Visions of Hope and Fear*, Thorn, Stud. Chr. Movement publication, and *From Daniel to St. John the Divine*, Ferrar, S.P.C.K.

*The debt of Revelation to the former books.*

This then is the literary pedigree of the book of Revelation. The writer, ' John ', is going to give the Christian version of the vision of the last days and of the future life, which has been seen fitfully and vaguely by many seers of the preceding three centuries. This writer's crowning addition is 'the Lamb triumphant'.

Some of their more materialistic ideas he perpetuates, as Christ and Paul did not. Their nationalism had demanded an earthly kingdom for Israel; Greece had reigned, Rome had reigned, Israel must reign. The writer of Revelation partly shares this nationalist hope, except that in the place of Israel it is the triumph of the Christian Church. Nothing could bring this about but a catastrophe sent from heaven, in which the stars would fall and the firmament be shaken. This would bring the doom of the wicked oppressors, and the reign of Israel's Messiah in a new earthly kingdom for 1,000 years. Certain woes, proclaimed by angels, must precede this day of the Lord, war, famine, plague, and ravages of the Beast or world powers (as in Daniel). These would end with the great battle, Armageddon. The problem of evil would be solved too. The dread cause of it, the Dragon, would be bound in the pit, and after a short release cast into the lake of burning brimstone.

All these rather solid and materialistic ideas the writer has inherited from the Apocalyptists. He makes them the preface to his vision of the New Jerusalem, where God and the Lamb finally triumphant would be worshipped by the saints. Even his picture of the new Heaven and the new earth he owes partly to the prophet Isaiah (lxv).

*New features.*

But there are fresh features about this Revelation, through which it quite eclipses its predecessors. No one would read with much pleasure the literature of which the seventh and eighth chapters of Daniel and the first and tenth chapters of Ezekiel are a type, with their long drawn-out symbolism and repetitions and sense of unreality. The good things in this literature are too rare. Revelation, on the other hand, is full of good things, and presents them better.

Out of familiar quotations, fragments from Daniel, Ezekiel, and other apocalyptic writings the writer makes a new unique book. He gives new turns to old sentences, adds new touches, gives a new application to old matter. He is a master of phrases, and the A.V. was never happier than in these particular reproductions.

'Be thou faithful unto death, and I will give thee a crown of life.' How much better, though the change is small, than the similar thought in James, 'For when he is tried, he shall receive the crown of life.'[1]
'Behold, I stand at the door and knock.'[2]

The idea is in Solomon's Song (ver. 2), 'the voice of my beloved that knocketh, "Open to me, my sister"...', but what a new thing it becomes in its new application, Christ outside the door of a church just condemned for purse-proud complacency, waiting for the door to open.

'I heard a voice from Heaven saying unto me, Write, "Blessed are the dead which die in the Lord, from henceforth. Yea, saith the Spirit, that they may rest from their labours, and their works do follow them".'[3]

If the author was recalling Ecclesiastes (iv. 1, 2), 'I praised the dead, which are already dead, more than the living', his new touches have changed it out of all recognition.

'I know thy tribulation and poverty, but thou art rich.'
'Thou hast a few names, which have not soiled their robes.'
'I counsel thee to buy of me gold tried in the fire.'
'Hold fast that which thou hast, that no one take thy crown.'[4]

Whether the ideas in these sentences are altogether new or not, they are certainly new great sayings. The ring of personal authority behind them is just that of 'Go ye into all the world', and 'Fear not, little flock'. We cannot conceive sentences in matter or style more fit for Christ to deliver, outside the Gospels.

Take another instance of a new whole finer than the parts

[1] James i. 12; cf. Rev. ii. 10.   [2] Rev. iii. 20.
[3] xiv. 13.   [4] ii. 9, iii. 4, 18, 11.

borrowed to compose it. Two passages are put together, one from Daniel (vii. 13):

'I saw in the night visions, and behold, one like a son of man came with the clouds of heaven',

the other from Zechariah (xii. 10):

'and they shall look upon me whom they have pierced.'

The second of these sentences occurs in a dull passage full of repetition on the subject of mourning (vv. 10–14). Put in its new setting it has a brilliant significance, combining the scene on Calvary with the coming in Heaven:

'Behold, he cometh with clouds, and every eye shall see him, they also who pierced him.'[1]

So this writer picks up precious stones that he finds lying in company with inferior ones, polishes and resets them and makes a fine new circlet.

### Descriptions of God and Christ.

The great problem of Isaiah and the prophets had been to explain what God was like. The writers of the new apocalyptic literature had to go further. They had to make pictures of God for their fellow sufferers to see, for they themselves 'saw' God. But once more He had to be described in terms of the human. They strain to go beyond it, but have to fall back on 'the appearance of a man'.[2] The writer of Daniel makes two such attempts to describe the Great One, in vii. 9 ff., and x. 5, 6. It is these two passages which the writer of Revelation combines with other Old Testament hints into one new complete picture of Christ in heaven.

It is new, because of the new touches introduced, the Son of man is not enthroned but moving in the midst of the objects of his care, the candlesticks, whose oil he renews, that is, the churches, and he has in his hand the seven stars or spirits of

---

[1] Cf. our Advent hymn, A. & M. 51:

'Those who set at nought and sold Him,
Pierced and nailed Him to the tree,
Deeply wailing,
Shall their true Messiah see.'

[2] Ezek. i. 26.

these churches, so that the Ancient of Days of Daniel is now much nearer to man. Isaiah puts 'the waters' in the hollow of God's hand as the mark of power, but this writer's symbol of the candlesticks in the hand of Christ is the mark of tenderness. The Great One here has also the long robe of a king, with the high girdle of High Priesthood, and two new simple phrases are used for his claim to eternity and to be lord of life and death, he is 'Alpha and Omega', and 'has the keys of Hades and death'.[1]

It is also complete, with the clothing of kingship, with head and hair white to suggest perhaps the Ancient of Days, eyes that burn and pierce like fire, feet of brass to tread down opposition, voice, hand, face, all symbolical of some attribute. Other details of Daniel are not here required, the throne, and its fiery stream, and the wheels. Christ is still serving humanity, so he is among the candlesticks. 'John' prefers the finer description of the voice from Ezekiel, 'the voice of many waters', to that of Daniel, 'the voice of a great multitude', and he prefers the countenance to be 'as the sun shineth in his strength' instead of 'as the lightning'. Both these fine phrases are a gain. And he has one more new touch. Isaiah has 'he hath made my mouth like a sharp sword', while Hebrews has 'the word of God is sharper than a two-edged sword'. John seizes this as a new detail for his picture, 'out of his mouth went a sharp two-edged sword', the Roman sword, the most efficient sword the world had known, with a point to thrust, and two cutting edges.

It may be daring to attempt even to symbolize the glorified Christ, but if it is done, it could hardly be done more majestically than by this writer. He has quite eclipsed his originals. All the symbols are imposing, and the phrasing is of the best:

| Rev. i. 13–16. | Dan. vii. 9, 10. |
|---|---|
| And in the midst of the seven candlesticks was one like unto the Son of man, clothed with a agarment down to the foot, and bgirt about the breast with a golden girdle. | The Ancient of days did sit, whose agarment was white as snow, and cthe hair of his head like pure wool; his throne was like the fiery |

[1] Cf. Isa. xxii. 22, the key of David, the treasurer's key, but the symbol as usual is charged by John with much more meaning.

His ᶜhead and his hairs were white like wool, as white as snow, and his ᵈeyes were as a flame of fire.

And his ᵉfeet like unto fine brass, as if they burned in a furnace, and his ᶠvoice as the sound of many waters.

And he had in his right hand seven stars, and out of his ᵍmouth went a sharp two-edged sword; and his ʰcountenance was as the sun shineth in his strength.

flame, and his wheels as burning fire.

A fiery stream issued and came forth before him. Thousand thousands ministered unto him, and ten thousand times ten thousand stood before him; the judgment was set, and the books were opened.[1]

Dan. x. 5, 6.

Behold, a certain man clothed in linen, whose loins were ᵇ*girded with fine gold* of Uphaz. His body also was like the beryl,[2] and his ʰ*face* as the appearance of lightning, and his ᵈ*eyes as lamps of fire*, and his arms and his ᵉ*feet like* in colour to *polished brass*, and the ᶠ*voice* of his words like the voice of a multitude.

Ezek. xliii. 2.

His ᶠ*voice* was like a *noise of many waters*.

Isa. xlix. 1.

He hath made my ᵍ*mouth* like a sharp sword (cf. Heb. iv. 12).

The effect of the vision and the speech that follows are worthy of the vision itself:

'And when I saw him, I fell at his feet as dead. And he laid his right hand upon me, saying unto me, Fear not, I am the first and the last: I am he that liveth and was dead, and behold, I am alive for evermore, and have the keys of Hades and of death. . . .'

In the subsequent pages it is the same being who in majesty rides in front of his hosts, winning victory through his angels,

[1] These symbols Revelation uses elsewhere in other pictures, v. 11, xx. 12. For the stream cf. xxii. 1.
[2] Cf. Rev. iv. 3.

and who in humility stands at the door and knocks, 'the Lamb before the throne, as it had been slain'.

## The letters to the Churches.

If only for the sake of its first three chapters, Revelation is worth the place in the New Testament that was assigned to it with some hesitation, when the Canon was being completed. It is these chapters that give a sense of reality to the vision. In the first place the book's immediate message was to a definite group of churches in Asia, the Roman province. 'What thou seest, write in a book, and send it to the seven churches that are in Asia.' These were in immediate danger, Domitian's demand[1] for emperor worship was forcing an issue even in the provinces, and informers took care that the issue should be raised. Then there was the hostility of the Jews, embittered more than ever since the fall of Jerusalem. Our interest in the book to-day centres in these seven flickering lights of the candlesticks, churches with bad and good points, lukewarmness, false teaching, complacency, even deadness, on the other hand, courage against persecution, and caution in face of heresies; one church growing in Christian qualities, another losing ground.

There is another feature which increases this sense of reality, namely, the allusions to the historical circumstances of these cities of Asia.[2] Laodicea was noted for its wealth. It refused a Roman subsidy after the earthquake of A.D. 60. 'Thou sayest, I am rich, and increased with goods, and have need of nothing.' It was a great banking centre, 'I counsel thee to buy of me *gold* tried in the fire'. It was noted for the black wool of a special breed of sheep, from which a cheap cloak was manufactured there. 'I counsel thee to buy *white raiment . . .*' It was famous for a particular eyesalve. 'Anoint thine eyes with *eyesalve*, that thou mayest see.' The hot springs of Hierapolis became lukewarm as they went over the plateau and the cliff

---

[1] On Domitian's demand for emperor worship see Prof. Merrill, *Essays on Early Church History*, ch. vi (Mason, 1924), and Streeter, *The Four Gospels*, p. 476.

[2] Dr. Crafer, *New Commentary*, Revelation, pp. 687 ff., also Peake's *Commentary*, p. 930–1.

opposite Laodicea. 'Thou art neither hot nor cold. . . . Therefore because thou art *lukewarm*. . . .' Smyrna had its stadium and games, the prize a fading garland. 'I will give a living *garland*.' There are other allusions less clear like 'the open door' of the Philadelphians, and the 'throne of Satan' at Pergamum, which may mean emperor worship or the serpent worship attached to the god Asclepius. The churches are given in the order in which a traveller from Ephesus would reach them.

Impressive as is the description of Christ in chapter i, the messages which he sends to the churches are just as greatly conceived and phrased, and even more original. We might wonder how the writer would compose seven different messages all up to the level of the description in chapter i, all fit for that mouth to deliver. How, for instance, would he express the majesty of Christ speaking from heaven?[1] He does it by the superscriptions to the messages, all different, each title being taken from the picture of Christ in chapter i:

'These things saith he, that holdeth the seven stars in his right hand, and walketh among the candlesticks . . .'
'These things saith he, that hath the sharp two-edged sword . . .'
'These things saith he, that hath the key of David . . .'

Besides giving dignity to the message, some of these titles lead up to the contents of the message itself, and are not chosen haphazard:

'I will remove thy *candlestick* . . .'
'I will fight against them with the *sword* of my mouth . . .'
'I have set before thee an open *door* . . .'

What sort of tone again should we expect Christ to adopt to erring and struggling churches? Surely the tone used here, tender, but stern on occasion, praise coming first, if possible, then, if needed, criticism: 'I know thy works, and tribulation, and poverty, (but thou art rich). . . .' If the church is condemned, the faithful few are not forgotten: 'Thou hast a few

---

[1] Compare the fine series of titles in ch. i. 5, 6: 'the prince of the kings of the earth, that loved us and washed us from our sins in his own blood, and hath made us kings and priests unto God and his Father.' No one has so well proclaimed like a herald the royal and yet redemptive power of Jesus.

names even in Sardis, which have not defiled their garments;
and they shall walk with me in white, for they are worthy.'
Even from Laodicea that is so sternly dealt with, hope is not
cut off; love, he says, is the cause of the rebuke: 'As many as
I love, I rebuke and chasten. Be zealous therefore and repent';
and one of the greatest images of love in the Bible follows:
'Behold, I stand at the door and knock.' However the church
has failed, the promise is never omitted.

The style also is the grand style. The solemn and dignified
repetitions aid the effect. Each message begins, 'I know thy
works . . .', and goes on, 'Nevertheless I have a few things
against thee'. Each message closes with the promise 'He that
overcometh . . .' or 'To him that overcometh . . .'. And after
each comes the refrain of warning: 'He that hath an ear, let
him hear what the spirit saith unto the churches.'

A special feature are the promises. All of them are different.
But none holds out material boons, except perhaps the one to
Thyatira; all, through a symbol, promise rewards for the spirit.
The symbol may be vague, but gives the notion of something
great and fine, something mysterious but satisfying:

'I will give him to eat of the tree of life' (which would be
among the mysteries of Paradise).

'I will give him the morning star' (a symbol of the fresh
splendour of the new life,[1] or of the presence of Christ who so
calls himself, xxii. 16).

'I will give him of the hidden manna,[2] and I will give him a
white stone, and on the stone a new name written, which no
one knoweth save him that receiveth it.' (A talisman is always
mysterious and full of hope. This one secures entry into the
kingdom. The hidden manna again suggests mystery and food
for the spirit.)

A hint can be more terrible than being explicit: 'Thou shalt
not know what hour I will come upon thee.' What conse-
quences the coming will have is left to the imagination.

One fiercer touch, a relapse into 'Judaism' rather mars the

[1] Andrews in Peake, *Commentary*.
[2] Cf. Baruch (ii): 'the treasury of the manna shall descend again from on
high, and they shall eat of it in those years.'

series, the promise of power over the nations, by which he 'shall shepherd them with a rod of iron as a potter's vessel, and they shall be broken in pieces', suggested by Ps. ii. 9. The last promise (iii. 21, 22), 'I will grant him to sit with me in my throne, even as I am set down with my Father in his throne', fits well with the next stage in iv. 1, where the throne of heaven is described and God upon it.

## Original genius of the writer of Revelation.

To realize the genius of the book of Revelation read the first chapter of Ezekiel and compare it with the fourth chapter of Revelation and subsequent chapters. Ezekiel attempted with the aid of figures from Assyrian and Babylonian sculptures to give 'the appearance of the likeness of the glory of the Lord'. The 'appearance' is naturally vague and obscure, but it is also a crude mixture, with its tiresome elaborate account of the 'four living creatures', their rings and wheels, and of the firmament, with its monotonous phrasing ('appearance' occurring fifteen times in the chapter), and its wordiness,

'As is the appearance of the bow that is in the cloud in the day of rain, so was the appearance of the brightness round about,'

which amounts to 'the brightness around was like a rainbow'.

Then compare the impression John has left with us. The 'four beasts full of eyes behind and before' he got from Ezekiel, but their description he wisely condenses. (Even the terrifying and fantastic in Nature is under God's control, and adds to his praise (iv. 8).) And naturally the 'One on the throne' can only be symbolized, but one symbol is enough for John, the brightness of a flashing jewel ('like a jasper or a sardine stone'). Yet the brilliance of the jasper and the red light of the sardine stone are mercifully relieved by the green of the emerald light that encircles the throne. By mere inference he leaves us in subsequent chapters an impression of complete divinity; of his supremacy, as he lets loose and binds Satan, of his majesty, as he is worshipped by all, of his justice, 'true and righteous are his judgments'. 'How long, O Lord, holy and true, dost thou not judge . . .?' of his tenderness, 'God shall wipe away all tears from their eyes'. All these qualities belong to him, who in his great phrase is 'the Alpha and Omega, which is, and which was, and which is to come, the Almighty'.

But when it comes to symbols, we can never get out of mind this writer's brief but always significant collection of phenomena in chapter iv: the rainbow round about, the lamps of fire before the throne, which 'are the seven spirits' or Holy Spirit, and the sea of glass 'clear as crystal', the lightnings and thunders from the throne, or the elders' harps and golden vials, full of odours, 'which are the prayers of the saints'. One of the best and most original touches this, the prayers of the saints preserved as a valuable fragrance for God's pleasure.

More effective perhaps than the symbols are the two doxologies at the end of chapters iv and v, the one, as has been said,[1] of creative power, the other of redemptive love, the hymn of the elders:

'Thou art worthy, O Lord, to receive glory and honour and power, for thou hast created all things, and for thy pleasure they are and were created,'

and the voice of the angels, ten thousand times ten thousand, and thousands of thousands, saying with a loud voice:

'Worthy is the Lamb that was slain to receive power and riches, and wisdom, and strength, and honour, and glory and blessing.'

No symbols impress us like these great proclamations. The vision of Ezek. i would make no one an optimist, but who can resist the appeal of this vision of the triumphant worship of the heavenly host?

If the Christians of the churches of Asia could resist that, John has yet another picture for them, effecting them more nearly. Every one will agree about the beauty of the vision in chapter vii, a picture that has taken the sting out of death for many generations of Christians.

The writer did not see this vision all at once. At first he thinks on Jewish lines, and confines the saved servants of

---

[1] Thorn, *Visions of Hope and Fear.*

God, 'sealed in their foreheads', to 12,000 from each tribe of Israel. Then he becomes really cosmopolitan in his view:

> 'A great multitude, which no man could number, of *all nations and kindreds and peoples and tongues*, stood before the throne and before the Lamb, clothed in white robes, and with palms in their hands.'

It must have cost a Jew some thought to see things like this, all nations and kindreds and tongues joining in a full chorus of worship and sharing the palms of victory with Israel.

As if Heaven were not full enough, the hosts of angels stand and increase the massed effect, and add their refrain. Note the sevenfold 'Blessing and glory', &c. Then the brief dialogue with the elder relieves the tenseness, as it were, of the scene, 'Who are these that are clad in white robes, and whence came they?' 'And I said, "Sir, thou knowest".' Then follows a matchless paragraph. The imagery is of the commonest, white robes, no thirst, no hunger; the diction of the simplest; one of the best verses is taken wholly from Isaiah, another almost so from another passage of Isaiah.[1] Yet all these simple and borrowed elements are fused in a new mould, to produce a new beauty, a new original whole. As regards its form and diction, the A.V. had nothing to do but translate it word for word as it stands, and as musical prose it is perfect. As to its matter, it has exquisite tenderness:

> 'He that sitteth on the throne shall spread his tent over them' (the A.V. misses this).

Cf. ver. 17. The paragraph runs:

14. 'These are they which have come out of the great tribulation, and have washed their robes and made them white in the blood of the Lamb.

15. Therefore are they before the throne of God, and serve him day and night in his temple: and he that sitteth on the throne shall spread his tent over them.

16. They shall hunger no more neither thirst any more, neither shall the sun light on them, nor any heat.

17. For the Lamb which is in the midst of the throne shall feed them, and shall lead them unto living fountains of waters, and God shall wipe away all tears from their eyes.'

[1] Isa. xxv. 8, xlix. 10.

It will help to show its greatness if we quote a passage from the previous apocalyptic writings, which hold out hopes to sufferers:

> 'But with the righteous he will make peace,
> And he will protect the elect,
> 3. And mercy shall be upon them.
> And they shall all belong to God,
> And they shall all be prospered.
> 6. And they shall all be blessed.
> And he will help them all.
> And light shall appear unto them,
> 9. And he shall make peace with them,'[1]

where vv. 7 and 9 add nothing to what has been said, where the phrasing is monotonous, and there is little or no imagery to relieve the flatness. This is the barren style which prevails in a large portion of the apocalyptic writings, which lacked the inspiration both of vision and literary form that moved John the Elder.

In the intervening chapters of the book its literary form is confused by interludes. The visions are fragmentary and not in logical order.[2] Much fantastic imagery is borrowed to describe spiritual enemies, monstrous locusts emerging from a pit unlocked by a star, which is a fallen angel, and beings riding on horses with lion heads and serpent tails, 200,000,000 in number, familiar ideas to the Jews when trying to express the mysterious powers of evil. There is also a terrible picture of the reaping of the earth in xiv. 14–20, and the wine of the wrath of God and the winepress trodden in blood are two Jewish images. But there are some touches of the writer's own:

> 'They sang a new song before the throne, and no man could learn that song but the redeemed',

a truth that all sufferers that have come into their own would

---

[1] 1 Enoch i. 8 ff.

[2] There are three interruptions to the tale of the last things, vii, x. 1 to xi. 13, and xii, xiii. After the seventh seal is broken, one would expect the climax of the judgments, but instead a new series begins, heralded by seven trumpets. When the seventh trumpet sounds, the climax is still delayed, and seven angels with seven bowls begin a new series of happenings. There is no certain explanation of the disorder, but one need not expect visions and dreams to be too logical.

recognize. And though the taunt song against Babylon in xviii is Jewish, it has a powerful interest in its real reference to the imperial city of Rome:

'Babylon is fallen, is fallen, that great city.'

That sentence in xiv. 8 is suggested by Isa. xxi. 9, but Revelation expands it, and draws a much more vivid picture suited to the greatness of Rome, the kings watching and lamenting the smoke rising, the merchants mourning the loss of their rich customer, the shipmasters and sailors their carrying profits, but not coming too close for fear of sharing her torments. 'In one hour so great riches are come to nought.' A specially fine touch concludes the rich tale of her merchandise, '. . . flour and wheat . . . and horses and chariots and slaves[1] and *souls*[2] *of men.*'

'Woe and alas for the great city,
Gone, gone, in one brief hour.' (Moffatt's translation.)

And the grand cause of her downfall is reserved for the end:

'In her was found the blood of the prophets and of saints, and of all that were slain upon the earth.'

## The New Jerusalem.

Pause for a moment before the picture of the 'great white throne',[3] and 'the dead, small and great, standing before God', and the books opened, . . . and the dead 'were judged out of those things, which were written in the books, according to their works'. 'And the sea gave up the dead that were in it. And death and Hades were cast into the lake of fire. This is the second death. And whosoever was not found written in the book of life was cast into the lake of fire.' Then pass to the last famous vision of the New Jerusalem or heaven. Hints for the description are taken from some verses of real poetry in Isaiah, and from the last eight chapters of Ezekiel. Three tedious chapters of measurements of Ezekiel are condensed to three verses in Revelation. The kernel is extracted, and the chief idea seized, which is that the city *has perfect proportions*, 'lieth *foursquare*'. The city must also have *perfect safety*, so we have

---

[1] Greek, 'bodies'.
[2] Ezekiel has 'persons of men', meaning slaves, xxvii. 13.     [3] xx. 11 ff.

the symbol of the *high wall*. It must be *easily approached* from all parts, and this is symbolized by the three *gates on each side, always open*.

Then the city has a tree of life and a river. Comparing Rev. xxii with Ezek. xlvii we find the same procedure as before. Ezekiel with tedious detail laboriously models his river upon the Euphrates. John quickly selects what he wants in two verses, touches it up, adds a new line or two and has soon produced charm:

> 'He shewed me a pure river of water of life, clear as crystal . . ., and on either side of the river was the tree of life . . . and the leaves of the tree were for the healing of the nations.'

The city must also have *beauty*. So its foundations are *jewels*, its gates *pearl*, and its streets *gold*, for the Oriental loves precious stones and is sensitive to colour.

But, as always, *light* is the highest possible symbol of the divine and spiritual, for light is life. So the city is to be one of radiant light, filled with the presence and glory of God. No temple is required, because the whole city is a temple, God everywhere, not localized. Man is to contribute to its glory, for 'all the best that the nations have to offer will go into it' (cf. Isa. lx. 11), and nothing unclean. They will 'serve God, see God, belong to God'. The description is preceded and followed by great proclamations:

> 'Behold, the tent of God is with men, and he will dwell with them' . . .
> 'Behold, I make all things new.' 'I will give him that is athirst of the fountain of the water of life freely.' 'Behold, I come quickly.'

Revelation has been called a 'tract for bad times', those of Domitian, but its symbolism may stand for years to come. The modern hymns based upon Revelation still stir us.

> 'Mine eyes have seen the glory of the coming of the Lord,
> He is trampling out the vintage where the grapes of wrath are stored;
> He hath loosed the fateful lightning of his terrible swift sword;
> His Truth is marching on.

'He has sounded forth the trumpet that shall never call
     retreat;
He is sifting out the hearts of men before his judgment-seat;
O, be swift, my soul, to answer him; be jubilant, my feet!
Our God is marching on.'[1]

People must always be looking away and seeing visions, especially in bad times. John Bunyan of Bedford is the literary
successor of 'John in Patmos'. He also gave us his 'apocalypse'
from prison:

> 'As I walked through the wilderness of this world, I lighted on
> a certain place where was a den, and I laid me down in that place
> to sleep, and as I slept, I dreamed a dream. I dreamed, and
> behold, I saw a man clothed with rags. . . .'

As John saw Domitian as the beast, so Bunyan saw the Pope
as the ogre, the enemy of religious liberty. He also saw the
Celestial City, and wrote with a pen as sure as that which wrote
Revelation, and though he borrowed so freely from this writer
and others he himself produced a new work, a new original
whole.

> 'Now you must note that the city stood upon a mighty hill,
> but the Pilgrims went up that hill with ease. . . . While they were
> thus drawing nigh towards the gate, behold a company of the
> heavenly host came out to meet them. . . . (And) I saw in my
> dream that these two men went in at the gate: and lo, as they
> entered, they were transfigured. . . .'

The struggle between good and evil is continuous. Revelation 'strips off the subtle disguises and thin films that obscure
it', and ranges Christ against Satan in a way we cannot forget.
The temptation to let things slide because 'forces are too strong
to contend with' is continuous. The writer of Revelation,
when Christians were very few, sees the forces for good un-
questionably greater, ten thousand times ten thousand and
thousands of thousands, ranged with Christ. Who can feel
Providence weak after seeing through the eyes of John the One
that sits on the throne? The fight between law and conscience,
between the state and religion still crops up. Revelation puts
it in a concrete form, 'the Beast', 'Who is able to make war

---

[1] Julia Ward Howe, *Songs of Praise*, 304.

with him?' In our latest Armageddon the feeling was that we were fighting against the forces of the Beast, when the military ambition of a state went mad.

'Poetry is a greater thing than history.' We can well believe it as we read Revelation, for this poet of Revelation made men think of heaven and destiny in *his* way for centuries. The writers whose symbols he borrowed seem to have been making feeble guesses when compared with John. He gathers up their unequal fragments and welds them into an impressive whole. We are past argument in this last book of the New Testament. The forceful reasonings of Paul and the loving persuasiveness of John are left behind us. Revelation strikes at our instincts and emotions by vivid pictures. The mind goes back again and again to these visions of heaven. The battle with evil is already won. The spiritual power that is to triumph in the end has already been seen directing the fight.

There is a place in religious literature as in religion itself for vision of this kind. Its effect is instantaneous and lasting, if the writer writes with the restraint of John and with as sure a pen. For in this kind of speculation it is but a small step from the sublime to the ridiculous, and the thoughts of one looking into the unseen can only give satisfaction to others with the aid of the expression of well-chosen image and a delicate choice of phrase.

## XII

## TRANSLATIONS

PAUL directed that his letters should be read to the churches, that is to the assembled Christians in such places as Colosse and Corinth,[1] and the writer of Revelation contemplated that his work would be so read: 'What thou seest, write in a book, and send it to the seven churches...'.[2] We know that 'the memoirs of the Apostles' came to be read in the regular Christian services,[3] as the Law and the Prophets had been in the Jewish synagogues, and Matthew's Gospel is supposed to owe its arrangement to the plan of reading it in sections for lessons. Eventually the custom was established of reading lessons from the whole literature now known as the New Testament, a custom still in vogue.

It will be seen that if these church lessons are to remain a prominent item in the service, and to maintain their influence, an effective translation is of the highest importance. Fashions of speech change, and the old forms of the sixteenth and seventeenth centuries obscure the meaning for a congregation of the twentieth, and the modern hearer may be impatient of archaisms, such as 'howbeit', 'wherewith', 'after a godly sort', 'wrought for us the selfsame thing'. The plain man may prefer 'knowledge puffs up, love builds up' to 'knowledge puff*eth* up, *charity edifieth*'.

With the twentieth century have appeared at least three good new versions, Weymouth's, Moffatt's, and the *Twentieth-Century New Testament*. Their chief merit is that they allow the meaning of St. Paul's Letters to come through clearly, instead of through the fog of archaic English and classical syntax. Take for instance the following appeal of St. Paul as it is in the A.V.:

'O ye Corinthians, our mouth is open unto you, our heart is enlarged.' (An enlarged heart, now a physical derangement!) 'Ye are not straitened in us, ye are straitened in your own bowels. Now for a recompense in the same (I speak as unto *my* children), be ye also enlarged.'[4]

[1] Col. iv. 16.    [2] Rev. i. 11.    [3] Justin Apol. i. 65-7.    [4] 2 Cor. vi. 11 f.

What a strange jargon this must seem to any but close readers of the Bible! How would the plain man regard an appeal 'to be enlarged for a recompense in the same'? But see the fog cleared away:

> 'Corinthians, I am keeping nothing back from you; my heart is wide open for you. "Restraint?" That lies with you, not with me. A fair exchange now, as the children say! Open your hearts wide to me.'

This version of Moffatt's is clear and more accurate, and is the language of the people, and as simple, vigorous, concrete English will probably be so for years to come. Again, can one talk to the ordinary man like this?

> 'Now no chastening for the present seemeth to be joyous, but grievous: nevertheless afterwards it yieldeth the peaceable fruit of righteousness unto them that are exercised thereby.'[1]

That sentence will only too easily pass over the heads of the congregation, but the same idea in this form will strike the attention:

> 'No discipline at the time seems to be a thing of joy but of pain; but those who are trained by it reap the fruit of it afterwards in the peace of an upright life.'

The words make an instant appeal, and the English is unexceptionable. The R.V. published as late as 1881 dealt with these archaisms feebly. 'Say I these things *as a man*?' becomes in the R.V. 'Do I speak these things *after the manner of men*?'[2] and leaves us worse off than we were. But hear the lively Moffatt: 'Human arguments, you say? But does not scripture urge the same?' The R.V. keeps that archaic bit of English of the A.V. where Paul is recommending Titus to the Corinthians, 'His inward affection is more abundant toward you.'[3] What is 'inward affection' to the average man nowadays? Probably something demanding an operation. The plain English of it is, 'His own heart goes out to you more and more' (Moffatt).

Where the obscurity is increased by error in the A.V. the result in Moffatt is happier still. 'Now concerning virgins I have no commandment of the Lord, but I give my judgement as one that hath obtained mercy of the Lord to be faithful.'[4]

[1] Heb. xii. 11. [2] 1 Cor. ix. 8. [3] 2 Cor. vii. 15. [4] 1 Cor. vii. 25.

'Faithful' is not the meaning of the Greek word that is required here, but 'trustworthy', 'able to be believed'. So Moffatt says, 'I have no orders from the Lord for unmarried women, but I will give you *the opinion of one whom you can trust after all the Lord's mercy to him*'. This is excellent. Paul is allowed to speak naturally and clearly.

The drift of an argument is often difficult to follow in the A.V. for the lack of modern connecting words and phrases, which Moffatt so happily supplies. The faithful literalness of the A.V. does not suit Paul's advanced style as it does the simpler style of the Gospels. In the opening chapter of the Ephesians Paul's exuberance leaves his syntax extremely loose. In twelve verses the sentence is carried on eight times by a loose relative pronoun, and in the same twelve verses there are thirty-four prepositional phrases! These are most confusing for an English reader if translated literally. Such a passage (and it is a fine one) is only intelligible as handled by a modern version.

In the simpler narrative of the Gospels we have a different proposition. Here the A.V. needs little alteration to make it sufficiently modern, and it may easily be changed for the worse. Weymouth and the *Twentieth-Century New Testament*, though less vigorous and fresh than Moffatt's version, are sounder in the treatment of the Gospels. One dislikes such unnecessary alterations as 'Realm of Heaven' for the familiar and even more modern 'Kingdom of Heaven'. 'Realm', besides being more uncommon, often spoils the rhythm, too. Alterations of this kind merely shock the reader. They include many unhappy instances. The baby Jesus no longer lies in the well-known 'manger' but in a 'stall for cattle'. The famous saying of Pilate 'Behold the Man' becomes the rather feeble 'Here the man is!' The words of Jesus are unwisely treated. In the Beatitudes it is no gain to hear 'Blessed are they that mourn, for they will be *consoled*' instead of 'comforted', which is equally modern and better for the rhythm. 'Ranked' is an unnecessary change for 'called' in 'they shall be ranked sons of God' and it sounds less pleasantly. 'Wilt thou be made whole?' could easily be modernized as 'Do you want to be made well?' but Moffatt gives us 'Do you want your health restored?' He could not even let alone 'Even Solomon in all his glory was not arrayed like one of these'. Altering 'arrayed' to 'robed' he found the rhythm spoiled, and changed 'not' to 'never': 'Even Solomon in all his glory was never robed like one of these'. But 'arrayed' is the finer word, and Moffatt keeps it strangely enough in Acts xii, in the same sense, 'Herod arrayed himself in royal robes'. There is a proverbial ring about the words of Christ, to which the A.V. rarely fails to do justice by its rhythm:

'Where your treasure is, there will your heart be also.'

This is modern enough, simple in the extreme, and musical, a saying with a ring about it. Not so Moffatt's 'Where your treasure lies, your heart will lie there too'. (The Greek has 'is', not 'lies'.)

'Offended' is a difficult word, and not used now in the sense of 'made to stumble', 'caused to go wrong': 'All ye shall be offended because of me this night'. But Moffatt's substitution is a still more terrible Latinism, 'You will all be *disconcerted*', Peter replying, 'Though all be *disconcerted* . . .'. And did Moffatt really think 'parabolic saying' was more modern and simple than 'parable'?

This sort of change the *Twentieth-Century New Testament* avoids, as it does the slang and undignified words of which Moffatt is sometimes guilty: '*barring* these chains' (Paul before Agrippa), 'does this *upset* you?' (said by Jesus), 'they treated Jesus to *cuffs* and *slaps*', 'I will *up and off* to my Father' for 'arise and go to my Father', where 'arise and go' corresponds to really dignified verbs used in the Greek. It avoids also such loose idiom as '*Who* are you looking for?', '*Who* are we to go to?', 'people *got* baptized', and, further, the wrong tone of 'Are we to drown for all you care?' which gives a too insolent turn to the despairing, 'Master, don't you care if we perish?' Nor is it guilty of such exaggeration as 'Cease *clinging to* me' for 'Touch me not', said by Jesus to Mary. By no conceivable strain can the Greek words be made to mean that.

When we come to St. John's Gospel we shall find special care needed. It is the bounden duty of the translator to preserve John's simple diction, or he will destroy one of its three great qualities—simplicity, subtlety, and sublimity. He must also remember the peculiar method of John, who uses the same simple word several times and comes back to it, so as to keep the drift of his argument clear and let the meaning penetrate subtly and surely by the repetition of the chief ideas. It is on these word-echoes that the musical quality of John's style depends. For instance we have:

> 'He came for a *witness*, to bear *witness* to the *Light*. . . . He was not that *Light*, but came to bear *witness* to the *Light*. . . . And this is the *witness* of John.'

The last sentence, coming much later in ver. 19, picks up John's thread, and the effect is spoilt by the substitution of 'testimony', as in one version. Or again, 'He came unto *his own*, and *his own received* him not, but as many as *received* him . . .', the music of which Moffatt spoils unnecessarily by altering to, 'Yet his own folk did not *welcome* him. On those who *accepted* him, however . . .'.

A version of the Gospels giving wider satisfaction would probably be on such cautious lines as the following, where an attempt is made to keep the best features of the A.V., and when correcting it, either for the removal of archaisms or for greater accuracy, to adopt words and idioms that are likely to remain in common use and yet rank as good simple English:

Luke xv. 11–18.

*Suggested new version for modern readers.*      *Authorized Version.*

11. And he said, A certain man had two sons.

12. And the younger of them said unto his father, Father, give me the *share* of the *property* that fal*l*s to me. — 'portion of goods'. 'fall*eth*'.
And he *gave them their shares* of his living. — 'divided unto them', which might imply that he parted with all his property. 'after'.

13. And not many days *later* the younger son gathered all together and *went abroad* to a *distant land*, and there wasted his *money* in riotous living. — 'took his journey'. 'far country'. 'substance'. Or '*a life of debauchery*', but the A.V. 'riotous' is expressive and a simpler word.

14. And when he had spent all, there *befell* a mighty famine in that *land*, and he began to be in want. — 'arose'. 'country'.

15. And he went and *joined a citizen* of that land, and he sent him into his fields to feed swine.

16. And he *longed to fill himself* with the *pods* that the swine *were eating*, and no man gave *him anything*.

17. And when he came to himself, he said, 'How many hired servants of my father have bread enough and to spare, while I perish with hunger!

18. I will arise and go to my father, and will say *to* him, Father, I sinned against heaven and before you, and am no *longer* worthy to be called your son. Make me one of your hired servants.'

'joined himself to'.

'would fain have filled his belly'.
'husks'. 'did eat'. A.V. omits 'anything', as if they were expected to offer him 'pods'.

'unto'.

'more'.

Of the words altered above in the A.V. some are archaic like 'portion of goods', 'would fain have filled his belly' ('belly' is not in the Greek), others are less accurate, as 'husks'. 'Swine', on the other hand, is actually kept by Moffatt, who aims at complete modernization, and may be justified perhaps here as semi-poetical, and more impressive than 'pigs'. In the modern versions there are changes which seem unnecessary, such as 'attached himself' for 'joined himself' in the A.V. (Moffatt, who yet keeps 'was *fain* to fill his belly'!); '*squandered* his inheritance' for '*wasted* his goods' (*Twentieth-Century New Testament*, which also inserts '*actual*' before 'want' quite unnecessarily). The main alterations in such a version as the above would be the change of old suffixes like -eth and -est, the abandonment of old-fashioned conjunctions like 'wherewith', of adverbs such as 'forthwith' and 'hereafter', of 'which' for 'who', 'whatsoever' for 'whatever', and of 'thou' and 'thee' except in direct address to God himself, as in prayers.

A further instance of needless upsetting of the rhythm of the A.V. occurs in the modern versions of ver. 24 of this passage. The rhythm of this verse and its vowel play have been much praised:

'For this my son was dead and is alive again; he was lost and is found.'

There is no archaism here except 'this my son' for 'this son of mine', but we get the following versions:

> Moffatt: 'For *my son here* was dead, and *he has come to life*, he was lost and *he* is found.'

Here '*he*' comes twice too often for the rhythm, and is not wanted; '*my son here*' is not so close to the Greek nor so musical as 'this son of mine'; and 'he has come to life' is a needless refinement, and less accurate, for the Greek word means 'came to life *again*' or 'lives again'. One has only to quote the other two versions to see how needlessly they alter without adding to clearness or even to the modern ring of the sentence:

> *Twentieth-Century New Testament*: 'For *here is my son*, who was dead and is alive again, was lost and is found.'
> Weymouth: 'For *my son here* was dead, and *has come to life* again; he was lost and *has been* found.'

The translator of Paul's letters for modern readers has two alternatives; he may follow the freer method of Moffatt, or he may offer something like this, keeping the phrasing and structure of Paul, as long as they are clear, and removing merely archaic forms and words and obscurities. He will also break up some rambling sentences, and connect them afresh.

### Philippians iii.

1. Lastly, my brothers, rejoice in the Lord. To write the same things to you is *no trouble to me*,[a] and *it is safe for you*.[b]

2. Beware of *the* 'dogs', beware of evil workers, beware of the 'concision'.

3. For we are the circumcision, *who serve the spirit of God*,[c] and *boast*[d] in Jesus Christ, and *do not trust*[e] in the flesh.

4. *And yet* I have reason to trust in the flesh; if any one *thinks he can*[f] trust in the flesh, I *can* more *certainly*;

5. circumcised the eighth day, of the race of Israel, of the tribe of Benjamin; a Hebrew of the Hebrews; *in* law a Pharisee, in[g]

[a] A.V. 'is not grievous'.
[b] 'for you it is safe'.

[c] A.V., less accurately, 'worship God in the spirit'. [d] 'rejoice'.
[e] 'have no confidence' (less direct).

[f] 'thinketh *that he hath whereof he might* trust' (unusually long for the A.V.).

[g] The Greek repeats the same

6. zeal a persecutor of the church, *in* righteousness, *as the law accounts it,*[h] blameless.

7. But what was gain to me, I counted loss for Christ.

8. *Yes,*[i] and I count *everything*[j] a loss *compared with* the excell*ence* of *knowing*[k] Christ Jesus my Lord; for *whose sake* I *lost my all,*[l] and count it as *refuse,*[m] that I may gain Christ,

9. and be found in him, not having a righteousness *of my own, derived from* the law, but that which *comes from faith in Christ,* the righteousness *from God, which rests on faith.*[n]

10. *My aim is*[o] to know him and the power of his resurrection, and fellowship of his sufferings, *making myself like him in his death,*[p]

11. *in the hope that* I may *possibly*[q] attain to the resurrection of the dead.

[preposition. A.V. has 'concerning' and 'as touching'. [h] 'which is in the law'.

[i] 'yea'.
[j] Omitting 'doubtless'. A.V. 'all things'. [k] 'for the excellency of the knowledge of'. [l] 'for whom I suffered the loss of all things'. [m] 'dung'.

[n] 'not having mine own righteousness, which is of the law, but that which is through the faith of Christ, the righteousness which is of God by faith' (less clear and less close to the Greek).
[o] 'that I may know him . . .' but the sentence must here have a fresh start.
[p] 'being made conformable unto his death' (which does not make the Greek clear).
[q] 'if by any means I might . . .'.

The above is translated afresh from the Greek, but coincides with the modern versions constantly, first with one, then another, on the whole tending to be more concise. Compare, for instance, 'it is safe for you' with 'while so far as you are concerned it is a safe precaution' (Weymouth). It is not the business of the translator to paraphrase like a commentary, unless the literal translation is unintelligible, else one might translate Paul's phrase 'in the *flesh*' by 'external privileges', as the modern versions do. But most people still know what 'trust in the flesh' means. On the other hand 'being made conformable unto his death' (A.V.) may be improved in many ways without going farther from the Greek. Moffatt's is perhaps the best, though rather free, 'with my nature transformed to die as he died', but 'moulding myself in the spirit of his death' would perhaps render the idiom of the Greek best.

# INDEX

Acts of Apostles, dramatic features, 114 ff., 125; exact terminology, 124 f.; historical value, 112 ff.; Roman officials, 125; speeches, 125; subject-matter, 105 ff.; syntax, 123 ff. See also under Luke, and synopsis of chapter viii.
adjurations, 153.
Agabus, 114.
Agrippa, 115 ff.
allegory, 75, 88 ff.
antithesis, *see* balance.
Apocalyptic literature, 183, 185 f.
apostrophe, 76, 81, 141.

balance, 72, 81, 84, 135, 145 f.
Barnabas, 107, 109.
Bartimaeus, 6, 15.
beatitudes, 27, 78.
blind man healed, 15, 60.

church organization, 108.
citizenship, 133.
climax, 77 f., 82, 94, 139, 167.
collections of alms, 107.
Colosse, 131.
concentration upon one idea, 155, 168.
Corinth, church at, 143, 147, 157 f., 166, 168; games at, 136.
crowd, in Mark, 15; in Luke, 32, 97.

Daniel, influence on Revelation, 185, 188 f., 190, 192.
deaf and dumb man healed, 11.
diction, of John, 72 ff.; of Paul, 139, 141, 144, 148, 153 ff.; of Revelation, 198.
'direct' speech, 17 f., 71, 87.
disciples, picture of, 20 ff.
doxology, 141, 182, 197.
dramatic irony, 95.
dreams in Matthew, 30.

elegy, 97.
elevation of theme, 133 ff.
ellipses, 166.
Enoch, book of, 185 f., 199.

Ephesians, Epistle to, 165 f.
Ephesus, riot at, 113.
epigrams, of Jesus, 76; of Paul, 134, 144, 148 ff.
eunuch, 111.
Eutychus, 112.
exaggeration, *see* hyperbole.
exclamations, 135, 139.
Ezekiel, influence on Revelation, 191 f., 196 f., 200 f.

Festus, 117 ff.

Galations, Epistle to, 130, 159, 166.
genealogy in Matthew and Luke, 29.
Gentile question, 163.
Gethsemane, 94, 98.
'great refusal', the, 16.

Hebrews, Epistle to, 164, 171 ff.
hyperbole, 75, 77, 135.

imagery, of Jesus, 75 ff., 81; of Paul, 136 f.; in Revelation, 198 f.
irony, 75, 135, 159, 162.
Isaiah, influence on Revelation, 191, 198, 200.

James, Epistle of, 175, 177.
Jesus, actions of, 14; actual words, 17, 33, 119; bearing, 100 f.; diction, 87; great sayings, 90; human feelings, 13, 65 ff., 94; looks and gestures, 14; movements in travel, 22; oratory, 28 f., 75 ff., 78 ff., 82; personality, 4; power, 18; temptation, 23; thoughtfulness, 97.
John, Epistle of, 179 ff.
John, Gospel of; correcting Mark, 100; dramatic feeling, 98 f.; Greek style, 72 ff. See also synopsis of chapter v.
John the Baptist, 34, 79.
John the Elder, 47.
Jude, Epistle of, 181 f.